THE COMPLETE
IDIOT'S
GUIDE® TO

WordPress

D1301180

by Susan Gunelius

ALPHA

A member of Penguin Group (USA) Inc.

To Scott, for supporting everything I do without question and for always making me laugh, even when I'm at my height of stress.

ALPHA BOOKS

Published by the Penguin Group

Penguin Group (USA) Inc., 375 Hudson Street, New York, New York 10014, USA

Penguin Group (Canada), 90 Eglinton Avenue East, Suite 700, Toronto, Ontario M4P 2Y3, Canada (a division of Pearson Penguin Canada Inc.)

Penguin Books Ltd., 80 Strand, London WC2R 0RL, England

Penguin Ireland, 25 St. Stephen's Green, Dublin 2, Ireland (a division of Penguin Books Ltd.)

Penguin Group (Australia), 250 Camberwell Road, Camberwell, Victoria 3124, Australia (a division of Pearson Australia Group Pty. Ltd.)

Penguin Books India Pvt. Ltd., 11 Community Centre, Panchsheel Park, New Delhi—110 017, India

Penguin Group (NZ), 67 Apollo Drive, Rosedale, North Shore, Auckland 1311, New Zealand (a division of Pearson New Zealand Ltd.)

Penguin Books (South Africa) (Pty.) Ltd., 24 Sturdee Avenue, Rosebank, Johannesburg 2196, South Africa

Penguin Books Ltd., Registered Offices: 80 Strand, London WC2R 0RL, England

International Standard Book Number: 978-1-61564-072-0
Library of Congress Catalog Card Number: 2010913770

13 12 11   8 7 6 5 4 3 2 1

Interpretation of the printing code: The rightmost number of the first series of numbers is the year of the book's printing; the rightmost number of the second series of numbers is the number of the book's printing. For example, a printing code of 11-1 shows that the first printing occurred in 2011.

Printed in the United States of America

Note: This publication contains the opinions and ideas of its author. It is intended to provide helpful and informative material on the subject matter covered. It is sold with the understanding that the author and publisher are not engaged in rendering professional services in the book. If the reader requires personal assistance or advice, a competent professional should be consulted.

The author and publisher specifically disclaim any responsibility for any liability, loss, or risk, personal or otherwise, which is incurred as a consequence, directly or indirectly, of the use and application of any of the contents of this book.

Most Alpha books are available at special quantity discounts for bulk purchases for sales promotions, premiums, fund-raising, or educational use. Special books, or book excerpts, can also be created to fit specific needs.

For details, write: Special Markets, Alpha Books, 375 Hudson Street, New York, NY 10014.

Publisher: *Marie Butler-Knight*

Associate Publisher: *Mike Sanders*

Senior Managing Editor: *Billy Fields*

Senior Development Editor: *Christy Wagner*

Production Editor: *Kayla Dugger*

Copy Editor: *Amy Borrelli*

Cover Designer: *William Thomas*

Book Designers: *William Thomas, Rebecca Batchelor*

Indexer: *Tonya Heard*

Layout: *Ayanna Lacey*

Proofreader: *Laura Caddell*

Contents

Introduction

Congratulations! You made an excellent decision in choosing WordPress as your blogging application. Becoming a part of the social web as a blogger is exciting and surprising, and you won't regret your choice to establish your own space in the online world.

You've made another great decision by picking up this book. *The Complete Idiot's Guide to WordPress* takes you through the process of setting your blogging goals, choosing the right version of WordPress for you, setting up your blog, publishing content, changing the design, adding extra features, growing your audience, and making money. In other words, if you read this book cover to cover, you'll find no stone left unturned that a beginner WordPress user needs to know to become a blogger.

Reading this book front to back is recommended to ensure you know everything you need to effectively use WordPress and join the blogosphere, but I wrote the book in a manner that allows you to skip chapters or parts and focus only on the areas you need help with. For example, if you're not interested in using the self-hosted version of WordPress, you can skip Part 4 entirely. Similarly, if you have no desire in making money from your blog, you don't have to read Part 6. However, throughout the book, when it would be useful for you to read another chapter for additional information, I refer you to that chapter.

One of the aspects of *The Complete Idiot's Guide to WordPress* that sets it apart from other beginner's guides to WordPress is that in addition to teaching you *how* to use WordPress, this book also focuses on teaching you *why* you should or should not configure your blog in certain ways or use specific tools. Throughout the book, you'll find deeper discussion related to decisions you'll need to make as a WordPress blogger, and Appendix B includes additional answers to frequently asked questions about the *whys* of WordPress blog configuration and design.

The Sum of Its Parts

This book is divided into six parts:

Part 1, Welcome to the World of WordPress, starts at the very beginning by helping you ensure you've picked the right topic for your blog, checking out the competition, and setting appropriate goals for your blogging experience. Only after completing these tasks effectively can you make an intelligent decision about which version of WordPress is best for you. This part shows you how to do it by clearly explaining the differences between the application available to you at WordPress.com versus the application at WordPress.org.

Not only does **Part 2, Writing for the Blogosphere,** teach you how to write for the web, but it also teaches you how to find blog post ideas and how to follow the written and unwritten rules of online publishing, including legalities. Pleading ignorance won't work in a court of law, so be sure you read and understand the contents of this part before you publish your first blog post!

Part 3, Starting Your Blog with WordPress.com, offers the step-by-step instructions you need to start a new blog using the application available to you at WordPress.com. You learn what all the parts and pieces of a WordPress blog and account dashboard are used for, how to configure them to meet your goals, and how to publish a variety of content on your blog.

Part 4, Using WordPress.org, covers everything you need to know about using the self-hosted version of WordPress available at WordPress.org. Anything that's different or new in WordPress.org from what you learned in Part 3 about WordPress.com is highlighted in this part. For example, you learn about domain registration, web hosting, the FTP process, themes, plug-ins, and more.

Part 5, Attracting an Audience, takes you to the next step of blogging with WordPress—growing your audience and analyzing your blog's performance so you can continue to attract more visitors. After reading this part, you'll be able to link your WordPress blog to your Twitter, Facebook, and LinkedIn accounts. You'll also be able to add Google Analytics code to your blog, so you can track performance.

Part 6, Blogging for Big Bucks, is a must-read for those who want to make money from their WordPress blogging efforts. In this part, you learn about a variety of popular blog monetization opportunities, as well as how to place ads in your blog, sell ad space, and more.

At the back of the book, I've included a glossary, answers to many frequently asked questions, and a comprehensive list of resources to help you take your learning to the next level.

Extras You Don't Want to Miss

The Complete Idiot's Guide to WordPress includes a variety of helpful sidebars to draw attention to important tips, definitions, warnings, and other fun information that can help make your life as a WordPress user easier and more enjoyable:

DEFINITION

As you read this book, you'll inevitably come across words related to blogging you're unfamiliar with. Those words are defined in these sidebars.

INSIDER SECRET

These sidebars contain helpful information you definitely should check out.

QUICK TIP

Quick Tip offers helpful ways to save time or money or just make your WordPress experience easier.

PROCEED WITH CAUTION

If you see a Proceed with Caution sidebar, stop and read it immediately. These convey information related to impending peril and should not be ignored.

Acknowledgments

Foremost, I want to thank my family for supporting me while I wrote this book. The timing for writing landed during the summer after my triplets completed kindergarten, and writing a book while three 6-year-olds are home with you is challenging, to say the least. Add managing the house, my company, and all of my regular clients to my list of daily priorities, and the summer of 2010 became a crazy one for my family. Scott, Brynn, Daniel, and Ryan, thanks for putting up with me (or perhaps I should say the *lack* of me) while I wrote this book. And thank you to my parents, Bill and Carol Ann Henry, for offering to watch my children if I needed some extra time to write.

I also need to thank my literary agent, Bob Diforio, for bringing this project to me, and Mike Sanders at Alpha Books for offering it to me. Along those lines, I'd like to recognize and thank all of the editors, including my technical editor, Roberta Rosenberg, for helping ensure the final product is the best it can be. When it comes to writing about WordPress—or any online tool—changes happen in the blink of an eye. It takes more than one set of eyes and ears to stay on top of everything, and I thank you all!

And of course, thank you to everyone who reads my books, my blogs, and all my other online content as well as everyone who follows me on Twitter, Facebook, LinkedIn, and so on. Thank you for sharing content with me, conversing with me, and making the social web such an amazing place!

Special Thanks to the Technical Reviewer

The Complete Idiot's Guide to WordPress was reviewed by an expert who double-checked the accuracy of what you'll learn here, to help us ensure that this book gives you everything you need to know about starting and maintaining a blog with WordPress. Special thanks are extended to Roberta Rosenberg.

Roberta has 25+ years experience in the direct response marketing field. Roberta studied broadcast journalism at The Newhouse School of Public Communications at Syracuse University and earned her bachelor of science in radio/TV/film from University of Maryland/University College, College Park. Roberta has served as technical editor for numerous blog- and copy writing–related books. She blogs at CopywritingMaven.com and writes the popular Landing Page Makeover series at Copyblogger.com.

Trademarks

All terms mentioned in this book that are known to be or are suspected of being trademarks or service marks have been appropriately capitalized. Alpha Books and Penguin Group (USA) Inc. cannot attest to the accuracy of this information. Use of a term in this book should not be regarded as affecting the validity of any trademark or service mark.

All trademarks, terms, screenshots, and intellectual property referenced in this book are included for educational purposes and are the property of their respective owners. Furthermore, information discussed in this book was current at the time of writing. However, online technology changes quickly, and readers are encouraged to confirm the accuracy of all information included in this book by visiting the websites referenced herein to ensure updates or changes have not been made since this book was written.

Welcome to the World of WordPress

You've made the decision to start a blog, and you've decided that WordPress is the tool for you. Before you go any further, you need to take some time to evaluate your blogging goals so you can set your blog up for success from the start.

In Part 1, you learn how to establish your goals, ensure you've chosen the right blog topic, size up the competition, and choose the right version of WordPress to use for your blog. You also learn about the features and functionality available to you through each version of WordPress, so there's no question you're using the right tool from day one of your foray into the world of blogging and WordPress.

Blogging Basics

In This Chapter

- It all starts with a plan
- Give them something to talk about
- What it takes to be a great blogger
- The ugly side of blogging
- Tips for blogging success

It's hard to believe that just over a decade ago, *blogs* were little more than online diaries published by very few individuals. In the early years of the twenty-first century, blogs have become an integral part of daily communications between individuals, organizations, businesses, and more. In fact, blogs have become more than an outlet for expository writing and user-generated content. Today, hundreds of millions of blogs provide online destinations for marketing, publicity, reputation management, journalism, advocacy, and so much more. And many of those blogs are created and updated with WordPress.

In this chapter, you learn how to plan your entry into the *blogosphere* so you're positioned to successfully reach your blogging goals, which includes choosing the right version of WordPress for you and understanding the downsides to blogging.

Are you ready? It's time to blog!

Why Do You Want to Blog?

The blogosphere has grown into a global conversation anyone can join, for a few simple reasons. First, there are virtually no barriers to entry. *Blogging applications* and tools are easy to use. If you know how to use a word processing application and can navigate the web, you can become a *blogger*, publish a blog, and own your own space online.

> **DEFINITION**
>
> A **blog** (the fusion of the words *web* and *log*) is a website that includes written entries, called posts. Readers can publish comments on posts and access older posts through an archive. *Blog* as a verb refers to the act of writing content published on a blog. The **blogosphere** is the online blogging community. A **blogging application** is the tool you use to create and publish blog content—such as WordPress. Sometimes blogging applications are referred to as *blogging software* or *blogging platforms*. A **blogger** is a person who blogs.

Second, blogging doesn't have to cost you any money. You can find and use tools—like WordPress—to publish your own blog without spending a dime.

Third, there's room for everyone in the blogosphere. Regardless of who you are, where you live, and what you want to write about, you are welcome to publish a blog to meet your personal or business goals. The rules of blogging are fairly easy to follow, so anyone with Internet access and a desire to write can become a blogger.

Before you create a WordPress blog, you need to know why you want to blog in the first place. Each blogger has his own reasons for blogging and his own long-term goals for his efforts. It's essential that you take the time to evaluate your blogging objectives so you set up your WordPress blog for success from day one.

> **INSIDER SECRET**
>
> WordPress users refer to the two different versions of the WordPress blogging application as WordPress.org (the self-hosted WordPress application) and WordPress.com (the WordPress hosted application), which are the domains where you can access the respective applications.

For example, if your blogging goals include making money, you need to choose a blogging application like WordPress.org that allows you the freedom to monetize your blog. Similarly, if you want to build your brand through your blogging efforts, you need a blogging application like WordPress.org that offers a great deal of customization options. However, if you simply want to share your thoughts online with no set growth or monetization goals, WordPress.com might be the best choice for you.

You can learn more about the differences between WordPress.com and WordPress.org in Chapter 2. But for now, keep in mind that setting your goals upfront helps you not only choose the right version of WordPress, but also helps you focus your efforts on tasks necessary to achieving your own definition of blogging success, as well as in prioritizing those tasks and omitting extraneous tasks that steal time from more important activities.

Bottom line, blogs provide people with the ability to own a specific place on the World Wide Web, which they can use in their own ways and to meet their own objectives. Just choose your topic, establish your goals, and you're on your way to becoming a blogger!

QUICK TIP

It's possible to migrate your blog from one blogging application to another, but it's always best to think long term and begin with the best version of WordPress to help you meet your goals.

Refine Your Topic

Maybe you already know what you want to blog about—your hobby, your work, a cause you're passionate about, or another topic important to you. But what if you don't know what you want to blog about? How do you find the best topic for you?

Ultimately, the choice is yours, but your topic should help you meet the blogging goals you established for yourself. For example, if your primary blogging goal is to build your business, publishing a WordPress blog about a controversial topic unrelated to your business is unlikely to help you meet your goals. Your blogging goals and the subject matter of your blog should blend cohesively.

Furthermore, it's imperative that you choose a blog topic you're passionate about, have a deep interest in or knowledge of, and won't get bored with. Successful bloggers update their blogs with new posts frequently—sometimes multiple times a day. If you want to achieve similar success, you need to publish new content to your blog at least several times per week. You also need to respond to comments and participate in the conversations that happen on your blog, as well as on other blogs and sites related to your topic.

Not only do you need to be able to come up with numerous new post ideas for your blog if you want to be successful, but you also need to be social and become an active member of the community on and off your blog. That means you should pick a blog topic you have a lot to say about.

PROCEED WITH CAUTION

Remember, even though your WordPress blog is your own to control and use as you want, the blogosphere is not the Wild West. Even if you write and publish a blog anonymously, you're still bound by the law and WordPress's terms of use. Be sure to read Chapter 4 to learn about blogging rules and publishing laws. Claiming ignorance won't get you off the hook if you violate a law or contractual obligation.

Ultimately, the topic you choose to write about on your blog should help you carve out your own focused niche on the web. The scope of that niche depends entirely on your long-term goals.

Check Out the Competition

Before you make any final decisions on what you want your blog to be, take some time to check out your competition. Search for blogs related to the topics you're considering. Conduct a keyword search using a tool like Google Blog Search (blogsearch. google.com) or IceRocket.com. Read the posts on those blogs and see what topics elicit conversations that you can leverage on your own blog, or where there are gaps in information that you can fill on your own blog.

Here's how to conduct a blog search using Google Blog Search.

1. Visit blogsearch.google.com, shown in Figure 1-1, and select the **Advanced Blog Search** link at the top-right corner of the page, to the right of the search text box.

Figure 1-1 *The Google Blog Search page is easy to use.*

(Source: blogsearch.google.com)

2. On the Advanced Blog Search page (shown in Figure 1-2), enter the keyword or keyword phrase you want to search for in the text box to the right of the **In blogs/with these words in the blog title** heading to find blogs related to your chosen keyword.

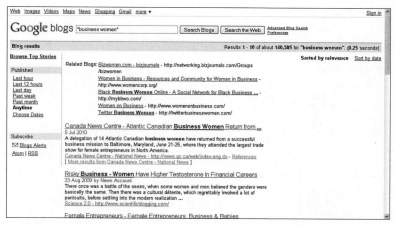

Figure 1-2 *The Advanced Blog Search page offers extensive search options.*
(Source: blogsearch.google.com/blogsearch/advanced_blog_search?hl=en)

3. Click the **Search Blogs** button on the top-right side of the page to access your search results, shown in Figure 1-3.

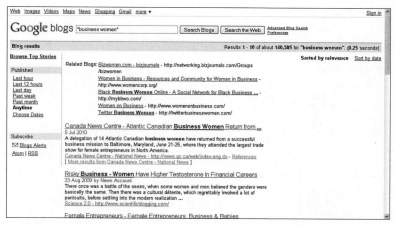

Figure 1-3 *Google Blog Search displays your search results based on your chosen keywords.*
(Courtesy of Google)

Visit the blogs found in your Google search results and read the content, looking for subjects that draw readers and comments as well as for missing content. This helps you determine how you can position your WordPress blog relative to the competition and deliver value beyond what's already being published online.

The key to blogging success is bringing something new, different, or extra to the table. In other words, how can you differentiate your WordPress blog from others already being published with existing audiences? Unless you can demonstrate through your content and conversations that your blog is worth reading over or in addition to others published about similar topics, you'll only be able to grow your blog's audience so much before you hit a roadblock.

You can learn more about growing your blog's audience in Part 5. For now, be sure you select a blog topic you can add value to within the online community.

Determine Your Blogging Application Needs

Once you define your blogging goals and refine your blog topic, it's time to think about your blogging application. Do you want something quick and easy, like WordPress.com, or something you can customize and dig a little deeper into, like WordPress.org?

Again, look to your blogging goals. For example, if your goal is simply to have fun, then WordPress.com, a free blogging application that offers limited functionality, is likely to suit your needs. However, if you plan to use your blog to build your business or generate an income, then you need something more along the lines of WordPress.org, a blogging application that offers advanced features and maximum customization.

WordPress.org offers lots of functionality and flexibility. In fact, many businesses use WordPress.org to create their entire websites, not just their blogs! You can see examples of websites built on WordPress.org in Chapter 16.

To help determine your blogging application needs, answer the following questions yes or no:

- Do you want to have a unique *domain* name for your blog?

DEFINITION

A **domain** is the part of a URL that represents a specific website. Domain names are typically preceded by *www.* and end with an extension such as *.com* or *.net*.

- Are you comfortable with technology and willing to try new things?

- Do you want to include ads and other monetization efforts on your blog?

- Do you want to have complete control over the ads that appear on your blog?

- Do you need your blog to have a unique design and appearance?

- Are you willing to spend some money (typically $20 or less per month) on your blog?

- Do you want to upload and publish audio and video content directly to your blog using another service such as YouTube?

- Do you want to use contact forms, search engine optimization enhancements (discussed in Chapter 19), spam blockers, and other advanced features on your blog?

- Do you plan to publish large images and content on your blog that require a lot of storage space?

- Do you want to have unrestricted control of your blog layout and content (of course, within the WordPress terms of use)?

If you answered yes to any of these questions, you need an advanced blogging application like WordPress.org. On the other hand, if your blogging application needs are less advanced and you didn't answer yes to any of these questions, WordPress.com should work for you. (Learn more about the differences between WordPress.com and WordPress.org in Chapter 2.)

 QUICK TIP

Create a list of the functions and features you want in your blog. Reference that list as you evaluate and compare WordPress.com versus WordPress.org.

Pitfalls to Avoid

Blogging is fun and useful, but it's not all wine and roses. Elements of blogging can cause concern, and you need to be aware of them before you become an online publisher. Before you join the blogosphere, you need to understand not only the steps required to meet your goals, but also the steps to avoid. Some blogging pitfalls can ruin your efforts faster than you can say, "I'm sorry." Chapter 4 offers an in-depth discussion about blogging do's and don'ts, but there are some considerations you need to make before you delve into blogging rules and ethics.

First, blogging exposes you to a global audience. Are you ready for that level of exposure? It's possible to write an anonymous blog, but most authoritative blogs are written by people who provide information about their backgrounds and experiences, as well as methods to contact them to ask questions or get additional information.

Before you set yourself up to become a big or small web celebrity, be sure you've considered and accepted the ramifications of blogging. If you're not ready to put yourself out there yet, WordPress does offer an option to keep your blog private, allowing you to control who sees it.

Second, as a blogger, you need to have a thick skin. Everyone who reads your WordPress blog won't agree with what you publish. It's highly likely that at some point, your posts will generate negative comments, and many people hide behind the anonymity of the web to publish offensive and even hateful comments about you and your blog.

You need to be prepared for the inevitable day when someone will publish something online that's hurtful about you. Have a plan for deleting or editing offensive comments on your blog by publishing a comment policy (a sample is offered in Chapter 4), and set up your WordPress blog's comment moderation settings so you can edit or delete comments that include offensive language (comment moderation is discussed in Chapter 7).

Third, to become a successful blogger, you need to publish content on your WordPress blog *and* participate in conversations happening both on and off your blog. Therefore, you need to be able to write about your blog topic *a lot*, and you need to keep up on developments related to your topic so you can write intelligently about them. If you publish outdated or inaccurate information, your credibility will be questioned and your blog's reputation—as well as your own—might get tarnished.

Secrets to Blogging Success

So you've determined what topic you want to blog about and what your goals are for your WordPress blog, and you're ready to get started. Now, let's review some of the secrets to blogging success so you can get a good start.

First of all, blog about a topic people are actually interested in. Your success can only grow as much as there are people interested in your blog's topic.

Blog about a topic that won't go away anytime soon. You might love a television program and want to blog about it, but eventually, that program will go off the air. What will happen to your blog then?

Be visible and promote your blog by being social both on and off your blog. No blog is an island. Just because you build your WordPress blog doesn't mean people will come to it. Join conversations on other blogs, forums, Facebook, Twitter, and so on, to build relationships with people and invite them to visit your blog for more great content.

Be willing to take risks and experiment with new tools and features to continually enhance and grow your blog. A blog shouldn't be static; it should change with the times and continually deliver relevant information to a modern audience.

 INSIDER SECRET

Just because another blogger is using a particular tool or technique doesn't mean that tool or technique is right for your goals and your WordPress blog. Always evaluate tools and techniques against your own objectives rather than simply copying what other bloggers are doing.

Commit to the long haul. Blogs don't grow overnight. If you want your WordPress blog to be successful, you need to be patient and continually work to grow your audience. To help with that, dedicate time to your blog. Updating your WordPress blog once a week won't help it grow. You need to spend time writing content and participating in conversations on and off your blog.

Create a reader experience on your WordPress blog that's inviting, nonthreatening, and enjoyable. Make it easy for visitors to find and read the content on your blog through your blog design and writing style. Use a comment policy so threatening or offensive comments and conversations don't appear on your blog.

Research and know your audience. Spend time learning what your audience wants and needs from your blog, and continually and consistently deliver that content to them. That includes adding value. No one will want to read your blog or interact with you if you don't publish useful, interesting, or entertaining content that actually adds value to the user experience.

Read and learn. The best bloggers spend as much time reading and learning about blogging and their topics as they do creating content.

Avoid self-promotion. If you spend all your time on and off your blog trying to sell your products and services, no one will want to read your content or interact with you. Be yourself. People recognize posers, liars, and frauds. Speak from your heart and share your passion for your subject, and people will respect you online.

Following the secrets to blogging success doesn't end when your WordPress blog debuts online. The exact opposite holds true. Continually evaluate your blogging efforts against these success factors to ensure you stay on your path to achieving the goals you originally established. Furthermore, you should reevaluate those goals periodically to determine where changes should be made.

The blogosphere changes quickly with new tools, features, and players introduced all the time. Your goals and blogging strategy today might not apply six months from now. Take the time to modify your goals and techniques every few months to be sure you stay on target to achieve your own blogging objectives.

The Least You Need to Know

- Analyze your blogging goals before you settle on a topic to write about on your new blog.
- Take some time to see what other people are publishing across the blogosphere before you jump in with both feet.
- Think in the long term if you want to set up your blog for success from the start.
- After you've thoroughly defined your blogging goals and needs, you'll have a better idea which WordPress—WordPress.com or WordPress.org—is right for you.

WordPress.com Versus WordPress.org

In This Chapter

- Uncovering the differences between WordPress versions
- Blogging for free with WordPress.com
- Maxing out the possibilities with WordPress.org
- Choosing the right WordPress for your blog

The team at Automattic launched WordPress in 2003, and in less than a decade, WordPress has become one of the most popular blogging applications in the world.

WordPress is an open source content management system, meaning it was developed by and for the community of users who create, publish, and manage content on their own blogs and websites with it. An open source application means two things to users: developers from around the world are welcome to work on the code and functionality of WordPress, and WordPress is free for anyone to use.

As the WordPress user audience grew, the team at Automattic realized there was demand for a second version of the application that would allow users with very little technical knowledge to create their own online destinations. Today, there are two versions of WordPress: WordPress.com and WordPress.org. This chapter explains the differences between the two versions so you can choose the right one for you and your blog.

What Is WordPress.com?

WordPress.com, launched in 2005, is the easiest-to-use version of WordPress. Blogs created using WordPress.com are hosted by WordPress, meaning WordPress stores the data and maintains all the behind-the-scenes technology necessary to display your blog online. All you have to do is log in to your WordPress.com account, create your content, and hit the publish button. WordPress.com takes care of everything else.

WordPress.com users have access to limited features and functionality for free, although those features are more than enough to publish a simple blog. Premium features that offer some advanced functionality and options are available for an annual fee.

In simplest terms, you can create a WordPress.com blog in just a few minutes by visiting WordPress.com, creating a free account, choosing a domain name, and clicking the sign up button.

What Is WordPress.org?

WordPress.org, offering the self-hosted WordPress application, is the most popular free, open source blogging application you can use to create a blog or website. To use WordPress.org as your blogging application, you need to pay for a *web host* to store and serve your content to your blog visitors. Once you secure a hosting account, you can register a domain name for your blog (also for a fee), upload the WordPress application from WordPress.org to your account, and publish your blog.

WordPress.org offers the most customization options of any blogging application by far. Users can access the *CSS* code and all the files needed to modify their WordPress.org blog design or its functionality, add plug-ins (extra features created to extend the abilities of WordPress), and more. The only limitations are your willingness to learn and try new things.

DEFINITION

A **web host,** also called a blog host, host, or hosting service, is the company that provides space to store website or blog data as well as the Internet connectivity to display that data to your blog visitors. **CSS** is an acronym for *cascading style sheets,* the programming language that defines the layout and design of a WordPress blog.

While WordPress.org offers extensive customization options, it's up to you to decide how far you want to dig into those options. Even a blogger with limited technical savvy can learn to use many of the advanced customization options available through WordPress.org, thanks to the active WordPress community and all the documentation WordPress provides through its Codex site (http://codex.wordpress.org/Main_Page), which is an open source help documentation resource.

Primary Differences

Many people are confused by the two different versions of WordPress, so don't worry if you're one of them right now. Most other blogging applications have just one version, so why does WordPress have two?

Think of WordPress.com as the *WordPress*-hosted version of the application and WordPress.org as the *self*-hosted version of the application. So when you create a blog using WordPress.com, you only have to worry about writing and publishing content. However, when you create a blog using WordPress.org, you need to find your own web host to store and serve your content.

Let's review some more differences between WordPress.com and WordPress.org, so you can better understand what each offers.

Cost: Both WordPress.com and WordPress.org are free to use, but as mentioned earlier, with WordPress.org, you need to pay for your own hosting account through a web host and register your own domain name. Neither costs are required if you use WordPress.com.

Themes: WordPress blogs are built on themes. A theme is basically a template made up of files that lay out the style, functionality, and parts of a blog created with that theme. WordPress.com users with free accounts have access to a library of themes, but that library is limited. WordPress.org users, on the other hand, can upload and modify themes from designers or, if they understand CSS, can create their own themes, which gives them far more design options.

Space: WordPress.com users with free accounts are given a limited amount of space—3 gigabytes (GB)—to store their blogs on WordPress-owned servers. However, that space is usually enough for the average blogger. Additional space is available for a fee as a premium WordPress.com feature. WordPress.org users are limited in terms of space based on the hosting account they purchase from a third-party host.

 INSIDER SECRET

WordPress.com users cannot upload audio or music files to their blogs without first purchasing additional space, a premium feature upgrade.

Monetization: WordPress.com users cannot currently display ads or other money-making features on their WordPress-hosted blogs. WordPress.org users, on the other hand, can monetize their blogs by displaying ads from third parties, selling products, and more.

Domain name: WordPress.com users with free accounts are given the domain names of their choice, if they're available, but the *.wordpress.com* extension is automatically added to the end of the domain. WordPress.com users can pay a fee to access a premium feature and use their own domain name. WordPress.org users must pay for and secure their own domain names, separate from WordPress. (Many hosting providers offer a free domain with the purchase of a hosting package.)

Customization: WordPress.com users with free accounts have access to limited customization options, but they can pay a fee to be able to modify the CSS files and, therefore, customize their blogs' appearances. WordPress.org users have complete access to all files and code related to their blogs and can customize them to their heart's content.

Control: To earn money, WordPress sometimes displays ads on WordPress.com blogs. You can eliminate those ads by paying for premium WordPress.com features. WordPress.org users never see these ads and have complete control of their blogs.

Users: WordPress.com users with free accounts can create an unlimited number of blogs, but each private blog created can only have up to 35 users. To give an unlimited number of users access to your private blog, you need to purchase a premium WordPress.com upgrade. WordPress.org users are not subjected to such restrictions.

Plug-ins: WordPress.com users aren't able to use third-party WordPress plug-ins, or add-ons that extend the functionality of their blogs. WordPress.org users can.

Which WordPress Is Right for Your Blog?

Now that you understand the differences between WordPress.com and WordPress.org, how do you know which one is right for you? Remember and keep in mind the goals you set in Chapter 1 as you review the features available for both versions of WordPress. Those, along with the following suggestions, should help you choose the right WordPress from the start.

Consider Your Budget

What are you willing to invest in your blog each month? The answer to that question has a direct impact on which version of WordPress you use.

As mentioned, WordPress.com users with free accounts have 3GB of space to store uploaded images and files. That's a lot of space for a small blogger, but if you need more, you can purchase an upgrade of an additional 5, 15, 25, 50, or 100GB with price tags ranging from approximately $20 a year all the way up to nearly $300.

INSIDER SECRET

WordPress.com space upgrades apply only to the blog they're purchased for, not any other blog you might maintain. And WordPress.com space upgrades must be renewed on an annual basis.

These days, hosting plans from popular web host services are quite inexpensive. If you choose WordPress.org, you'll need to secure your own hosting and domain name, both of which have a price tag attached to them with annual renewals required. However, you can secure a hosting plan with a provider like BlueHost.com or HostGator.com, including a free domain and unlimited space, for less than $10 per month. More restrictive plans in terms of space go for less than $5 per month.

If you're not as technically savvy as you'd like to be, you might want to hire someone to help you get your blog just the way you want it. That service comes with a cost.

Bottom line: if you plan to publish a simple blog and want to avoid paying any costs to do so, WordPress.com is a fine choice for you. However, if space is a concern for your blog, WordPress.org might be a better choice, depending on your budget.

What Features and Functionality Do You Need?

WordPress.com offers much more limited features than WordPress.org. Thanks to the huge number of custom themes and plug-ins available to WordPress.org users, there's practically nothing you can't do with a WordPress.org blog!

The WordPress.com upgrade, which allows you access to customize your blog's files and CSS, costs nearly $15 per year and nearly $15 more to register and map a domain name without the .wordpress.com extension. Adding even the most common features to a WordPress.com blog can get expensive.

If you don't want ads served by WordPress.com displaying on your blog, you'll have to pay nearly $30 more per year for that upgrade. These are costs you don't have to pay if you use WordPress.org.

Bottom line: WordPress.org is the choice for you if you need complete control and all the features you can possibly imagine. But if limited functionality suits your needs, WordPress.com should work for you.

What's Your Technical Ability?

The major reason many people choose WordPress.com rather than WordPress.org is because they're intimidated by WordPress.org. They think they don't have the technical knowledge or courage to learn how to use WordPress.org.

You actually don't need much technical knowledge to use WordPress.org, because web hosts make it very easy to get your WordPress.org blog online quickly and easily. Thanks to the helpful tools web hosts offer, uploading, installing, and using WordPress.org takes only a few minutes. You just need to know what to look for and the basic steps to get started—which I describe in detail in Part 4.

 QUICK TIP

Start a free test blog using WordPress.com to familiarize yourself with the basic features and functions available before you choose your blogging application and start your real blog.

You might be surprised to hear that many top bloggers have very little technical knowledge. That should prove you don't have to be a web designer or developer to use WordPress.org.

Technical knowledge can certainly help a WordPress blogger and can even save you money over the long term. However, it's not necessary to have a degree in computer science to use WordPress.org. WordPress.com certainly requires less technical knowledge than WordPress.org, which might be an important consideration for you as you select your blogging application, but don't be misled into thinking you need to be a technical guru to use WordPress.org. Like many other power WordPress.org users, I'm proof that's not the case.

If ease of use is most important to you, WordPress.com might be your best option. But if you're not afraid to experiment with new technology, WordPress.org will open up a world of opportunities and options to you.

What Are Your Long-Term Goals?

As with all choices related to your blog, your long-term blogging goals should rule your WordPress.com versus WordPress.org decision. The most important thing you can do as a blogger is decide why you want to blog in the first place and what you want to get out of your blogging experience before you even start your blog.

If you want to use your blog as a catalyst to grow a business, you need to set it up to accurately reflect your business's intended image and brand promise. For example, a .wordpress.com domain extension could be perceived by visitors as "small time" or unprofessional. Visitors might think, *This business doesn't even care enough to invest in its own domain name; how much could it care about me, and will it still be around a year from now?*

Similarly, a site built using WordPress.com and a standard theme people see on many other blogs sets a brand image similar to all the other sites using that same theme. That might not be the image you want associated with your brand. Many amazing business websites are built on WordPress, but most of those sites are built using customized themes that make those sites unique and create specific brand perceptions in consumers' minds when they visit.

Of course, you can always switch from one blogging application to another—WordPress makes it very easy to switch. But there are considerations that might not make switching in the future the ideal option for you. For example, if you switch from WordPress.com with a domain that uses a .wordpress.com extension to WordPress.org, you'll need to change your domain. That means all the incoming links to your blog will be affected and all the search engine rankings your blog has earned will be lost. If you're trying to grow your blog or a business through your WordPress site, changing your domain name could cause a problem in meeting your long-term goals.

Remember, your blog can only be what you want it to be and help you meet your goals if you're using the right tools and application. Weigh your options before making an educated decision and diving into the world of blogging with WordPress.com or WordPress.org.

The Least You Need to Know

- WordPress.com offers limited features for free. You can purchase some additional advanced features for a fee.
- WordPress.org offers maximum flexibility and functionality but requires more technical savvy and an investment in an account with a web hosting service.
- Consider your budget, customization needs, technical courage, and long-term goals before deciding on a WordPress version.
- You can switch WordPress versions after you start your blog but not without some potential negative effects.

Writing for the Blogosphere

You've chosen your WordPress application, decided on a blog topic, and established your goals. Now it's time to be sure you know how to write a blog people will actually want to read.

Part 2 teaches you how to find blog post ideas, write for the social web, and remain a welcome member of the larger blogging community. You also learn about the various rules and ethical considerations bloggers must be aware of in order to stay out of legal or personal trouble on the World Wide Web.

Creating Content

In This Chapter

- Finding inspiration for post ideas
- Developing the right style for you and your audience
- The elements of a blog post
- Tips for blog-writing success

There are no *real* rules for writing blog posts, but before you start typing anything and everything on your blog, some tips might be helpful before you get started—especially if you want to grow your blog's audience over time. Your WordPress blog is your own to write as you wish, but depending on your goals, you might want to put more thought into what you write, how you write it, and why you write it before you hit the publish button.

This chapter introduces you to the world of blog writing. You learn about the specific elements of blog posts you can use to make your posts even better, and the specific techniques you can use to format and write your posts to make them more enjoyable for your readers. We also look at some tricks to blog-writing success you might want to apply to your own blog.

Coming Up with Blog Post Ideas

Popular blogs are updated frequently, and that means they always include fresh content. Your posts should be current, and your content should be unique—no one wants to read a stale blog. That doesn't mean you have to be the *only* person who writes a blog post about a specific topic, but it does mean your take on that topic should be uniquely yours. In other words, you need to add value to the existing online conversation about that subject. This applies to writing your blog overall as well as writing individual blog posts.

WordPress gives you the tools you need to become a web publisher, but it's up to you to create the content that attracts and retains readers.

Getting Ideas from Other Blogs and Sources

The best bloggers read a lot. To keep a fresh list of blog post ideas coming, you should have a go-to list of blogs and sources you check periodically for new ideas to resolve an occasional bout of "blogger's block."

Following are several ideas to get your source list started:

Blog searches: Use Google Blog Search or IceRocket.com (discussed in Chapter 1) to find other blogs related to your own blog topic. Visit these blogs to see what bloggers are writing about. However, *never* copy and republish another person's content. Always write your own blog post, adding your own thoughts on a topic, and attribute the original story source with a link. (Learn more about attributing sources in Chapter 4.)

Blog feeds: Subscribe to the *feeds* of blogs you like and blogs related to your own blog topic. Check your *feed reader* to get post ideas.

News sites: Keep on top of daily news by visiting popular news sites to see what journalists are talking about.

Twitter streams: Follow people on *Twitter* who *tweet* about topics related to your blog, and check your Twitter stream to learn what people find interesting enough to tweet about each day.

> **DEFINITION**
>
> A **feed** is syndicated blog content. The most common format for blog feeds is RSS (Really Simple Syndication). **Feed readers** gather and display blog feeds for quick and easy viewing in one place, such as Google Reader. (See Chapter 19 for more on feeds.) **Twitter** is a popular microblogging application where users can publish short (140 characters or fewer) updates to their personal profiles. A **tweet** is an update published by a Twitter user.

Social networking sites: Poke around on Facebook (www.facebook.com) and LinkedIn (www.linkedin.com) to see what your friends and connections are posting about.

Social bookmarking sites: Check out the latest content shared on sites like Digg (digg. com), StumbleUpon (www.stumbleupon.com), and Yahoo! Buzz (buzz.yahoo.com) to see what people are sharing related to your blog topic.

For example, if you blog about baseball, you can select the Baseball category on Digg to view popular shared content, as shown in Figure 3-1. Just follow the links to view the content listed to help you get ideas for blog posts of your own.

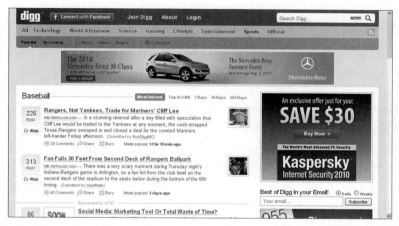

Figure 3-1 *You can view popular shared content by category on Digg.*
(Courtesy of Digg)

The more time you spend reading content online, the more sources you'll find. In time, you'll find favorite sources you check daily and others you only check on occasion.

Never stop looking for new sources, and always take the time to reach out to the people behind your favorite online sources in an effort to develop relationships with them. Leave comments on their blog posts, retweet their Twitter updates, send them an e-mail to introduce yourself, and so on. These are the types of relationships that can help you over your lifetime as a blogger.

Looking for "Link Bait"

An important part of building your WordPress blog is attracting incoming links, which help boost your search engine rankings. Search engines like Google build their algorithms around a variety of criteria, but one factor that can boost a page's ranking in keyword search results is incoming links. The theory is that no one will link to content that stinks. Therefore, a page that has a lot of incoming links, especially from popular sites, must have great content and should be rewarded with higher search rankings than substandard pages.

With that theory in mind, many bloggers try to publish posts for the sole purpose of attracting incoming links. These posts are called *link bait posts*.

PROCEED WITH CAUTION

Link bait posts can boost incoming links and drive short-term traffic spikes, but they do little in terms of creating loyal, long-term readers.

The trick to using link bait posts to grow your blog is to write about link bait topics your core audience is likely to be interested in. Then, people who find your blog through a link bait post that's directly related to your blog's topic are more likely to find even more content on your blog they'll be interested in. That means they'll linger, click around, and return later.

Here are some suggestions for places to find link bait post ideas:

Google Trends: Google Trends (google.com/trends/hottrends) is a great place to find link bait ideas because it enables you to find the most searched keyword phrases on any given day. Google Trends updates frequently each day. If you can catch the "lightning in a bottle" from one of these hot search topics, your blog could see a big spike in traffic. Figure 3-2 shows a list of hot searches on Google Trends.

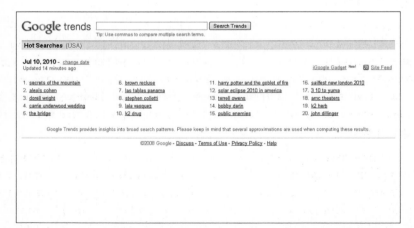

Figure 3-2   *Google Trends provides a list of hot searches updated throughout the day.*
(Courtesy of Google)

Twitter trending topics: Visit Twitter and view the scrolling bar near the top half of the page, shown in Figure 3-3, to see what topics people are talking about a lot at that moment. You can also view trending Twitter topics in the right sidebar of your Twitter profile when you're logged in to Twitter.

Figure 3-3   *Find hot Twitter topics on the Twitter home page.*
(Courtesy of Twitter)

Writing Posts

Once you determine the voice you want to write with, you need to consider the various elements that make up a blog post and decide which to include in your own posts based on your goals for your blog. A number of characteristics and techniques separate great bloggers from the rest of the pack, beginning with establishing a unique voice and adding value to the online conversation. However, the various pieces you include in your posts also make a difference. Let's take a look at some of the most important elements:

Voice   The best blogs are written by people who aren't afraid to let their personalities shine through in their posts. And because WordPress allows you to interact with your readers through the commenting feature, you can further express your personality as you engage in conversations with your readers. If you hope to build a successful blog, you need to let your audience know who you are and what they can expect from you and your blog by choosing and sticking with a distinct voice to use in your writing that your audience can rely on over the long term.

Length   Your posts should be long enough to get your point across and add some kind of value to the online conversation. Try to publish posts at least 250 characters long if you want to get any kind of search engine traffic. However, keep your blog posts under 800 words (I prefer under 600 words) to appeal to the majority of blog readers who want information quickly and succinctly.

INSIDER SECRET

Your blog posts can be however long you want them to be, but if you have bigger goals for your blog than simply having a personal creative outlet, you should think about the length of your posts as you write them.

Links   If your blogging goals are limited, using links isn't as important as it is if you want your blog to grow into a popular online destination. Links serve multiple purposes:

- Links from your posts to other blogs can send traffic their way and, therefore, put your blog on their radars, which could mean more traffic from their blogs to yours.

- Links within your own blog can help with search engine optimization (as discussed in Chapter 19), boost page views, and keep people on your blog longer.

- Strategic links can offer valuable information to your readers, who will appreciate when you point them in the right direction to learn more.

Don't stuff your blog posts full of links. Search engine optimization experts suggest including no more than one link for every 125 words.

Images   Taking a few minutes to find and add images to your blog posts is definitely worth it if you want to build a successful blog. Images serve a few purposes in your blog posts:

- Images add visual appeal and break up text-heavy pages.

- Images allow you to add supporting information such as charts, graphs, photos, and so on, which can clarify the points you make in your blog posts.

- Images can boost search engine traffic if you name the images you include in your blog posts with keywords and use those keywords in the HTML *Alt-tag* when you upload them to your WordPress account.

DEFINITION

The **Alt-tag** is a piece of HTML code used to identify the text that displays on-screen when a web browser cannot load the image that's supposed to display on a page. The Alt-tag name is short for Alternate Tag.

Before you publish images in a blog post, always resize, crop, and save them to a web-friendly resolution (72 dpi is usually adequate) and file format (.png, .jpg, and .gif are the most commonly used) to create the smallest file sizes possible. Larger images take up more storage space in your hosting account and take longer to load on-screen. Depending on your WordPress account and hosting limits, as discussed in Chapter 2, the amount of space available to you to store images can vary. Furthermore, visitors don't like to wait for large images to load on their screens. You can learn about several image editing tools in Chapter 10.

Only use images on your blog you have permission to publish. Otherwise, you run the risk of violating copyright laws. (Learn about copyright laws in Chapter 4.)

Frequency   If you're a casual blogger, you can publish new content whenever you want, as often or as infrequently as you like. If you want to develop a successful blog with a big audience, you need to publish new content frequently. If you want …

- Maximum growth potential, publish new content multiple times per day.

- Moderate growth potential, publish new content at least once per day.

- Slow growth potential, publish new content at least three times per week.

PROCEED WITH CAUTION

Growing your blog audience depends on more than just publishing new content. Be sure to read Part 5 to learn more about driving traffic to your blog.

Writing Tips

The ideas discussed throughout this chapter can help you write a better blog people will actually want to read. Here are additional quick tips that can make you a better blogger:

- Proofread your blog posts.

- Publish original content.

- Use keywords in your link text to increase search engine traffic.
- Write post titles that encourage or tease people to read more.
- Use keywords in your post titles to boost search traffic.
- Write in short paragraphs that are easier to read on-screen.
- Use bulleted lists and headings to break up text.
- Link to sources.
- Be consistent in voice and style.

Take some time to read a lot of blogs and analyze what other bloggers are doing that you like. Blogging isn't about reinventing the wheel; it's about bringing something new, different, or extra to the party. You can do that by writing great blog posts in your own unique voice.

The Least You Need to Know

- Finding ideas to keep your blog post writing flowing requires a lot of reading.
- The best blogs are written by bloggers with distinct and consistent styles and voices.
- Successful bloggers write posts that are easy to read in terms of length, tone, visual appeal, and format.
- To grow your blog's audience, you need to publish new content at least once a day.

Blogging by the Rules

In This Chapter

- Crediting your sources
- Understanding copyright laws
- Finding images you can use on your blog
- Creating your own blog policies
- Following WordPress's rules

When you start a blog using WordPress and join the world of online publishing, you must follow a variety of written and unwritten rules. Laws and ethics apply to every blogger, and you must follow them if you want to stay out of legal trouble and remain a welcome member of the blogging community.

This chapter introduces you to some of the legal and ethical considerations that affect you as a blogger. You also learn how to create your own blog policies and establish a user experience your visitors can rely on. Additionally, you learn what you need to do to avoid violating any WordPress policies.

Using Links and Providing Attribution

When you write a blog post about a topic you found via another blog or website, you should attribute your source with a link. Give credit where credit is due. Not only is it the right thing to do ethically, but it can help your blog grow, thanks to WordPress's *trackback* function.

DEFINITION

A **trackback** is a virtual shoulder tap from one blog to another. When you publish a blog post that includes a link to another blog that has enabled its trackback function, the link to your blog post is published within the comments section of the other blog.

An example of a trackback published in the comments section of a WordPress blog is shown in Figure 4-1. Some other blogging applications, like TypePad, publish trackbacks as well, but these trackbacks are not automated. You need to insert the source URL in the **Send Trackbacks To** field within your WordPress post editor in order for those trackbacks to publish on the source blog. (Don't worry about how to do this right now. I discuss it in detail in Chapter 9.)

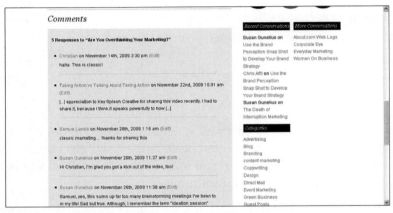

Figure 4-1 *A trackback publishes as a comment on a WordPress blog post.*
(Courtesy of KeySplashCreative.com)

Trackbacks can help boost traffic to your blog because people who read the other blog where the trackback is published can follow the link to read your blog post, too. The trackback also notifies the other blogger that you linked to his content in your own post. It's a great way to reach out to another blogger to show him you helped share his content and begin to form a relationship with him.

Following Copyright Laws

It bears repeating: you must link to and provide attribution for your sources. Bloggers who publish content on the public Internet are bound by copyright laws. You don't want to be accused of plagiarizing another person's work, so it's imperative that you always publish original content on your blog and properly cite your sources.

PROCEED WITH CAUTION

The WordPress.com Terms of Service prohibit copyright violations.

A gray area of copyright law, called fair use, affects bloggers. Under fair use, publishers can republish another person's content to add commentary or for educational purposes. However, the safest course of action for a blogger is to only republish snippets from other sources along with a link to that source. Also, add your own opinion to the snippet, so the vast majority of content on your blog is original.

Following this guideline will help you stay out of legal trouble and ensure your search engine rankings are not negatively affected, because sites that simply republish content from other sites are often penalized or banned from search engine results. (I discuss this in greater detail in Chapter 18.)

What Images Can You Use on Your Blog?

A very common question among bloggers—both beginner and seasoned bloggers—is related to using images on blogs and in blog posts. Copyright laws protect the original owner of any work, and images are protected by copyright laws just as words and music are. It might seem like a great idea to create a celebrity gossip blog and link to pictures you find on entertainment sites, but doing so is likely to be a violation of copyright laws.

To use an image on your blog without violating any laws, you need permission. You can get permission by requesting it from the image owner, or you can find sources that provide images with copyrights attached to them that allow you to republish them on your blog. The most common copyright licenses you need to understand are: rights-managed, royalty-free, and Creative Commons.

Rights-Managed

Rights-managed copyright licenses are based on usage and require that you either pay the owner for the rights to use the images on your blog or get permission to use the images on your blog. Typically, you must pay a fee each time you want to use a rights-managed image.

An example of a site that offers rights-managed images is Getty Images (www. gettyimages.com).

Royalty-Free

Royalty-free copyrighted images typically come with a price tag, but you can pay one time and use the purchased image again and again. Some royalty-free images don't have price tags but do come with restrictions that require you to credit the source or perform other actions in order to use them as dictated by the image owner. Royalty-free images are often referred to as *stock images*.

An example of a site that offers royalty-free images is stock.XCHNG (sxc.hu), which offers both images for free (with restrictions attached) and for a fee.

Creative Commons

Creative Commons (creativecommons.org) is an organization that helps owners of original works share those works in a less-restrictive manner than copyright laws allow. Creative Commons offers six types of licenses:

- *Attribution:* Anyone can republish the work with proper attribution to the owner.

- *Attribution Share Alike:* Anyone can modify the work in any way and republish it with proper attribution to the owner as long as the new version of the work is licensed using the same Creative Commons license as the original work.

- *Attribution No Derivatives:* Anyone can republish the work with proper attribution to the owner as long as no changes are made to the work.

- *Attribution Non-Commercial:* Anyone can republish the work for noncommercial purposes with proper attribution to the owner.

- *Attribution Non-Commercial Share Alike:* Anyone can modify the work in any way and republish it for noncommercial purposes with proper attribution to the owner as long as the new version of the work is licensed using the same Creative Commons license as the original work.

• *Attribution Non-Commercial No Derivatives:* Anyone can republish the image for noncommercial purposes with proper attribution to the owner and as long as no changes are made to the work.

You can learn more about finding images you can use on your blog and inserting them into your posts in Chapter 10.

Be Mindful of Spam

The last thing you want as a blogger is to earn a reputation as a *spammer*, which you can unintentionally do if you break some of the unwritten rules of WordPress or the blogosphere. The *social web* is a great place to promote yourself, your business, and so on, but members of the blogosphere don't like self-promoters. The key to growing your blog and your online reputation is to use *indirect* self-promotion. So then what's a blogger to do to promote her blog?

DEFINITION

A **spammer** is someone who floods the Internet with messages of a solicitous nature. This is particularly common on the **social web,** which is the term used to describe the evolution of the Internet where user-generated content and two-way conversations via the use of tools like blogs, Twitter, Facebook, and so on, became common means of global communications.

I tell you how to correctly promote you blog later in Chapter 21. But for now, let's look at what *not* to do. Following a few ground rules should keep you from being labeled as a spammer.

Don't leave comments on other blogs filled with links. It's tempting, but don't do it. Instead, use the URL field in the blog comment form for your self-promotional link.

Don't leave comments on other blogs that don't add value to the conversation. Be sure to say something interesting, or blog owners will think you're just trying to get a free link back to your own blog.

Don't clutter other bloggers' e-mail in-boxes with link requests and other self-promotional content. Instead of annoying other bloggers, send them information they'll find interesting and start to develop a relationship with them that will help you build your blog in the long term.

The more time you spend blogging and reading other blogs, the easier it will be for you to identify the tactics and behaviors members of the blogosphere frown upon. Once you gain a reputation as a spammer or a blogger who flouts the ethics of blogging, it's very difficult to get off the blogger blacklist.

Creating Policies

Your blog is your own space on the web, and depending on your goals, you can publish the type of content you want and not publish the type of content you don't want. That's where blog policies come into the picture. Policies are intended to protect you and your audience as well as set expectations about the type of content that will or will not be published on your blog.

You need to establish three primary types of blog policies:

- Comment policy
- Privacy policy
- Terms and conditions of use policy

There's no set format or text you're required to use in your blog policies—in fact, publishing blog policies is entirely up to you. But it's important to understand the basic purposes of blog policies and what information is typically found in them so you can create the most appropriate policies for your own blog.

Comment Policy

As your blog grows and your posts receive more and more comments, you'll undoubtedly receive comments you don't want to publish on your blog or that require minor editing before you'll publish them. For example, hateful comments that attack individuals usually aren't welcome on blogs, and comments that include obscenities could be offensive. Similarly, comments that might be spam can hurt the user experience on your blog and should be deleted.

A comment policy allows you to define what types of comments you will delete or edit using the comment moderation tools in your WordPress account. Your comment policy also protects you, so you can refer visitors whose comments are edited or deleted to your established policy to understand why their comments were revised or not published at all.

Following is a sample blog comment policy. It can help you get started in writing your own policy for your blog.

Comments submitted to this blog may be edited or deleted in the following situations:

1. Comments that are considered spam or potential spam will be deleted. This includes comments that are irrelevant or with multiple links that are irrelevant to the blog post to which they are attached.

2. Comments including profanity will be edited or deleted.

3. Comments that could be deemed offensive will be deleted.

4. Comments that attack a person or entity will be deleted.

The owner of this blog reserves the right to edit or delete any comments submitted to this blog at her own discretion and without notice. This comment policy is subject to change at any time and without notice.

Privacy Policy

A privacy policy is used to tell visitors to your blog about the kind of information you collect when they visit your blog and what information you share with third parties. For example, some blog advertising programs require that the advertiser be able to collect and store information about visitors to your blog in order to serve more appropriate ads in the future. If you participate in this type of program, it's likely that the advertising program will require you to publish a privacy policy on your blog explaining the type of information collected about each visitor and what that data is used for.

PROCEED WITH CAUTION

Be wary of publishing ads from advertisers that collect or share information about visitors to your blog but do not require that you publish a privacy policy outlining their tactics. If private information is collected about your blog visitors (even if it's done by a third-party advertiser), you are required by law to disclose that it's happening.

Similarly, if you use a web analytics tool like Google Analytics (google.com/analytics), StatCounter (statcounter.com), or Site Meter (sitemeter.com) to track your blog's performance based on visits to your blog, you're collecting information about visitors' travels across your blog. You should publish a privacy policy on your blog that explains the type of information collected and why.

Here's a sample, generic privacy policy for a blog that does track analytics but does not collect or share any other kind of visitor data. Use it to help you get started in creating your own policy for your blog.

> *We do not share personal information or behavioral information with third parties. We do not store information we collect about your visit to this blog for use other than to analyze content performance through the use of cookies, which you can turn off at any time by modifying your web browser's settings. We are not responsible for the republishing of the content found on this blog on other websites or media without our permission. This privacy policy is subject to change at any time and without notice.*

Terms and Conditions of Use Policy

You should publish a terms and conditions of use policy on your blog to protect you. It outlines everything people agree to by visiting your blog.

> **QUICK TIP**
>
> You may want to consult with an attorney to ensure your blog policies fully protect you from potential lawsuits and other threats.

Following is a generic sample terms and conditions of use policy you can use to write your own.

> *The content provided on this blog is for informational purposes only. The owner of this blog makes no representations as to the accuracy or completeness of any information on this site or found by following any link on this site. The owner will not be liable for any errors or omissions in the information available on this site or by following any link on this site nor for the availability of this information. The owner will not be liable for any losses, injuries, or damages from the display or use of this information. These terms and conditions of use are subject to change at any time and without notice.*

Keep in mind that blog policies are meant to accomplish two primary goals: establish visitor expectations and protect you. Take some time to read policies on other blogs, create your own to meet your needs, and provide the full disclosures and protection you require.

WordPress Policies

WordPress has its own policies users must adhere to or risk having their blogs deleted. This primarily applies to WordPress.com users, but WordPress.org users must follow policies related to using the WordPress application as well as policies from their web hosting providers.

QUICK TIP

Most blog hosting providers publish their terms of service on their sites. For example, check out the policies for two popular blog hosting providers, BlueHost (www.bluehost.com/cgi/info/terms.html) and HostGator (www. hostgator.com/tos/tos.php).

You can view the WordPress policies at these pages:

- WordPress.com Terms of Service: en.wordpress.com/tos
- WordPress.com Privacy Policy: automattic.com/privacy
- WordPress.org Privacy Policy: wordpress.org/about/privacy/

The WordPress privacy policies apply to you, personally, and your rights as a WordPress.com or WordPress.org visitor or user. The WordPress.com Terms of Service applies to anyone who creates a blog using WordPress.com.

While these policies seem lengthy and complicated, they're actually fairly easy to understand. Take the time to read through the policies that apply to you, depending on the version of WordPress you use, and adhere to them at all times.

The Least You Need to Know

- You must credit your sources and avoid violating copyright laws on your blog.
- Avoid being labeled a spammer or publishing spam on your own blog. If you don't, you risk gaining a negative reputation among the blogging community or violating WordPress policies.
- Publishing your own blog policies can protect you from some ethical and legal entanglements.
- If you use WordPress, you must read and adhere to WordPress's policies at all times.

Starting Your Blog with WordPress.com

It's time to blog! Part 3 is for people who have chosen WordPress.com for their blogging tool. (However, much of the content related to creating posts and pages and configuring settings applies to WordPress.org users, too.) I recommend all bloggers start a free test blog on WordPress.com to become familiar with the features and capabilities before investing the time and money into creating a WordPress.org blog to ensure they like to blog and like WordPress. Therefore, Part 3 is important for all WordPress bloggers.

In Part 3, you learn how to create an account at WordPress.com and what all the boxes and links are for you to see on your screen when you log in to your account. I take you through each screen and each function step by step, so you can set up your blog, customize your settings to your liking, modify your blog's design, write blog posts, add pages to your blog, and try all the various options and features available to you. In addition, you learn what upgrades are available to you.

The Nuts and Bolts of a WordPress Blog

In This Chapter

* Understanding WordPress blog domain names
* Learning the parts of a WordPress blog
* The invisible extras of a WordPress blog

WordPress blogs contain lots of parts and pieces. Some are easily identifiable to the novice user, while others are a bit more difficult to understand. This chapter clears up all the confusion, starting with domain names and moving through the visible and invisible parts of a WordPress blog so you know what's what.

If you're moving to WordPress from another blogging application such as Google Blogger, you need to learn some new terms and some new definitions for terms you might already know. WordPress offers additional functionality some other blogging applications don't, and some terms have different meanings from one blogging application to another, even though they're basically the same things. Don't let this intimidate you. The following pages explain it all. Read this chapter thoroughly, and soon you'll understand what everything means and does.

The Domain Name Challenge

There are two "names" related to your blog. First, there's the title of your blog. For example, I own a blog called "Women on Business." That's the title of the blog. I can use that title in many ways in my blog's WordPress design, when I refer to my blog in communications, and so on, but that's not the only name for my blog. I can also refer to it by its domain name, which is WomenOnBusiness.com.

Every site on the Internet has a unique domain name, which is part of the address, or URL (Uniform Resource Locator), you type into your web browser to go to a specific web page. A URL includes three main parts:

- *Access protocol:* The generic access protocol for most URLs in the United States is *http*.

- *Domain name:* The domain name for my blog is *www.WomenOnBusiness.com.* It includes three elements: *www, site name* (WomenOnBusiness), and *.com.* (Some sites use *.net, .biz, .org,* etc., at the end.)

- *Extension:* One example of a specific page address within a website is */pagename.htm.* The / and extension are tacked on to the end of the main page's URL, so visitors can navigate to individual pages within that site.

You need to think about two things when you start a new blog: the title and the domain name you want to use. Coming up with a title depends entirely on how you want to uniquely brand your blog. (Learn more about choosing your blog title in Chapter 6.)

 INSIDER SECRET

If your blog is hosted by WordPress, your blog's URL automatically includes .wordpress.com at the end of the domain name. If you want, you can pay for an upgrade to your account to remove it and use your own registered domain name instead.

Choosing your blog's domain can be a challenge. Because so many websites already exist, the domain name you want might already be taken. To avoid getting your heart set on one name and it not being available, before you even create your blog, make a list of domain name options you'd be happy with. Then see what's still available. (Chapter 6 offers more tips and suggestions to help you choose and find the best domain name for your blog.)

The Parts of a Blog

It's fairly safe to say that no two WordPress blogs look exactly alike. Not only does the content of a blog make it unique, but the design can give it a distinct brand persona as well. However, despite the design nuances from one blog to the next, the vast majority of WordPress blogs are made up of the same basic elements.

Themes

A theme is a template that gives you the skeleton design and layout of your WordPress blog. All you have to do is choose a theme, input your content, and your blog is ready! Of course, you can also customize elements in your WordPress theme to make it stand out from the crowd.

One of the reasons it's so easy to make your WordPress blog unique is because WordPress offers so many theme options to choose from. If you use the free WordPress.com application, you have a lot of themes to choose from, and you can customize them in a variety of ways. If you use WordPress.org, the options are practically limitless!

Three types of WordPress themes are available:

- Free
- Premium
- Custom

Free WordPress themes are available to WordPress.com users through their WordPress dashboards and to WordPress.org users through designers found across the web.

Premium WordPress themes are available to WordPress.org users and are typically offered for a reasonable price through third-party designers. You can purchase premium themes by the theme, in bundled packages, or through annual memberships, depending on which one you choose.

Custom WordPress themes are available to WordPress.org users and are developed by designers from the ground up, specifically for the sites they'll be used on. Custom themes are by far the most expensive option.

For example, take a look at Figure 5-1, which shows three of my own sites, each built using a different premium WordPress theme on WordPress.org. Notice how different the sites look from each other. Each was easy to build, thanks to the well-coded premium WordPress themes the sites started with.

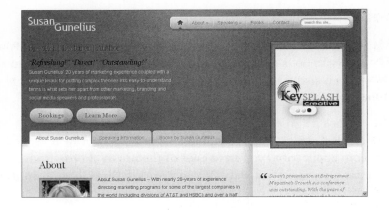

Figure 5-1   *These websites were all built with different WordPress themes, and each looks very unique.*

The Header

Most blogs include a header, which is similar to the top of the front page of a newspaper. The header spans the top of the blog and usually includes a title and an image. Sometimes a blog header includes additional elements such as changing images, clickable buttons and icons, and more.

INSIDER SECRET

If you create a free blog hosted on WordPress.com, the edits you can make to your blog's sidebar depend on the theme you choose. The changes you're allowed to make are more limited than for WordPress.org users, who have complete control over their header design.

Above or below the header, you'll often find navigation bars with links to the various pages within the blog. You can see an example of a blog header with a navigation bar beneath it in Figure 5-2.

Figure 5-2 *The blog header from the KeySplash Creative blog.*
(Courtesy of KeySplashCreative.com)

Your blog's header is the first element visitors see when they arrive at your blog. It should help readers immediately understand what your blog is about and visually draw them in. If you want your blog to be successful, take some time to create a header that uniquely brands your blog.

Pages

WordPress not only enables you to create pages on your blog, but also makes it very easy to do so. (Not all blogs have pages, and not all blogging applications give users the option to create pages on their blogs.)

A typical website is made up of multiple pages, each identified by the / and extension used in the site's URL, as explained earlier in this chapter. WordPress blogs can also have pages, which are different from blog posts. Pages live on your blog outside your chronological blog post archives and are often accessible through the top navigation bar. Notice the links in the top navigation bar in the WordPress blog shown in Figure 5-2. Each of those links takes you to a different page on that site.

You can create any pages you want on your blog. Common ones include the following:

- About page
- Contact page
- Privacy policy page

Unlike posts, WordPress pages are not interactive, and visitors cannot publish comments on pages. Pages also cannot be categorized, and tags cannot be included with pages. (More on posts, comments, categories, and tags coming right up.)

Posts

Your blog posts, or the individual entries you write and publish, are the heart of your blog. Your blog posts prompt a two-way conversation between you and your readers, who can then interact with you and other readers via comments and trackbacks on your posts.

Your blog posts are typically published in reverse-chronological order, with older posts available through your archives. Posts are usually categorized so people can find them in your archives by date or by category.

WordPress also allows you to write blog posts now and schedule them for publishing later. You can also add keyword tags to your posts that serve multiple purposes, as explained later in this chapter.

Comments

Comments are what make a blog truly interactive and foster the conversations that will make your blog successful. With WordPress, you can choose to allow comments on all, some, or none of your posts. You can also set up comment moderation settings so you can preview comments before you publish them. You can even edit, delete, or flag comments as spam before they're published for your audience to see.

Comments are published in chronological order, so the most recent comment is published at the end of the comment string.

INSIDER SECRET

A variety of WordPress settings and plug-ins (for WordPress.org users) enable you to change how the comments on your blog posts are displayed. These settings and plug-ins could affect the order of comments, the type of information included with comments, and more.

An example of a blog post comment submission form is shown in Figure 5-3.

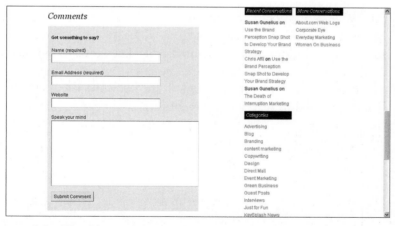

Figure 5-3 *Your blog readers can submit comments on blog posts.*
(Courtesy of KeySplashCreative.com)

The comments section can also include trackback links, other links, and updates, depending on how you configure your comment settings. (Take some time to read Chapter 7 to learn all about comment configuration.)

Categories

Categories provide an organizational system for your blog archives. The categories you use on your WordPress blog are completely up to you, and you can create new categories when you need them. As you write blog posts, you can identify one or more categories for posts to help you and your readers find related content in your archives.

QUICK TIP

Many WordPress bloggers include a list of their blog post categories in a sidebar on their main page to make it easy for readers to find more of the kind of content they want.

When a visitor to your blog clicks on a category link, as shown on the bottom right side of Figure 5-3, they are taken to a page that looks just like your main blog page, but instead of containing all your blog posts in reverse-chronological order, it contains only the posts archived in that specific category. (I discuss archives in more detail later in this chapter.)

Tags

WordPress enables you to tag your blog posts with keywords to aid search engine optimization. Technorati (technorati.com), one of the original blog search engines, originally used tags to deliver relevant content for keyword searches performed on that site. Today, tags aid in search engine optimization beyond just Technorati.com.

It's important to understand that tags are not categories and categories are not tags. Categories group like entries in your blog post archives, while tags help with search engine optimization. It's not unusual to see a blog post with multiple tags but only one category.

Think of it this way: categories live and work on your blog, but tags live and work on *and* off your blog.

Sidebars

Most WordPress themes include a sidebar where you can include just about any kind of links, videos, images, etc., you want—even a list of categories, as mentioned earlier. Common WordPress theme designs include one or two sidebars. These are either flanking or on the left or right side of your blog post column, which is almost always the widest column on your blog.

Most WordPress themes are widget ready, which means you can simply click and drag to add content to your blog sidebars. Each widget includes a different element in your sidebar, such as text, links to categories, links to recent posts, ads, and so on.

Widgets

As discussed in the previous section, widgets are the elements you use to populate your blog's sidebars. Depending on the WordPress theme you choose, the default widgets available to you may vary, but you're almost always going to find widgets that enable you to easily add text, your blog's subscription feed, recent posts, recent comments, and categories to your blog's sidebar. For example, take a look at Figure 5-4 to see a variety of common widgets available to a WordPress user.

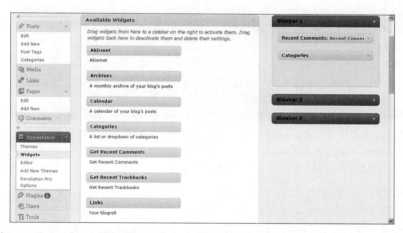

Figure 5-4 *Some WordPress themes offer a huge selection of widgets!*
(Courtesy of KeySplashCreative.com)

If you have limited technical abilities and little programming knowledge, widgets make it easy for you to customize your blog sidebars quickly—and without having to invest in hiring a developer to help! Widgets also enable you to make changes to your blog on the fly.

The Footer

Your blog's footer is the section at the bottom of your blog that appears on all (or most) of your blog pages and archives. Your blog's footer is a great place to include your copyright notice, links to your blog policies, and a handy link to your contact page.

If your WordPress theme allows it, your footer could be widgetized, making it easy to customize, like the one shown in Figure 5-5.

Figure 5-5 *A widgetized WordPress footer is easy to customize.*
(Courtesy of SusanGunelius.com)

Archives

Your blog archives are like a filing system for your older blog posts. Imagine if you publish a new blog post every day for a year. That's 365 blog posts a visitor has to scroll through if she's looking for a specific post. Archives make it easy to find that older post by cataloging posts by date and category. You can even publish links to your archives by category or date in your WordPress blog's sidebar.

Blog post archives also give blogs a search lift because older content is always available for search engines to find! Additionally, people can always find your older posts via historical links from other sites and blogs because they live forever (or until you delete them) in your blog archives.

PROCEED WITH CAUTION

Your blog posts live online indefinitely through your blog archives, so what you publish today will be available through searches and links for years to come. Be sure your archives don't damage your current reputation or brand!

Subscriptions and Feeds

When people like your blog, they can subscribe to it. That means they can choose to have your new blog posts delivered to them via e-mail or their preferred feed readers (such as Google Reader). The process of creating your blog's feed using RSS (Really Simple Syndication) is discussed in detail in Chapter 19.

You can promote your blog's feed and encourage people to subscribe to it in your blog's sidebar, as shown in Figure 5-1. Most WordPress themes make it very easy to add a subscription widget to your blog's sidebar.

The Least You Need to Know

- Creating a blog starts with understanding the difference between your blog's title and domain name.
- Before you create a WordPress blog, you need to learn the parts of a blog and terms specific to WordPress.
- WordPress uses categories, tags, widgets, and archives to turn ordinary blogs into powerful social web tools.
- Offering feed subscriptions to your blog content creates another way for people to read your posts.

Creating a WordPress.com Blog

In This Chapter

- Creating your WordPress account
- Starting your first WordPress blog
- Getting to know the WordPress dashboard

You're ready to start your first blog, and you've chosen to use the free WordPress.com blogging application. Congratulations and welcome to the blogosphere! You're sure to meet new people from around the world here—and have a lot of fun!

The first step to launching your WordPress-hosted blog is to create a WordPress.com account. In this chapter, I teach you how to create your own account and start your first blog with WordPress.com. I also introduce you to the WordPress dashboard, the place online where you'll do everything to manage your blog, including writing and publishing posts, configuring your sidebars, setting up comment moderation, and much more!

There's a lot to learn, but don't feel overwhelmed! This chapter breaks down what could feel daunting into easily digestible pieces. Let's get blogging!

Establishing Your WordPress.com Account

Your new life as a blogger begins with a visit to WordPress.com, as shown in Figure 6-1. To create your own WordPress account, click the **Sign up now** button in the upper-right side of the page.

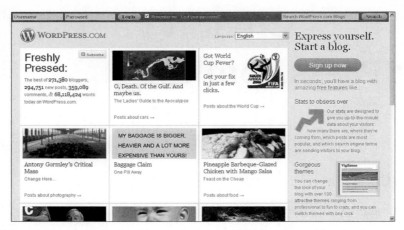

Figure 6-1 *Visit the WordPress.com home page to start your blog.*
(Courtesy of WordPress.com)

A form opens, as shown in Figure 6-2, where you are asked to enter a blog address, username, and password as well as your e-mail address. You can't change your username once you select it, so try to choose one you'll be happy with for the long haul. Furthermore, your e-mail address is imperative, because after you submit your completed form, WordPress sends you an automated e-mail with your WordPress account activation link. You must click on the link in the e-mail to activate your account. Be sure the e-mail address you enter in this form is accurate!

PROCEED WITH CAUTION

The username and e-mail address you enter in the sign-up form cannot already be used by another WordPress account or you'll receive an error message prompting you to select an alternative.

Finally, it's a good idea to click the link below the **Sign up** button to read the **fascinating terms of service**, which you automatically agree to by submitting the form.

After you've completed the form, click the **Sign up** button to register your new account and blog. When you do so, a page opens like the one shown in Figure 6-3. This notifies you that an e-mail has been sent to the address you provided when you registered your account with a link you need to follow to activate your new WordPress account.

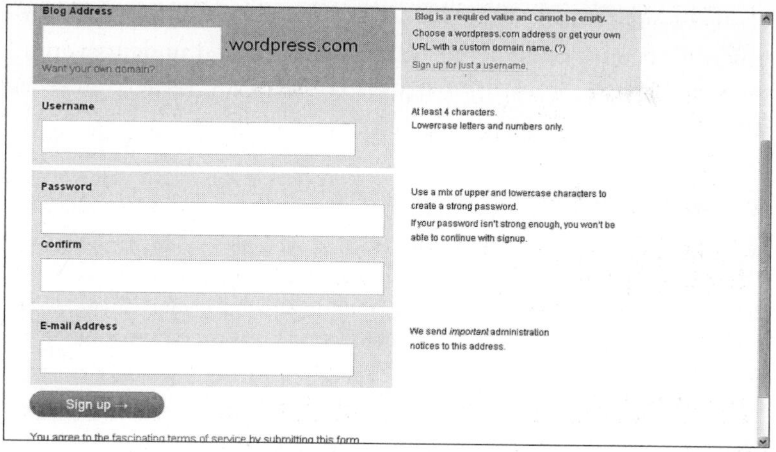

Figure 6-2 *Complete this form to create your WordPress account.*
(Courtesy of WordPress.com)

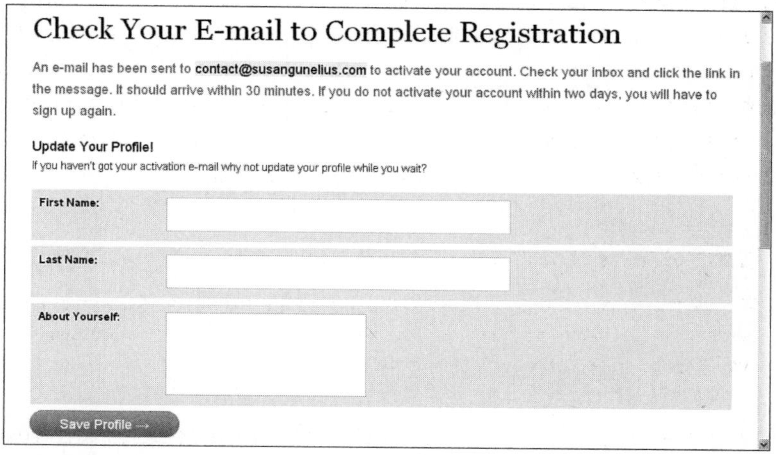

Figure 6-3 *Registration and activation of your blog is not complete until you receive the registration e-mail.*
(Courtesy of WordPress.com)

Notice in Figure 6-3 that you're given two choices to proceed. You can either wait to receive the e-mail from WordPress to activate your account and blog, which typically only takes a few minutes to arrive, or you can make some basic entries to your *profile* first. I recommend waiting to create your personal profile until you activate your account via the e-mail you receive from WordPress. You'll need to visit this section of your WordPress account once it's activated to access and update even more settings. To save time, you can do it all at once after your account is activated, as described later in this chapter.

DEFINITION

Your WordPress **profile** is similar to a short biography you create by filling in fields from the My Profile section of your WordPress dashboard. It can include your name, contact information, and other details about yourself you want to share. If you prefer, you can also publish your personal information on a separate "About" page on your WordPress blog.

If you choose this option, you don't have to do anything on the WordPress registration completion page shown in Figure 6-3. Instead, click the link in the activation e-mail shown in Figure 6-4 to activate your new WordPress.com blog.

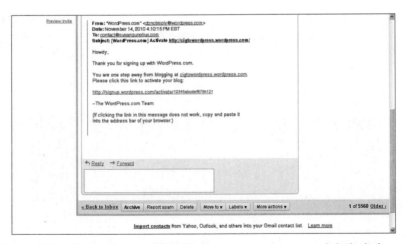

Figure 6-4 *To complete your WordPress account registration, click the link sent in your activation e-mail.*
(Courtesy of WordPress.com)

Once you click the activation link in your registration e-mail from WordPress, you'll be taken to the **Your account is now active!** page, shown in Figure 6-5, where you can log in to your new account.

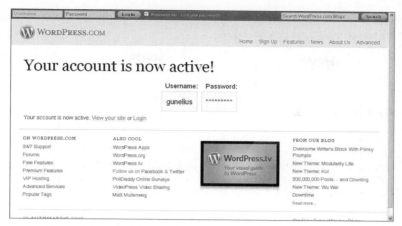

Figure 6-5 *When your account is active, you can view your WordPress blog or log in to your account.*
(Courtesy of WordPress.com)

Notice on this page that you can follow a link to **View your site** or **Login** to your WordPress account. Click the **View your site** link near the center of the page, so you can see your new blog. It should look just like the one in Figure 6-6.

Figure 6-6 *A new WordPress blog looks good right out of the gate!*

It's that easy to create your own WordPress blog shell. Now, you just have to customize it and add content! To get started, click the **Login** link in the center of the page, as shown in Figure 6-5, to open the login page for your blog, shown in Figure 6-7. Enter your username and password.

QUICK TIP

Bookmark the WordPress login page in your web browser so it's easy to find when you need to log in to your WordPress account later.

Figure 6-7   *Enter your username and password to log in to your WordPress dashboard.*

(Courtesy of WordPress.com)

Click the **Log In** button to open your WordPress account and go to your WordPress dashboard, shown in Figure 6-8. Your WordPress dashboard is where you can make all the changes, enter all the content, and do all the things you want to do to your blog. If your dashboard doesn't open automatically, click the **Dashboard** link in the My Blog drop-down list in the top navigation bar that appears after you log in.

The remainder of this chapter helps you understand what all those links and sections on your WordPress dashboard are about, and in later chapters, you learn how to use the majority of these components to personalize your blog.

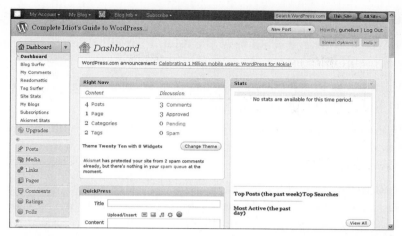

Figure 6-8 *All your blog-management tasks are easily accessible from your WordPress dashboard.*
(Courtesy of WordPress.com)

Your Dashboard's Admin Bar

The easiest place to start is with the Admin Bar, the navigation bar that spans the width of your WordPress dashboard. This navigation bar, visible above all WordPress.com-hosted blogs when you're logged in to your WordPress account, includes four primary links with drop-down menus providing additional links:

- My Account
- My Blog
- Blog Info
- Subscribe

In addition, to the right of the Admin Bar, you'll see a search box. Here you can input keywords to search within your own blog or to find other WordPress.com-hosted blogs related to topics of interest to you.

My Account

The My Account link and sublinks in the Admin Bar allow you to navigate to a number of useful features.

New Quick Press Post This link opens a rudimentary blog post editor where you can input and publish blog posts quickly.

Edit My Profile Your Public Profile is available to anyone with Internet access. You can add as much or as little information to this profile as you want to help people get to know you.

Read Freshly Pressed Quickly navigate to the Freshly Pressed section of WordPress.com, which shows the 10 handpicked posts published by WordPress.com users each day as chosen by the WordPress.com staff.

Read Posts I Like When you visit other WordPress.com blogs, you can click the **Like** button in the top navigation bar of any blog post on WordPress.com to add that post to your list of Likes accessible through your WordPress dashboard. Once you "like" them, you can easily find them again later.

Read My Subscriptions To quickly access and read WordPress.com-hosted blogs you enjoy, you can subscribe to and read them in this section of your account.

Manage My Subscriptions If you want to receive e-mail messages when specific WordPress.com-hosted blogs are updated with new posts, you can add and manage e-mail subscriptions in this section of your account.

Track My Comments See when people reply to comments you've left on WordPress.com blogs in this section of your account.

Global Dashboard This page provides information from WordPress, as well as links to new and popular posts from other WordPress.com-hosted blogs.

Get Support This link provides information about all aspects of the WordPress.com application.

Log Out You can log out of your WordPress account by clicking this link in the My Account menu.

 INSIDER SECRET

To reveal a list of links to specific sections of the Support site, as shown in Figure 6-9, click the **Help** link on the right side of your main WordPress dashboard screen located directly beneath the **Log Out** link.

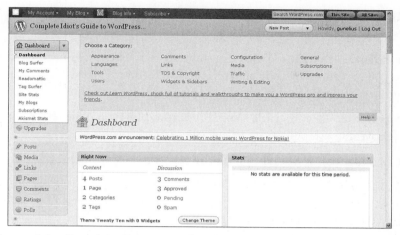

Figure 6-9 *Reveal the **Help** links in your WordPress.com dashboard to quickly access the WordPress.com Support site.*

My Blog

The My Blog link and sublinks in the Admin Bar allow you to navigate to a number of useful features and frequently used features related to your own blog.

Dashboard You can quickly navigate to the main page of your WordPress blog's dashboard by clicking the **Dashboard** link.

New Post When you log in to your WordPress account, this link makes it easy for you to quickly navigate to the new post section of your dashboard.

Site Stats Here you can access high-level statistics related to your blog's performance.

Manage Comments Quickly navigate to your comments screen to moderate, edit, approve, or delete comments submitted to your blog posts.

Read Blog Click on this link to visit your blog's live home page.

Register a New Blog It's very easy to create a brand-new blog. Just click this link!

Blog Info

The Blog Info drop-down menu includes links you might use when you're visiting other WordPress.com-hosted blogs.

Random Post   Select this link to view a randomly selected post on the WordPress.com-hosted blog you're visiting.

Get Shortlink   If you use Twitter or another tool where you need to shorten URLs to links, you can automatically shorten the URL to any WordPress.com blog page by selecting **Get Shortlink** from the Blog Info drop-down menu.

Report as Spam   If you visit a WordPress.com blog you believe is spam, click this link to report it.

Report as Mature   If you visit a WordPress.com blog you think is only appropriate for adult audiences, click this link to report it as such.

Subscribe

If you find a WordPress.com blog you enjoy, you can subscribe to it and receive e-mail messages when that blog is updated with new posts. Just click the **Subscribe** link to add and manage your e-mail subscriptions.

INSIDER SECRET

When you're actually navigating your WordPress account dashboard, you're far more likely to access features and tools using the links in the left menu, rather than through the Admin Bar.

Navigating the WordPress.com Dashboard

The first thing you're likely to notice when you arrive at your WordPress dashboard (shown in Figure 6-8) are the many boxes of information, called modules, across the largest part of the page. You can completely customize this section, and you can show a huge amount of information about your blog here, depending on the boxes you choose to display and where you display them.

You can click on the header of any module on your dashboard to drag it to another area of the page, so the modules you're most interested in are visible *above the fold*. If you prefer, you can minimize or maximize sections by clicking on the drop-down arrow in the right corner of each module's title bar.

DEFINITION

The content visible on a web page without requiring scrolling is referred to as being **above the fold,** similar to how information in the top half of a folded newspaper's front page is visible without having to unfold or flip the newspaper to view it.

You can also click on the **Screen Options** link near the top-right side of your dashboard to reveal a hidden menu of options, shown in Figure 6-10. These options let you configure the layout of your dashboard modules in a 1-, 2-, 3-, or 4-column layout.

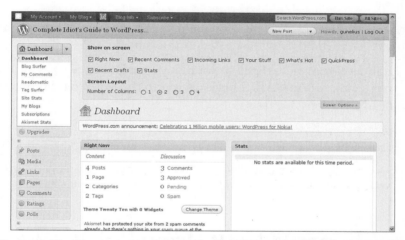

Figure 6-10 *You can customize your dashboard layout by selecting or unselecting what options you show on-screen.*

The modules available on the Screen Options section of your dashboard include the following:

Right Now This module gives you a quick snapshot of your blog's setup and content with links to access additional information within specific sections of your WordPress dashboard. For example, you can see how many posts, pages, and comments have been published, if any posts or comments are pending review before being published, and more.

Recent Comments This module shows you the five most recent comments submitted to your blog so you can review and respond to them accordingly, without having to navigate to the Comments section.

Incoming Links   This module uses Google Blog Search to generate a list of the most recent links from other blogs to yours with the active URL the links came from, so you can visit those blogs.

Your Stuff   This module shows a snapshot of your recent WordPress.com activity, both on your own blog and any comments you've submitted to other WordPress.com-hosted blogs.

What's Hot   This module includes the same news and information from across WordPress.com.

QuickPress   If you want to write a rudimentary blog post, you can do so easily from this module.

Recent Drafts   If you wrote any blog posts and saved them as drafts until you're ready to publish them, they will be listed in this module.

Stats   High-level statistics related to your blog's performance are provided in this module with a link to **View All**. This leads you to the **My Blog**, **Stats** section, as discussed earlier in this chapter.

QUICK TIP

Over time, you'll learn which modules of the dashboard you use most frequently and can configure your dashboard to look and work the way you want it to.

The Dashboard's Left Menu

The left menu of your WordPress.com dashboard gets the most use as you configure your blog and publish content. In this section, I introduce you to what you can find in the left menu so you can make sense of all those links!

The Dashboard

Many of the links available under the Dashboard section of the left menu are also available from the My Account link in the Admin Bar. The following links are *not* available through the Admin Bar:

Blog Surfer   You can keep track of blogs you like using here.

My Comments   Whenever you submit comments to WordPress.com blogs, they're also listed in this section.

Readomattic   You can subscribe to the feeds of blogs you enjoy and read them without leaving your WordPress account. You can even subscribe to Twitter profile feeds and view them here.

Tag Surfer   Enter keywords in this section's text field to view posts related to those keywords published on other WordPress.com-hosted blogs.

Site Stats   You can access high-level blog stats for your WordPress.com blog here.

My Blogs   This section gives you access to all the blogs you write for. Just click the **Register Another Blog** button to add new blogs to your list. You can also change the order, hide, view statistics, or choose your primary blog from this list. If you have multiple WordPress.com blogs that you registered here, you can also access them through the **My Dashboard** link in the Admin Bar.

Subscriptions   If you want to receive e-mail messages when specific WordPress.com-hosted blogs are updated with new posts, you can add and manage e-mail subscriptions in this section of your account. Site subscriptions can now be managed under the Subscriptions tab on the WordPress.com home page.

Akismet Stats   Akismet is a comment spam detector and blocker software that comes with WordPress.com. You can view statistics related to the comment spam Akismet has detected on your blog here.

Upgrades

When you click on the **Upgrades** link in the left menu of your WordPress dashboard, you're taken to a page that lists the types of upgrades you can purchase for your WordPress account, along with pricing.

This is the section in which you can add a domain name to your blog, and drop the .wordpress.com extension on your blog's URL. Click the **Domains** link in the Upgrades section of the left menu to do this. (These features are discussed in more detail in Chapter 13.)

Posts

You can manage all your blog post activities from the Posts section of your WordPress dashboard left menu. You can add new posts, edit existing posts, add or delete categories, and add or delete tags. (These options are discussed in detail in Chapters 9 and 10.)

Media

The Media section provides access to the library of all the images you've uploaded to your WordPress.com account to use in your blog posts or pages. You can also add new images by clicking on the **Add New** link in the Media section of the left menu.

INSIDER SECRET

You can upload .jpg, .jpeg, .png, .gif, .pdf, .doc, .ppt, .odt, .pptx, and .docx files to your free WordPress account. You can't upload video files unless you pay for an upgrade to your WordPress account. Audio files require a separate space upgrade as well.

Links

The Links section of the left menu is where you can manage lists of links to blogs and websites you like, including your blogroll. You can add new links, manage existing links, and create categories to group your links lists, which you can easily add to your blog's sidebar, as discussed in Chapter 8.

Pages

You can add, edit, delete, and manage the pages included in your blog through the Pages section of the left menu. (Pages are explained in detail in Chapter 11.)

Comments

In the Comments section of the left menu, you can access, moderate, edit, and quickly reply to all comments submitted to your blog. (Comment settings are explained in Chapter 7, and comment management is discussed in Chapter 12.)

Ratings

Through the Ratings section of the left menu, you can allow visitors to your blog to rate your blog posts, pages, or comments using a star rating system or a voting (thumbs up or thumbs down) system. (Ratings are discussed in detail in Chapter 12.)

Polls

You can quickly and easily use the Polls section of the left menu to create custom polls to publish on your blog. (For details, be sure to read Chapter 12.)

Appearance

You're likely to spend a lot of time using the Appearance section of your WordPress account, because it's through these links that you can change your blog's theme, header, sidebar, and so much more (as discussed in Chapter 8).

Users

From the Users section of the left menu, you can add new users to your WordPress.com account. This enables them to access your blog to publish posts and perform other tasks you require of them. (You can learn to send invitations to join your blog and configure access settings in Chapter 12.)

Tools

You can access a number of features through the Tools section of the left menu of your WordPress dashboard. These features help you easily perform tasks like publishing content via e-mail, importing blogs to your WordPress account, or exporting blogs to another platform. You can even delete your entire site through the Tools section of your account. (Each of these capabilities is described in Chapter 12.)

Settings

The Settings section of your account is where you configure all your global WordPress account settings that affect multiple parts of your blog's functionality. Configuring your blog settings is the first thing you should take time to do after you create your blog. (Each setting is discussed in detail in Chapter 7.)

The Least You Need to Know

- Creating a new WordPress.com account and blog takes just a few minutes.
- You can use the links in the WordPress Admin Bar and WordPress dashboard to configure your blog, publish content, and network with the WordPress user community.
- Many of the same settings and features can be accessed from multiple links and sections of your WordPress account dashboard. It's not as confusing as it might look at first.
- It's unlikely that you'll use every link and feature available through your WordPress.com account and dashboard, so don't feel like you have to memorize everything right now.

Customizing Your Blog's Settings

In This Chapter

- Building your WordPress profile
- Personalizing your blog's settings
- Getting your blog ready for the world to see

After you create your WordPress.com account and your first blog, it's time to configure all your blog's settings so it works exactly the way you want it to. Fortunately, it's very easy to set up your blog's functionality through the WordPress dashboard, and this chapter shows you how to do it.

As you read this chapter, you learn how to create your personal profile and set up your blog's writing, reading, comments, media, privacy, and other important settings, so you're ready to start publishing content on your blog and attract an audience.

Creating Your Profile

The first settings you need to configure are the ones that tell the world who you are when they visit your blog. That means you need to share a bit of information about yourself and be sure that information is displayed the way you prefer.

Start by updating your Public Profile, which is visible to anyone with Internet access. With that in mind, add or delete information from this profile based on personal information you want to publicly share.

First, log in to your WordPress.com account and select the **User, My Profile** link from the left menu, which opens the My Public Profile page shown in Figure 7-1.

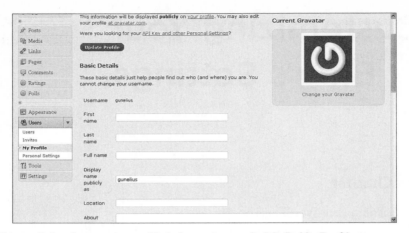

Figure 7-1 *Set up your profile information on the My Public Profile page.*

INSIDER SECRET

As you navigate through the various settings accessible through your WordPress dashboard, you'll find references to your "API key," which you might be asked to provide to activate some features. This is a unique string of 12 letters and numbers every WordPress.com account holder automatically has assigned to his or her account. You can access your API key by selecting the **Personal Settings** link in the Users section of your dashboard's left menu.

The **Basic Details** section includes fields where you can enter your name, location, and a brief biography. Filling in these fields is optional. The only required field is the **Display name publicly as** field because this is the name people across the web will see associated with your WordPress.com account, blog, and comments. Be sure you enter the name you want to use publicly in this field.

QUICK TIP

Anytime you make a change to your profile, be sure to click the **Update Profile** button to save your changes.

In the upper-right corner of the **My Public Profile** configuration page is an image labeled **Current Gravatar** with a **Change your Gravatar** link below it. *Gravatar*, or Globally Recognized Avatar, is a feature provided by Automattic (the same company that owns WordPress). Blogs that enable the gravatar feature display your gravatar image alongside comments you submit to those blogs.

The **Contacts** section of the My Public Profile page, shown in Figure 7-2, includes fields where you can enter any of your personal contact information you want to include with your profile and share publicly.

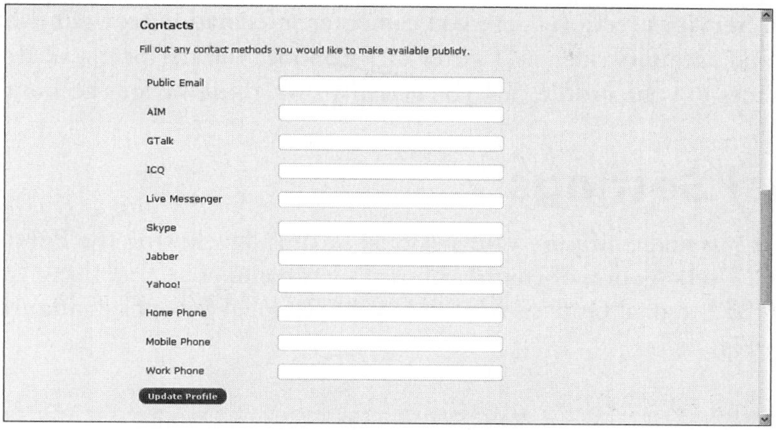

Figure 7-2   *Enter the contact information you want to share in your public profile.*

Figure 7-3 shows the remaining information you can configure in the My Public Profile page. In the **Photos** section, you can upload multiple images to appear with your profile using Gravatar. To upload your images, click the **Add photo through Gravatar...** button. You'll be prompted to choose a file to upload from your hard drive to save as part of your public profile.

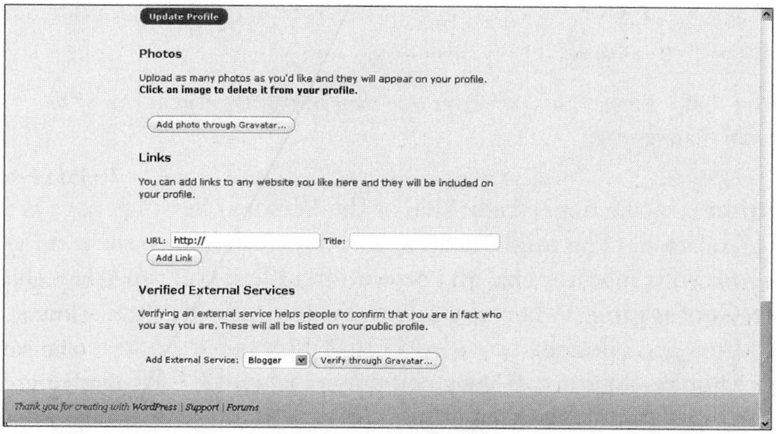

Figure 7-3   *Add photos, links, and verified accounts to your public profile.*

The **Links** section of your public profile is where you can publish links to any other blogs, websites, Twitter profiles, and so on, that you want to share publicly. You can include a title for each link in the **Title** field next to each URL you enter.

The final section in the My Public Profile configuration page is the **Verified External Services** section. Here you can enter information for your other online services and accounts, such as Twitter or Facebook, and perform a verification to show visitors to your profile that you actually own those various accounts.

Personal Settings

You can access and configure your personal settings by clicking the **Personal Settings** link in the Users section of your dashboard's left menu. The first thing you see on your screen is the Personal Options section of your Personal Settings configuration page, as shown in Figure 7-4.

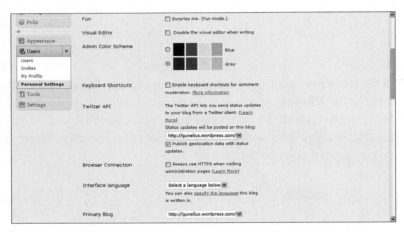

Figure 7-4 *Enter your preferences into the Personal Options section of the Personal Settings page.*

My Location In the upper-right side of the Personal Settings page is a feature called My Location. (You might need to scroll to the right to see it on your screen, depending on your monitor size and resolution.) Here you can select the check box to **Enable Geotagging**. When you select this box, a field opens where you can type in your address and click the provided **Find Address** button to identify the location from where you're blogging. If your computer includes a GPS tracking device, you have the option to click on the **Auto Detect** button and allow your location to be detected automatically. Using the geotagging feature, you can select check boxes to make your location public or your posts' locations public. (You can tag each post with a location, separate from your profile location.)

While geotagging information is currently only machine readable (meaning it's hidden from view and only WordPress and possibly search engines can see it), WordPress plans to launch tools in the future that will enable human-readable geotagging (so people can view geographical tags), as well as a search directory based on geotagging to make it easy to find "local" posts.

The following options are available for you to configure within the Personal Options section of the Personal Settings page:

Fun   The fun mode adds no real value to the WordPress experience except some fun surprises. If you check this box, you reveal a new **Humanize** section within the Blog Stats section of your WordPress dashboard comparing your traffic stats to real-town populations (with photos). You'll also see a larger **Publish** button in your blog post editor, and you'll receive positive reinforcements in the form of text or videos after you publish posts. It's fun to play with if you have extra time.

Visual Editor   If you want to enter your blog posts in HTML format rather than through the visual editor that simulates popular word processing software, check this box to disable the visual editor.

PROCEED WITH CAUTION

Don't check the box to disable the visual editor unless you know HTML.

Admin Color Scheme   If you want to change the colors used in your WordPress dashboard, this is where you do it. Two options are available.

Keyboard Shortcuts   If you want to speed up comment moderation tasks by applying keyboard shortcuts to those tasks, you can check this box and create your own shortcuts.

Twitter API   Using a Twitter client (such as Tweetie2 on Apple's iPhone), you can follow WordPress blogs just like you'd follow Twitter users. Note, this does not work with Twitter. If you want to follow blogs and see updates from those blogs using a Twitter client on your phone or other device, click on the **Learn More** link for instructions.

Browser Connection If you access your WordPress account from public Wi-Fi connections that might cause you concern over the security of your connection, you can check this box so you always log in using a secure connection. WordPress recommends this setting be activated, but it's not required.

Interface Language From the drop-down menu, select the language you want to use for your WordPress dashboard.

Primary Blog If you have more than one WordPress.com blog, you can specify which is your primary blog here.

The next section of the Personal Settings page includes proofreading options, as shown in Figure 7-5. WordPress proofreading functionality is provided by After the Deadline (afterthedeadline.com).

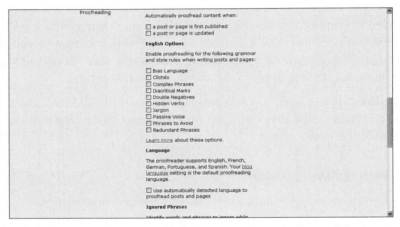

Figure 7-5 *You can configure proofreading options on the Personal Settings page.*

If you want to use the proofreading function in WordPress to proofread your blog posts and pages, you can set it up in the Personal Settings page. The following options are available:

Automatically proofread content when: If you want WordPress to automatically proofread your posts and pages without having to click a button as you're writing or publishing them, you can set that here. Check the corresponding box to have WordPress automatically proofread your posts and pages the first time they're published only or every time they're updated.

English Options   The WordPress proofreading function allows you to flag a few grammar and style rules you want the proofreader function to recognize. If you're not confident in your grammar skills or writing ability, you might want to check these boxes so you get extra help. However, no grammar editor is perfect, and you'll need to review each flagged item in your posts and pages to ensure you agree with the proofreader function results.

English options you can check so the proofreading function looks for them and flags them include the following:

- **Bias Language**   Language that could be offensive to some people.
- **Clichés**   Overused phrases.
- **Complex Phrases**   Words or phrases that could be replaced with simpler alternatives.
- **Diacritical Marks**   Accents and marks used in foreign words the proofreader detects and adds.
- **Double Negative**   Successive negative phrases that are confusing to readers.
- **Hidden Verbs**   A verb that's -*ed* into a noun and requires additional verbs to make sense.
- **Jargon**   Phrases and words, such as technical terms, that only make sense to specific groups of people who use them frequently.
- **Passive Voice**   Sentences written in the passive voice are not as strong as sentences written in the active voice where the subject of the sentence is actually performing the action.
- **Phrases to Avoid**   Indecisive or weak phrases.
- **Redundant Phrases**   Repetitive words and phrases.

Language   The proofreading functionality is based on the language you've set to write your blog content. However, if you write posts in multiple languages on the same blog, you can check the box next to **Use automatically detected language to proofread posts and pages** so the proofreader function matches the language to each individual post.

Ignored Phrases   If the proofreader function repeatedly flags any words or phrases that are correct (or acceptable to publish in your blog content), you can add them here so the proofreader function skips them in the future. Just type them into the text box and click the **Add** button.

Finally, the **Account Details** section of the Personal Settings page, shown in Figure 7-6, is where you can configure several pieces of information that you might want to change in the future.

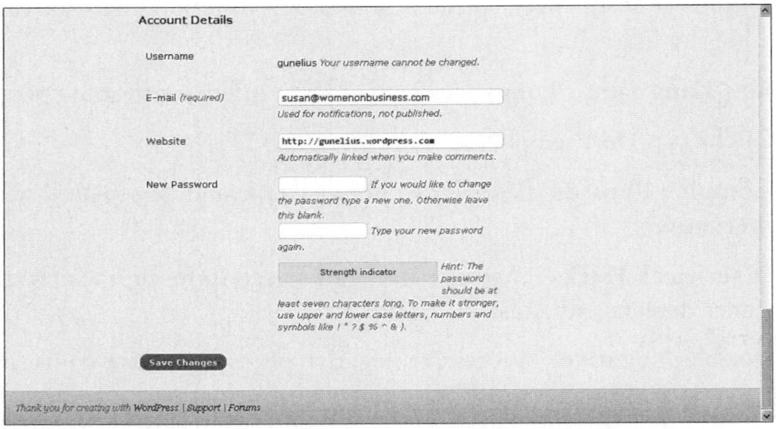

Figure 7-6 *Enter your account details in the Personal Settings page.*

Username   Your username is the name connected to your WordPress.com account. It's the one you enter to log in to your dashboard. You cannot change it.

E-mail   This e-mail address is used for notifications from WordPress.com, so be sure to keep this address current. For example, if you forget your password and request a reminder, that reminder will be sent to the e-mail address entered here. It's not visible publicly.

New Password   There may come a time when you want to change your WordPress.com password. You can enter a new password here, and WordPress will automatically tell you how secure that password is before you save it.

Click **Save Changes** before you leave this page, or none of your changes will be saved.

General Settings

The General Settings page of your WordPress.com dashboard, shown in Figures 7-7 and 7-8, is where you configure some of the functionality that affects your entire blog. You can access this page by clicking the right drop-down arrow in the **Settings** section of your WordPress dashboard left menu and then clicking the **General** link.

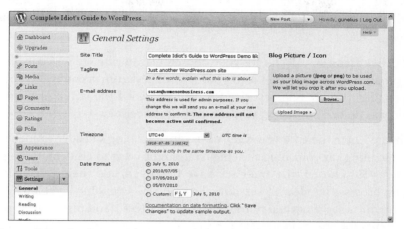

Figure 7-7   *Configure global settings from the General Settings page.*

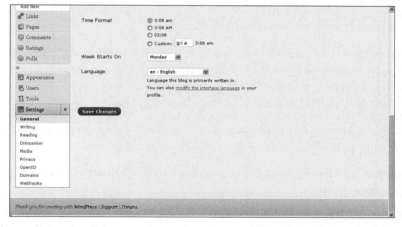

Figure 7-8   *Scroll down to view and configure additional settings on the General Settings page.*

Blog Picture/Icon   WordPress refers to the blog picture as a *blavatar*, which is a fusion of the words *blog* and *avatar*. The blavatar is used to identify your blog in a variety of places. It's used as your blog's *favicon*, with your blog pingbacks, and as an icon when your blog is added as a shortcut favorite on devices like Apple's iPhone.

You can click **Browse…** to locate your chosen blavatar image on your hard drive, and click **Upload Image** to upload it to your WordPress.com account. It should be saved in jpeg or png format. The best size for your uploaded file is 128 pixels × 128 pixels, but once you upload an image, you can crop it if necessary.

Site Title   Enter the title you want to use in your blog's header to identify your blog. Depending on your blog's theme, you might want to edit the title used in this box. Enter your chosen title and click **Save Changes**, and then view your blog in a separate browser window to see how the title looks on your live blog. (Be sure to refresh the browser if necessary to view your changes.) You might want to make some changes after you see it on-screen.

Tagline   Enter a tagline for your blog in this box. Your tagline could be a subtitle or an additional description of what your blog is about. The choice is entirely up to you. Depending on the theme you've chosen for your blog, the tagline may or may not appear in your live blog's header or sidebar.

E-Mail Address   The e-mail address you enter here can be different from the one you used in your profile. This address is where e-mails related to comment moderation are sent if you configure your discussion settings to require comment moderation. (See the "Discussion Settings" section later in this chapter.)

Timezone   Choose your time zone from the drop-down menu so your posts and the comments published on your blog match your time zone.

Date Format   Choose the radio button next to the format you want dates to appear in on your blog posts.

Time Format   Choose the radio button next to the format you want times to appear in on your blog.

Week Starts On   Use the drop-down menu to choose the day you want WordPress to identify as the first day of the week.

Language   Use the drop-down menu to choose the language you primarily write in on your blog.

Click the **Save Changes** button, or your selections will not go into effect.

Writing Settings

When you select the **Writing** link within the Settings section of your WordPress dashboard left menu, the Writing Settings page, shown in Figure 7-9, opens. Here you can configure how you want settings related to the actual writing of posts and pages on your blog to look and act.

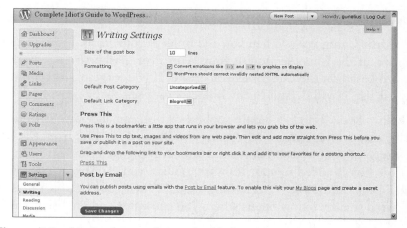

Figure 7-9 *It's simple to configure your blog's writing settings.*

Size of the Post Box Here you can change the number of text lines visible in the blog post editor when you're entering a new blog post. Simply enter into the text box the number of lines you want to be able to view at once without scrolling.

Formatting Check the box next to **Convert *emoticons* like :-) and :-P to graphics on display** if you want those commonly used emoticons to appear as smiley face images and so on in your blog content.

> **DEFINITION**
>
> An **emoticon** is a visual representation of a facial expression (such as a smiley face or a sad face) that is created by typing a series of characters. For example, a colon can be used to represent eyes and a closing parenthesis can be used to represent a smile. When emoticons are converted to graphics display, they appear as actual facial icon images.

Also, you can check the box next to **WordPress should correct invalidly nested XHTML automatically,** which means any content published on your blog using the

XHTML programming language invalidly will automatically be corrected for you. It's a good idea to check this box, particularly if you don't know XHTML, because invalidly nested XHTML can cause problems with your blog's layout and design.

Default Post Category   As you write blog posts, you can save them to categories to make it easier to find them in your archives later. If you forget to select a category for your post, it's automatically saved in the category specified here. Use the drop-down menu to select the category you want posts to default to if you forget to select a category before publishing.

Default Link Category   When you add links to your list of links using the **Add New** option in the Links section of your WordPress dashboard left menu, they can be grouped based on the categories you create. If you forget to categorize a link you add to your list, it will default to the link category selected here.

Press This   Press This is a handy application you can add to your web browser's toolbar by simply dragging and dropping the **Press This** link from the Writing Settings page of your WordPress.com dashboard to your browser toolbar. Once the **Press This** link is added to your browser toolbar, you can simply click it anytime you find a page online you want to blog about. When you click on **Press This** from the toolbar, a small window opens where you can enter and publish a quick blog post about that page.

> **PROCEED WITH CAUTION**
>
> If you have trouble installing the Press This tool, check the WordPress.com Support site for current compatibility issues and instructions.

Post by Email   You can e-mail blog posts and publish them on your WordPress. com blog. This option is mentioned on the Writing Settings page, but it can only be set up from the **Dashboard, My Blogs** section of your WordPress account. To set it up, simply enter a secret e-mail address to send blog posts for publishing to your blog in that section of your account.

Be sure to click **Save Changes** before you leave the Writing Settings page in your WordPress account, or your configurations won't be saved and activated on your blog.

Reading Settings

By selecting the **Reading** link in the Settings section of your WordPress dashboard's left menu, you open the Reading Settings page, shown in Figures 7-10 and 7-11. Here you can configure how your blog readers view your content.

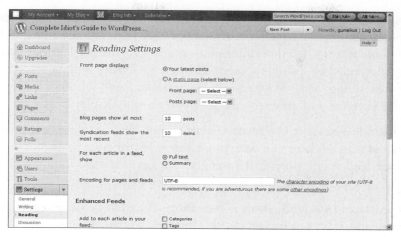

Figure 7-10 *You can quickly configure the reading settings for your WordPress blog.*

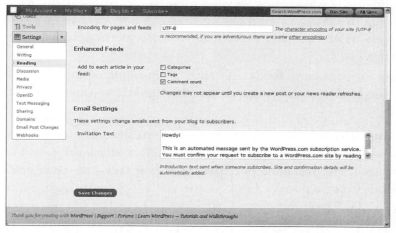

Figure 7-11 *Scroll down to view and configure additional reading settings.*

Front page displays When you create a blog with WordPress.com, you can have your recent blog posts appear on your blog's home page, or you can choose a static page to be your blog's home page. To show your latest blog posts on your blog's home page, select the radio button next to **Your latest posts**. To display a static page on your blog's home page, select the radio button next to **A static page**, and use the drop-down menus to select the page you want to use.

Blog pages show at most   This setting determines how many blog posts visitors to your blog can see on a single screen before they have to click a link to view more content. This setting also determines how much a visitor needs to scroll to view all the posts displayed on a single screen. The default setting is 10 posts, but that leads to a lot of scrolling. Most bloggers display between 5 and 7 posts on a single page, but the choice is yours. Just enter the number you want to display in the text box.

Syndication feeds show the most recent   Your blog's feed includes your recent content, and this is where you determine how many of your most recent posts to send out in your feed at one time. Just enter the number you want to use in this text box. (You can learn more about blog feeds in Chapter 19.)

For each article in a feed, show   Your blog's feed can be delivered to feed readers and e-mail subscribers in full or in part. In other words, you can send the full content from your most recent blog posts or partial content only. Depending on your choice, select the appropriate radio button in this section.

 INSIDER SECRET

The debate between which option is better has been going on for years, and you can learn more about which option is best for your blog in Appendix B.

Encoding for pages and feeds   A variety of encoding options are available for web content, but UTF-8 is the most common. It's unlikely you'd need to change this setting.

Add to each article in your feed   Some feed readers allow subscribers to view more than just blog post titles and content. You can select additional items to send with your blog feed here, including post categories, post tags, and the number of comments published on a post.

Email Settings   When other WordPress.com users subscribe to your blog using the Subscriptions option found in the Dashboard section of their WordPress dashboards, they'll automatically receive an e-mail from you with the text displayed in the Invitation Text box within the Email Settings section or your Reading Settings configuration page. You can enter any text you'd like to use in this text box, or use the default text provided.

Remember, your changes will not be saved unless you click the **Save Changes** button prior to navigating away from the Reading Settings.

Discussion Settings

Your blog's Discussion Settings are very important because they affect how people interact with you and each other—both vital aspects of developing a successful blog. You can modify these settings by selecting the **Discussion** link in the Settings section from the left menu of your WordPress dashboard. You'll see the Discussion Settings page shown in Figures 7-12, 7-13, and 7-14.

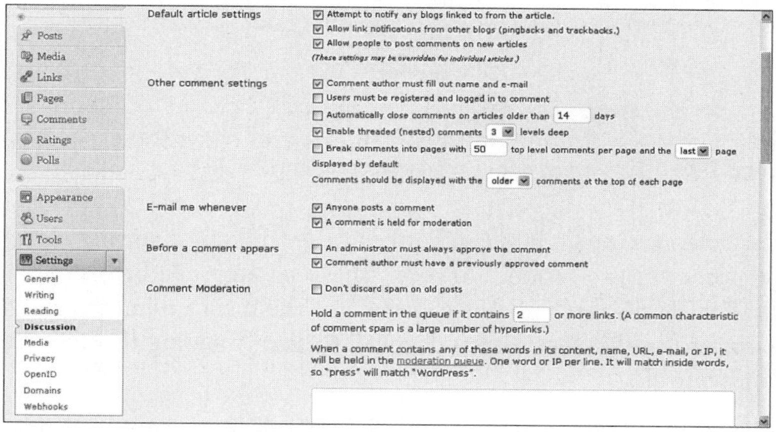

Figure 7-12   *Configure your comment and discussion settings here.*

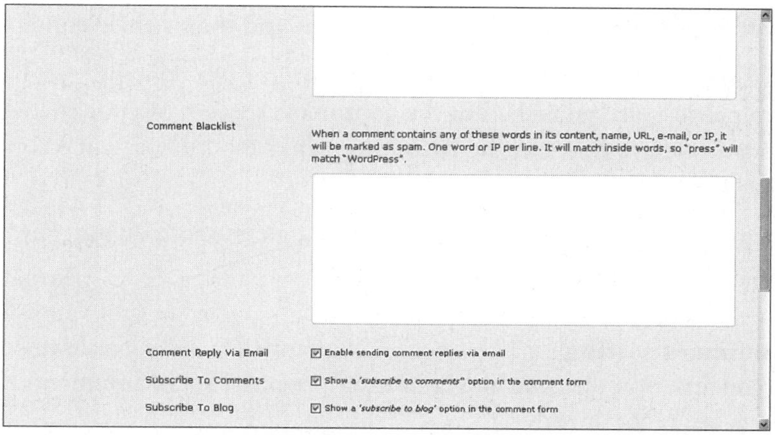

Figure 7-13   *Scroll down to view and configure additional discussion settings.*

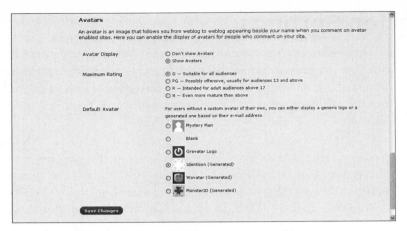

Figure 7-14   *You can enable or disable avatars on your blog.*

Default article settings   You can configure several commenting settings that apply to all new posts in this section. However, these settings can be overridden within each individual post's settings if necessary. For the most interactive blog, be sure all three options in this section are checked so the following three things happen globally on your blog:

1. WordPress notifies other blogs when you link to them in your content. If pingbacks and trackbacks are enabled on those blogs, a link to your content could be published on those blogs. Also, those bloggers might see your incoming links within their analytics programs or blog dashboards, putting you on their radar as someone who likes and shares their content.

2. When other blogs link to your blog within their content, pingbacks and trackbacks are published in the comments section of your corresponding posts and are listed in the Incoming Links module of your WordPress dashboard.

3. Anyone who visits your blog can submit a comment on any new post you publish.

Other comment settings   This section is intended to help you have some control over the conversation on your blog and limit potential spam comments. The following settings are recommended:

Comment author must fill out name and e-mail   Check this box. It's possible for people to submit comments with fake names and e-mail addresses, but checking this box can cut back on some spam and offensive comments.

Users must be registered and logged in to comment   Do not select this check box unless you want to severely limit the conversation on your blog. When checked, visitors cannot comment on your posts unless they're logged in to WordPress.com.

Automatically close comments on articles older than 14 days   This setting is intended to reduce spam because older posts have a tendency to attract spam bots and automated comment spam. If you find your older posts get a lot of spam comments, check this box and enter the number of days you want a post to live before comments are closed. Consider 30, 60, or 90 days, depending on the spam traffic you experience.

Enable threaded (nested) comments 3 levels deep   Sometimes people leave a new comment on one of your blog posts that's not related to a previous comment published on the same post. However, sometimes people submit comments in response to a previous comment published on the same post. To make it easier to follow those conversations, WordPress.com allows you to publish related comments in a comment thread. If you want to enable threaded comments, check this box and enter the number of levels you want threaded comments to be identified.

Break comments into pages with 50 top level comments per page and the last page displayed by default   This setting configures how many comments are shown on a single page before a visitor needs to click a link to view more. It also determines whether comments are shown with the last page (most recent comments) first or the first page (oldest comments) first.

Comments should be displayed with the older comments at the top of each page   The previous setting determines the order comments that span multiple pages should be displayed, page by page. This setting determines the order comments are displayed within each page. You can choose to have oldest comments or newest comments displayed first on a page.

E-mail me whenever   Here you can set up your e-mail notifications. Check the box to be notified anytime someone publishes a comment on your blog. This helps you keep on top of the conversations happening on your blog and respond. Also, check the box to be notified anytime a comment is held for moderation based on the settings you'll configure in the next section.

Before a comment appears   This section offers two comment moderation settings. Check the first if you want all comments to be held for moderation and review by you or another administrator before they're published on your blog. Check the second if you'd rather only hold comments for moderation that are left by visitors who have never submitted an approved comment to your blog before. I recommend the second option to reduce the amount of moderation you have to do as your blog traffic grows.

INSIDER SECRET

Once a person submits an approved comment to your blog, it's usually safe to assume they'll play nice and submit legitimate comments in the future.

Comment Moderation If the **Don't discard spam on old posts** box is checked, Akismet saves comments marked as spam until you manually delete them. To have Akismet automatically delete comments detected as spam after 30 days, leave this box unchecked. I recommend leaving this box unchecked. If you haven't missed a comment in 30 days, you probably don't need it anymore.

I recommend leaving the **Hold a comment in the queue if it contains 2 or more links** setting at 2. This way, all comments that include two or more links are automatically held for moderation no matter who submits them. Spam comments are often filled with links, so this is a great way to flag and filter potential spam comments from your blog that Akismet misses.

Enter words you want to flag within comments into the text box labeled **When a comment contains any of these words in its content, name, URL, e-mail, or IP, it will be held in the moderation queue. One word or IP per line. It will match inside words, so "press" will match "WordPress"**.

You can also blacklist words, so when they appear in comments, those comments are automatically marked as spam. Enter the offending words in the **Comment Blacklist** text box. Be sure to enter one word or IP per line, and be aware that words within words will be flagged as matches. That means if you enter *sex*, words like *sexy* or *Essex* will also be flagged as spam.

Comment Reply Via Email If you want to be able to reply to comments submitted to your blog quickly via e-mail, check this box.

Subscribe To Comments This is an important setting to enable if you want to build a successful blog with an ongoing conversation. When you check this box (which is the default setting), an option appears in the comment section of your blog posts inviting people who submitted comments to subscribe to the comments on that post. Once a user subscribes, they receive an e-mail each time a new comment is published on the same post.

Subscribe To Blog   If you want to make it easy for other WordPress.com users to subscribe to your blog so they can view it through the **Dashboard, Subscriptions** section of their own WordPress accounts, check this box. When enabled, a subscription option appears in the comment form of your blog posts.

QUICK TIP

Including the Subscribe To Blog option in the comment form of your blog posts only helps logged-in WordPress.com users and might even confuse some users who don't understand the difference between WordPress.com blog subscriptions and true RSS feed subscriptions, which are viewed using feed readers or via e-mail feed subscriptions. You might want to disable this option on your blog to avoid confusion.

Avatar Display   This setting refers to avatar images that can appear alongside comments published on your blog posts. If a person who submits a comment on one of your blog posts identifies her name and URL within the comment form and has previously set up an avatar image, this setting allows you to display those avatars on your blog next to the visitor's comment. To enable this feature, select the radio button next to **Show Avatars**.

Maximum Rating   Here you can decide what kinds of avatars you're willing to display on your blog by selecting ratings, similar to movie ratings used throughout the United States. Select the radio button next to the highest rating you're willing to display on your blog.

PROCEED WITH CAUTION

Consider your audience and your goals before you enable avatars on your blog. Not everyone uses avatars appropriate for all audiences, and even the rating configuration isn't 100 percent accurate in preventing inappropriate avatars from displaying on your blog.

Default Avatar   Not everyone who publishes a comment on your blog will have an avatar. Here you can select an image to display when a user does not have a set avatar. If you enable avatars on your blog, be sure to select a default avatar that matches your blog's image.

Click **Save Changes** before you leave this page, or your new settings will be lost.

Media Settings

You can configure several global settings related to the media files you upload and publish on your blog from the Media Settings page, shown in Figure 7-15. This page is accessible through the **Settings**, **Media** link in the left menu of your WordPress dashboard.

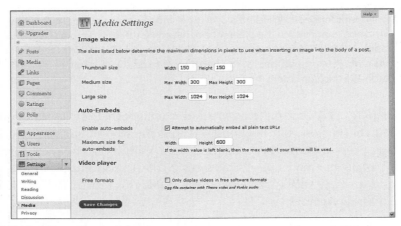

Figure 7-15 *Configure global settings for media files used in your blog.*

Image sizes When you upload images to insert into your posts and pages, you can choose to display them at full size, medium size, or as thumbnails. Enter values for the maximum width and height for each size option. WordPress will auto-size your uploaded images.

QUICK TIP

Take some time to publish content to your blog and see what image sizes work best with your theme and design preferences before you finalize the image size settings for your blog.

Auto-Embeds If you want WordPress to automatically convert URLs typed into your blog posts and pages into active links, check the **Enable auto-embeds** box. You can also configure the **Maximum size for auto-embeds** so links to media files (like videos) are resized to the size you specify. Note that if you keep the **Width** field blank here, WordPress will resize the media to fit the maximum width defined in your blog's theme.

Video player   If you want the video content on your blog only to display if the video player it plays in is free to use, check the **Free Formats** box. This is a good precaution.

Be sure to click the **Save Changes** button to activate your new settings before you leave this page.

Privacy Settings

You can configure your blog's privacy settings by selecting the **Privacy** link within the Settings section of the left menu of your WordPress dashboard. This opens the Privacy Settings page, shown in Figure 7-16.

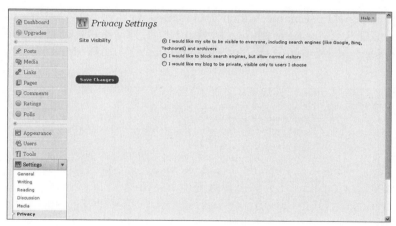

Figure 7-16   *Configure your blog's privacy settings on this page.*

You can set three options related to your site's privacy within the Site Visibility section of this page:

I would like my site to be visible to everyone, including search engines (like Google, Bing, Technorati) and archivers   Select this radio button if you want search engines to index your blog content and deliver it in keyword search results. This is important to increase traffic to your blog.

I would like to block search engines, but allow normal visitors   If you want everyone online to be able to view your blog but don't want search engines to find it, select this radio button. This is not a commonly selected setting.

I would like my blog to be private, visible only to users I choose If your blog is meant to be private, you can select this radio button and only give access to the people you choose. Set those users through the Users section of your WordPress dashboard (see Chapter 12).

Be sure to click the **Save Changes** button to save your privacy configurations.

OpenID Settings

WordPress.com supports the OpenID standard (OpenID.com), which is an open standard created to allow people to log in to multiple sites quickly without the need for multiple usernames and passwords. You can log in to other sites that support the OpenID standard with your WordPress.com username and password.

Find your OpenID username, which you created with your WordPress account, on your OpenID Settings page (shown in Figure 7-17) by selecting the **OpenID** link from the Settings section of the left menu on your WordPress dashboard.

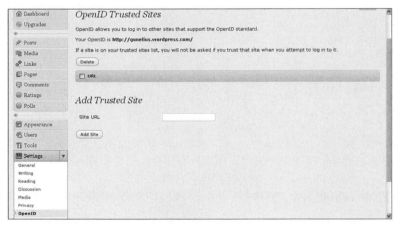

Figure 7-17 *Find your OpenID username and add trusted sites to your WordPress account on this page.*

You can also add other sites that support the OpenID standard to your list of trusted sites so you don't have to click through warnings asking you if you trust the site next time you try to log in to it with your WordPress.com OpenID. Just click the **Add Site** button to add new trusted sites or the **Delete** button to remove sites from your list.

Sharing

The new social sharing options for WordPress.com blogs allow you to provide links or buttons readers can click to share your posts to their own online audiences on Twitter, Facebook, and more. The most current information about the sharing features available in WordPress.com can be found in the WordPress Support site at en.support.wordpress.com/sharing.

Using a simple drag-and-drop system, as shown in Figure 7-18, you can drag social buttons from the **Available Services** section of the Sharing page to the **Enabled Services** section of the page to add them to your live posts.

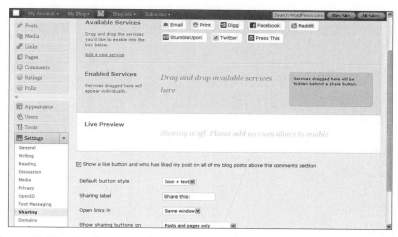

Figure 7-18 *Configure social sharing buttons and links on the Sharing page.*

QUICK TIP

Some social buttons include a drop-down arrow when dragged into the Enabled Services section, where you can activate smart buttons that display the number of people who shared your posts.

If you'd rather not display all the enabled sharing links and buttons, you can drag them into the **Services dragged here will be hidden behind a share button** area, which means they'll only be visible if a visitor hovers his mouse over a generic share button that will appear with your post.

You can also add more sharing services by clicking the **Add a new service** link and providing the requested information. Customizing the way your sharing buttons and links work is easy to configure using the drop-down menus at the bottom of the Sharing Settings page, shown in Figure 7-18.

Domains Settings

You can access the Domains Settings page of your WordPress account, shown in Figure 7-19, by selecting the **Domains** link within the Settings section of your WordPress dashboard.

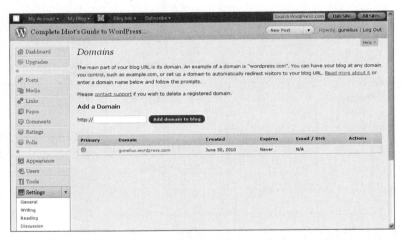

Figure 7-19   *Configure domains for your blog on the Domains Settings page.*

If you want to drop the .wordpress.com extension from your blog's URL, you can do so on this page or through the **Upgrades** link accessible from the left menu of your WordPress dashboard. That's because, to add a domain to your existing WordPress.com blog, you need to purchase an upgrade (see Chapter 13).

Email Post Changes

If your blog is written by multiple authors, then the Email Post Changes settings section of your WordPress.com account might be very useful to you. As shown in

Figure 7-20, you can check the box next to **Enable** to send an e-mail when a post or page changes on your blog.

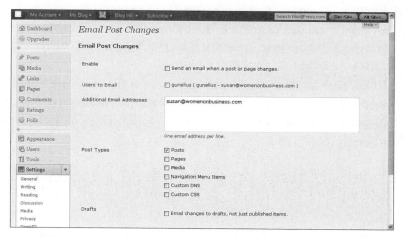

Figure 7-20   *Receive e-mail notification when posts or pages on your blog change on the Domains Settings page.*

You can also input e-mail addresses for anyone you want to receive e-mails whenever posts, pages, media, navigation menu items, custom DNS (if you paid for the domain upgrade), or custom CSS (if you paid for the CSS upgrade) are edited on your blog—including drafts, if you so choose.

Your Webhooks Settings

Webhooks are notifications that are pushed to you when a specific action related to your blog occurs. You can set up webhooks through the **Settings**, **Webhooks** link in the left menu of your WordPress dashboard.

Typically only developers use webhooks because they require more coding and technical knowledge than most beginner and even many advanced WordPress users have. If you're brave enough to tackle webhooks, you can learn more by visiting en.support. wordpress.com/webhooks or hiring a developer to help you.

The Least You Need to Know

- Take the time to configure your blog's settings before you start publishing content.
- The longer you use WordPress, the more you'll understand how your blog performs and how your audience responds to it, which could motivate you to adjust your blog's settings in the future.
- Just because another WordPress.com user has his blog configured in a specific way doesn't mean that configuration is right for your blog.
- Not all settings options will apply to your blog. In fact, you'll never touch some settings.

Modifying Your Blog's Appearance

8

In This Chapter

* Choosing a WordPress theme
* Adding widgets to your blog
* Configuring your blog's menus
* Changing your blog's background and header
* Adding fonts and editing your blog's style sheets

Your settings are configured, thanks to your work in Chapter 7, and your blog is ready to function the way you want it to. Now, it's time to make your blog *look* the way you want it to by modifying its design and appearance.

This chapter shows you how to pick a theme for your WordPress blog, add additional widgets and menus to it, and make your header and background look great. I also introduce you to some of the more advanced design options available if you're ready to take your blog to the next level of customization.

Themes

WordPress.com blogs are built from skeleton layouts called themes. You can access approximately 100 free themes through the Themes link in the Appearance section of your WordPress dashboard left menu, as shown in Figure 8-1.

At the top of the Manage Themes page, you see the theme that's currently activated on your blog. To change your blog's theme, you can browse through the various themes available using the links under the Browse Themes heading. You can list themes in random order, alphabetically by theme name, by popularity, or from newest to oldest based on when they were added to the directory. You can also enter keywords in the search bar on the right to search themes that have been keyword-tagged.

Figure 8-1 *Select your blog's theme from the Manage Themes page of your WordPress dashboard.*

WordPress offers several primary theme layouts: 1 column, 2 column, and 3 column. When you preview different themes, take some time to click the different links and view how different pages, posts, and parts of your blog would look using that theme. You might fall in love with a particular WordPress theme's home page layout, but you might not like the layout of the interior pages, posts, sidebars, or footer.

When you find a theme you like, click the **Preview** link beneath the thumbnail image of the theme to view it, as shown in Figure 8-2.

Figure 8-2 *You can preview any theme before selecting and activating it on your blog.*

QUICK TIP

Click the X in the upper-left corner of the preview window to close it and return to the Manage Themes page of your WordPress dashboard.

When you find the theme you want to use on your blog, click the **Activate** link under the theme's thumbnail image. Once you activate a theme, it's automatically live on your blog. When you visit your blog, a message appears at the top of the Manage Themes page of your WordPress account that says **New theme activated. Visit site**, as shown in Figure 8-3. Click the **Visit site** link to view your new blog look. Your newly activated theme is also displayed under the Current Theme heading on the Manage Themes page.

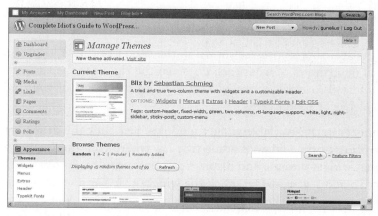

Figure 8-3 *When you activate a new theme, it immediately appears as your Current Theme in your WordPress account.*

Widgets

Depending on the WordPress theme you choose, you can add widgets to a variety of places on your blog. For example, some themes allow you to add widgets in multiple sidebars, while others only offer one sidebar. Furthermore, some themes provide widget-ready footers, but others do not.

Regardless of what theme you use on your blog, the process of adding widgets to your blog is always the same, thanks to the easy drag-and-drop function you can access through the **Widgets** link in the Appearance section of your WordPress dashboard left menu, as shown in Figure 8-4.

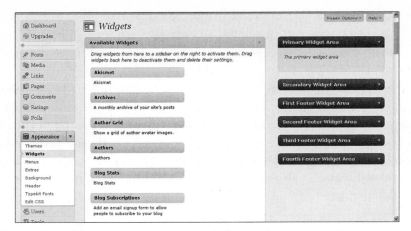

Figure 8-4 *Drag-and-drop widgets to add functionality to your blog.*

The widgets available to you are shown in the center of the Widgets page, along with a brief description of what each does. To the right are the various widget-ready sections, referred to as *widget modules* throughout this book, of your blog. These are typically sidebar or footer areas.

To add widgets to the available widget modules, just click the drop-down arrow in the right corner of the widget module title bar where you want to add a widget. This expands that widget module and displays any widgets already active in that section of your blog. To add a new widget, click the widget title bar and drag it to the widget module where you want the widget to appear on your blog. You can change the order of your widgets by dragging and dropping them to new locations within the widget module.

Then you need to configure the new widget. For example, you can create custom titles on most widgets. For others, you can add links, images, and more.

 INSIDER SECRET

Take some time to experiment with the various widgets available. You can't break your blog by adding them, and you can always delete them if they don't work for you and your blog.

To edit a widget that's already active in a widget module, simply click the drop-down arrow in the right corner of the widget module title bar and then do the same on the specific widget title bar you want to edit. This expands it and reveals the available configuration options. After you make your changes, you must click **Save** for your edits to go into effect. You can also remove widgets by clicking the **Delete** link.

Sometimes you might want to remove a widget from your blog temporarily. To avoid re-creating the configurations of that widget again when you want to reactivate it later, simply drag and drop it from your active widget module to the **Inactive Widgets** section of your Widgets settings page, as shown in Figure 8-5. (You might have to scroll down to see this area of the page on your screen.) All your settings will be saved, and you can simply drag and drop the widget back to the appropriate widget module later to re-activate it.

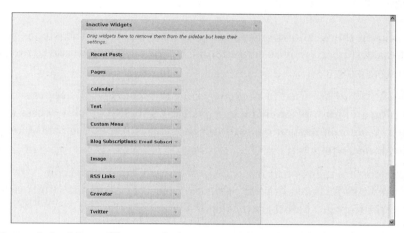

Figure 8-5   *Move widgets you don't want to use but may want to re-activate later to the Inactive Widgets area.*

The widgets you use on your blog are entirely up to you, but you can learn more about choosing widgets in Appendix B.

Menus

Some WordPress themes allow you to publish custom menus using the **Menus** link in the Appearances section of your WordPress left menu, as shown in Figure 8-6.

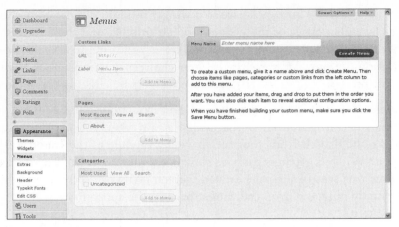

Figure 8-6 *You can create custom menus for your WordPress blog.*

If your chosen theme allows custom menus, the features on the Menus page of your WordPress dashboard will be active. Some themes even allow you to create primary and secondary menus!

Your blog's menus are used in the navigation bar that typically appears at the top of your blog and most often includes links for visitors to quickly access the pages of your blog. Common navigation bar links include an About page and Contact page, as mentioned in Chapter 5.

Using the custom menus feature available through WordPress.com, you can easily change the links included in your navigation bar, add or remove links, and even include links to pages on other websites.

To create a custom menu for your blog, open the **Menus** page from your WordPress dashboard (shown in Figure 8-6), enter a name for your new menu in the **Menu Name** text box, and click the **Create Menu** button. Once your menu is created, you can access the various modules to configure it, as shown in Figure 8-7.

To add links to your menu, use the **Custom Links**, **Pages**, and **Categories** modules. Simply enter a URL and label for the new menu item in the **Custom Links** module to add a link to an external website in your menu. Click **Add to Menu** to add the link to your custom menu.

To add pages to your menu, click on the tabs in the **Pages** module to find the specific pages you want to add. Check the boxes next to pages you want to add to your menu, and click **Add to Menu** to add them to your custom menu.

Figure 8-7   *Once you create a new menu, you can customize it by adding links, pages, and more.*

To add links to categories of posts on your blog, click on the tabs in the **Categories** module and check the boxes next to the categories you want to include in your menu. Click **Add to Menu** to add the selected category links to your menu.

If you want to change the label used for the link for an item in your menu, you can click on the drop-down arrow on the right side of the menu item's title bar to expand it. Just enter the new label in the **Navigation Label** text box. The only place this new title will appear is in the actual navigation bar.

Once you have all the links added to your menu, you can drag and drop them to change the order they'll appear in on your blog navigation bar. You can also drag and drop menu items to the left and right to create submenus within your navigation bar.

Extras

In the **Extras** link in the Appearance section of your WordPress dashboard, you have three settings you can configure for your blog, as shown in Figure 8-8.

The first option allows you to **Enable *mShots* site previews on this blog**. mShots are little pop-up preview windows that open when visitors to your blog hover their mouse arrow over links in your content.

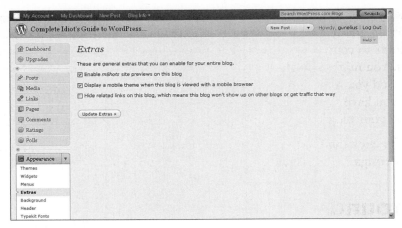

Figure 8-8 *Select your preferred options from the Extras settings page.*

There are two disparate opinions about preview windows. Some people think they're useful because they can eliminate the need to click through to visit sites people aren't interested in. However, some people find them intrusive and annoying. It's up to you to decide whether or not you want to use mShots on your blog.

> **QUICK TIP**
>
> To help you decide for or against mShots, enable them and then visit your blog to get an idea of how they affect the user experience. If you find you don't like mShots, return to the Extras settings page in your WordPress account and uncheck this box.

The second option on the Extras page allows you to **Display a mobile theme when this blog is viewed with a mobile browser**. When this box is checked, people who view your blog through mobile devices will see it in a stripped-down, mobile-friendly layout, which increases load times and can make it easier for more people to easily view your blog on new and old mobile devices. If you want visitors to see your blog in its original online format when they access it from mobile devices, uncheck this option.

The final option on the Extras settings page allows you to show or **Hide related links on this blog, which means this blog won't show up on other blogs or get traffic that way**. When this option is unchecked, posts across the WordPress.com user community that are automatically deemed to be related to your own blog post will be listed at the end of your post with links to visit those other blogs. Additionally, your own posts might appear as related links on other WordPress.com blogs.

Whether you enable or disable this option depends on your goals for your blog. You can't control the related links that are published on your blog, nor can you control where links to your blog posts are published across the WordPress.com community of blogs. You might not like the related links published on your blog through this feature, and you might not like where links to your content are published on other sites. If you have those concerns, check this box. Related links will be hidden on your blog, and your blog links are not published on other blogs.

Be sure to click the **Update Extras** button to save the changes you make to your Extras settings.

Background

Some WordPress themes give you the option to change your blog's background, or the area that appears on-screen to the left and right of your actual blog posts. To do this, select the **Background** link from the Appearance section of your WordPress dashboard left menu. This opens the Custom Background page of your WordPress account, as shown in Figure 8-9.

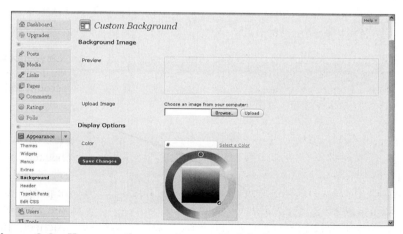

Figure 8-9   *You can easily customize your blog's background color or image.*

You have two options to customize your blog's background. You can either upload an image, or you can select a color. To upload an image, simply select the **Browse** button in the Upload Image section of the Custom Background page to find the image on your hard drive. Once you select the image file, click **Upload** to upload it to your WordPress account and set it as your blog background. You can see how your background will look in the Preview section of the Custom Background page.

QUICK TIP

Images must be in .jpg, .jpeg, .png, or .gif format and under 1GB in size.

To select a color for your blog background, click the **Select a Color** link in the Display Options section of the Custom Background page and use your mouse to select the color you want to use. Alternatively, you can type the HTML color code into the text box if you know it.

Click the **Save Changes** button to immediately activate your blog's new background.

Header

Some WordPress themes include an image in the header area, and you can change this default image to one of your choice. Changing your blog's header is easy and can make a big difference in personalizing your blog. To do so, select the **Header** link from the Appearance section of your WordPress dashboard left menu to open the Custom Header page, as shown in Figure 8-10.

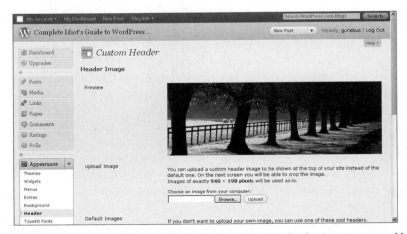

Figure 8-10   *WordPress makes it easy to add a custom header image to your blog.*

The Custom Header page is divided into several sections:

Preview   In the preview area, you can view your selected blog header to get an idea of what it will look like on your live blog.

Upload Image   If you want to upload an image from your computer to use as your blog's header, you can click on the **Browse** button to find it on your hard drive. Then click **Upload** to load it to your WordPress account and activate it as your header.

 INSIDER SECRET

Depending on your chosen theme, the perfect size for your header image can vary. Typically, that size is provided in the Upload Image area of the Custom Header page. However, you are given the option to crop your uploaded image if necessary.

Default Images   Some WordPress themes come with several different default images you can choose from to use in your blog's header, as shown in Figure 8-11. To select a default image, just click on the radio button next to the image you want to use.

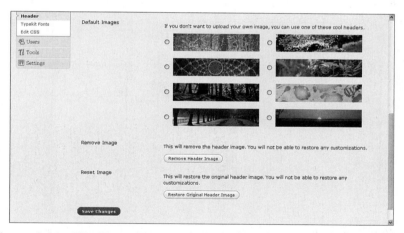

Figure 8-11   *WordPress offers you several header images to customize your blog.*

Remove Image   If you want to remove an image from your header, you can do that by clicking **Remove Header Image**. When you remove a header image, any customization settings you created previously are deleted and cannot be restored unless you re-create them.

Reset Image   If you want to restore the original header image and configurations that came with your chosen WordPress theme, click the **Reset Image** button. Keep in mind that you can't restore any customization settings once you reset your header image.

Some themes might offer additional options you can configure. If so, you might find a **Theme Options** section or other links within the Appearance menu. If the theme you choose offers more personalization options, take some time to test them out and truly make your blog your own!

Typekit Fonts

The WordPress theme you choose to use for your blog comes with specific fonts by default. What if you want to change those fonts or add new ones? You're limited in the amount of changes you can make to your blog's design unless you pay for a CSS upgrade (discussed in Chapter 13), but you can add some fonts through the **Typekit Fonts** link in the Appearance section of your WordPress dashboard left menu, shown in Figure 8-12. Click the **Sign up in seconds** button to create your own free trial account at Typekit.com.

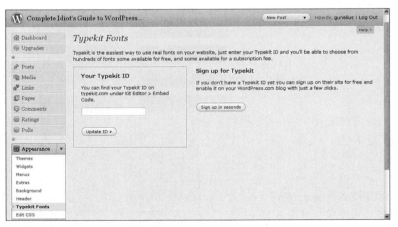

Figure 8-12   *It's simple to access and add Typekit fonts to your blog.*

Once you have a Typekit.com account, you can enter your Typekit ID into the **Your Typekit ID** text box and click **Update ID** to link your WordPress.com blog with your Typekit account. From there, you need to add your WordPress.com account information into your Typekit account and configure settings from that site.

It's important to point out that at the time of this book's writing, the free version of Typekit only allows one site (or blog) and two fonts on that site. You also have to display the Typekit badge on your blog when you use it. To access more fonts or use Typekit on more than one site, you have to pay for a personal account, which currently costs $24.99 per year. It might be more economical to purchase a CSS upgrade for your WordPress account so you get access to modify far more than just fonts in your blog's design. Take the time to research what's available and what works best for you before you pursue either option.

Edit CSS

You can access the CSS coding for your blog by selecting the **Edit CSS** link from the Appearance section of your WordPress dashboard left menu, as shown in Figure 8-13.

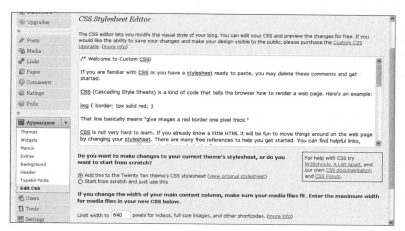

Figure 8-13   *Make changes to your blog's CSS style sheet to modify your blog design.*

Unless you pay for the **Custom CSS Upgrade** option from WordPress.com (discussed in Chapter 13), any changes you make on this page can be previewed by selecting the **Preview** button, but you can't save or activate them on your live blog.

It's important to point out that if you want to edit your blog's CSS, you might want to consider using WordPress.org, which offers complete CSS control and blog customization, rather than WordPress.com. You can learn more about using WordPress.org in Part 4.

The Least You Need to Know

- You can choose from approximately 100 free WordPress themes to make your blog look unique.
- Widget-ready themes make it easy to add more features to your blog.
- You can customize your blog's navigation bar labels and settings using WordPress's menus function.
- Some themes allow you to upload your own header and background images for additional customization.
- Extensive customization may require a monetary investment in additional functionality and features.

Creating Blog Posts

In This Chapter

- Penning a new blog post
- Editing with the post editor
- Adding categories, tags, and excerpts
- Configuring your blog post functionality
- Scheduling and publishing blog posts

Once your blog is live on the web, it looks the way you want it to, and it's configured to work the way you want it to, it's time to start publishing content.

Your posts are the heart of your blog. When blogs first hit the scene, they were little more than online diaries, but today, you can write blog posts about anything you want. WordPress.com makes it easy to be an online publisher because the process of writing and publishing blog posts takes a matter of minutes. If you can use a traditional word processing program like Microsoft Word, you can create and publish blog posts using WordPress.com.

In this chapter, you learn how to create a very basic new blog post (you learn to add bells and whistles in Chapter 10) and what all the boxes, links, and buttons you see when you add a new post actually mean. As with most aspects of WordPress, you might find that you don't even use some of the tools available to you, but they're there if you need them. This chapter teaches you what to do with them when that day comes.

Writing a New Post

The first step to publishing a new blog post is to log in to your WordPress.com account and click the **New Post** link in your top navigation bar. Or you can navigate to any page within your WordPress dashboard and click the right drop-down arrow in the **Posts** section from the left menu to reveal the link options available to you, as shown in Figure 9-1. Click the **Add New** link to open the Add New Post page, shown in Figures 9-2 and 9-3.

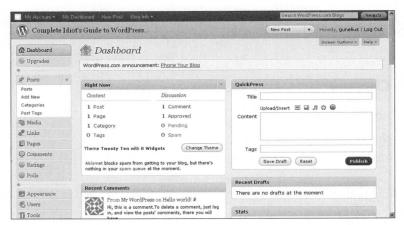

Figure 9-1 *You can start a new blog post by clicking the **New Post** link or the **Add New** link.*

The Add New Post page is where you create and publish new blog posts. Your screen is divided into a number of modules in which you can enter your post title and body as well as configure settings and options for that specific post.

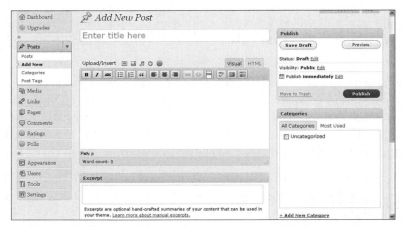

Figure 9-2 *You can create a new blog post on the Add New Post page.*

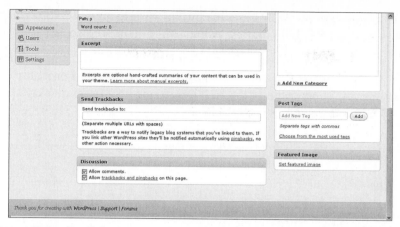

Figure 9-3 *Scroll down to reveal more options on the Add New Post page.*

 INSIDER SECRET

Depending on your WordPress theme, you might see more modules on your screen than what's shown in these screenshots, but the primary modules discussed here should always be visible.

The text box located directly beneath the Add New Posts heading is the title box, where you type the title of your blog post. Try to make the title interesting to entice readers to keep reading. Also, you can include keywords in your title to boost search engine rankings.

When you've added a title for your post, you can move on to the first module, located directly below the title box. This is your post editor, and it's where you'll enter the body of your new post.

Along the top of the post editor, you can see a number of icons and links. Each of these can help you create or modify your blog post. Hover your mouse over each icon to get a pop-up that tells you what that icon is for.

Choosing a Post Editor

In the upper-right side of the post editor you'll see two tabs: **Visual** and **HTML**. When you click on these tabs, you switch back and forth between the Visual post editor mode and the HTML post editor mode. You can see how the Visual post editor mode looks in Figure 9-2. Notice that the various icons in the Visual editor toolbar look like icons you're probably already familiar with from your word processing software—for example, bold, italics, bullets, alignment, and so on.

When you click on the HTML tab and switch to the HTML post editor (shown in Figure 9-4), the icons at the top of the post editor change and probably aren't familiar to you unless you know some HTML. These icons help users quickly apply HTML codes to the text in their blog posts.

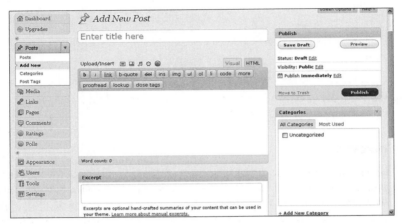

Figure 9-4   *The HTML post editor is best for people who know some HTML.*

Most people use the Visual editor, even if they know some HTML, because it's faster. However, the HTML editor is extremely helpful in enabling you to add far more enhancements and customization to your blog post content than you can achieve with the Visual editor. That's just one reason why learning some HTML can help you as a blogger. While it's certainly not essential, it can make your life easier to know some HTML.

Entering Your Post Body Content

Click on the **Visual** tab on the Add New Post page to be sure you're using the Visual post editor, as shown in Figure 9-2. It's time to enter the content for your first blog post! Go ahead and start typing your content into the post editor. Use the icons in the menu bar to add text enhancements. To reveal additional icons, click on the icon with the various colored squares on it (when you hover over it, the pop-up says **Show/Hide Kitchen Sink**) to reveal even more icons, as shown in Figure 9-5.

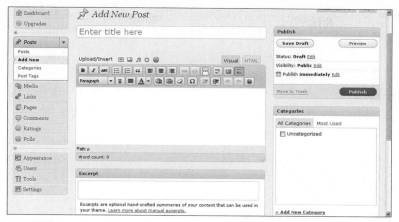

Figure 9-5 *Reveal the post editor "kitchen sink" for formatting options.*

> **QUICK TIP**
>
> As you type your post, there's always the possibility that your Internet connection could go down or your electricity could go out. You don't want to lose your work. WordPress.com does have an autosave feature, but it's a good idea to get into the habit of clicking the **Save Draft** button as you're writing. Find it in the **Publish** module located in the upper-right side of the Add New Post page.

As you're typing your blog post, you can click the **Preview** button in the Publish module located in the upper-right side of your screen to see how your post will look on your blog when you publish it. This is a great way to be sure your posts look perfect before you publish them, because what you see in your post editor isn't always exactly what you'll see when your post is live on your blog.

Applying Categories

Once your post is written, you can assign a category to it to make it easier for visitors to find other content similar to this post in other posts in your archives. Locate the **Categories** module on the right side of your screen. To add a new category, click the **+ Add New Category** link at the bottom of the module, as shown in Figure 9-6, and type a name for your new category. If you want the new category to be a subcategory of an existing category, click the drop-down menu and select that parent category. Click the **Add New Category** button to save that category to your existing list of categories.

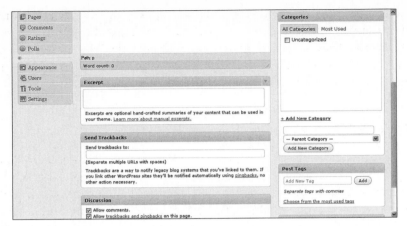

Figure 9-6 *You can add as many categories to your blog post as you want.*

To add a post to an existing category, check the box to the left of that category in the category list to select it.

Tagging Posts

When you use WordPress as your blogging application, you have the option of adding tags to your posts, which helps drive search engine traffic to your blog. Take a few minutes to type in a series of keyword tags into the text box in the **Tags** module located on the right side of your screen, as shown in Figure 9-3.

You can add as many tags as you want, but avoid adding an overwhelming number of keyword tags because search engines might view that as a form of spam. Include a comma after each keyword tag, and click **Add** to attach them to your post.

INSIDER SECRET

Depending on the WordPress theme you're using for your blog, the tags you add to posts may or may not be visible on your live blog. That's okay. They're saved with your blog post when you click the **Add** button.

Writing an Excerpt

Directly beneath the blog post editor module is the Excerpt module, shown in Figure 9-3, where you can enter a summary of your blog post.

Entering an excerpt in this text box is entirely up to you. The excerpt can be used as the description in search engine results pages, so it can be helpful to take a few minutes to write a well-crafted, intriguing excerpt to try to convince people who find your post via keyword searches to click through and visit your blog to read the complete post.

Sending Trackbacks

Trackbacks, introduced in Chapter 4, are virtual shoulder taps to other bloggers letting them know you linked to their content on your blog. When another blog accepts your trackback, a link to your post is published in the comments section of the other blogger's post. Furthermore, when other bloggers link to your content and send a trackback to you, links to their posts are included in the comments section of your posts, if your blog is configured to accept trackbacks (as discussed in Chapter 7).

Trackbacks are a great way to increase potential traffic to your blog and get on the radar screens of other bloggers who accept trackbacks. With that in mind, it's a good idea to send trackbacks to other bloggers when you link to their content by copying and pasting the URL for the page you linked to in your post in the Send Trackbacks box before you publish your blog post. If the other blogger accepts trackbacks, a link to your post will automatically be published in the comments section on that blogger's post, giving your post additional exposure to a new audience.

 QUICK TIP

If you're linking to another WordPress.com blog, you don't need to enter the URL you linked to in the Send Trackbacks box. Trackbacks are automatically sent between WordPress.com blogs.

Configuring Discussion Settings

The Discussion module, shown in Figure 9-3, is where you can make changes to your global discussion settings (discussed in Chapter 7) for a specific blog post. If you want to allow comments on your post, check the **Allow comments** box.

Similarly, if you want trackbacks from other blogs to be published in the comments section of your post, check the **Allow trackbacks and *pingbacks* on this page** box.

> **DEFINITION**
>
> A **pingback,** or ping, is an automated verification from one website to another, which typically happens behind the scenes and confirms that a site exists and accepts notifications (such as trackback notifications).

For maximum blog growth and exposure, check both of the boxes in the Discussion module.

Scheduling and Publishing

Your post is written, categorized, and tagged, and you've sent any trackbacks you want to send to other bloggers. The final step is to publish your post for the world to see! You can do that with a click of the mouse by selecting the **Publish** button from the Publish module in the upper right of your screen, as shown in Figure 9-2.

If you're not ready to publish your post immediately, a few additional options are available in the Publish module, shown in Figure 9-7.

First, you can click the **Edit** link after **Status: Draft** to reveal the drop-down menu shown in Figure 9-7. Here you can select whether you want to save the post as a draft to finish later or as **Pending Review**, meaning it can't be published until another person with access to your WordPress account approves it. Unless you write a blog for another person, it's unlikely you'll use the Pending Review status.

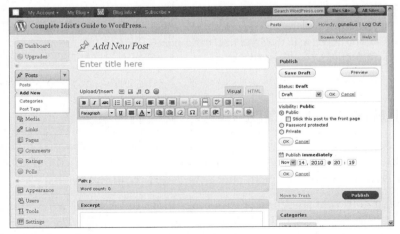

Figure 9-7 *Expand the Publish module to reveal more options.*

Next, you can adjust the privacy settings on specific posts by clicking the **Edit** link next to **Visibility: Public** to reveal the options available to you, as shown in Figure 9-7. Choose a setting that matches your requirements for that post. Selecting the **Public** radio button allows anyone who visits your blog to see your post in the natural order it was published.

Stick this post to the front page makes it a sticky post, which means it will always appear as the top post on your blog (typically at the top of the home page).

If you don't want anyone with Internet access to be able to see your blog post, you can select the radio button next to **Password protected** and type in a password of your choice so only people you give the password to can see the post.

You can make the post completely private and visible to no one by choosing the radio button next to **Private**.

Once you've chosen the visibility settings for your post, you can click the **Edit** link next to **Publish immediately** to reveal additional options, as shown in Figure 9-7. These options allow you to set a future date and time for your post to go live on your blog rather than publishing immediately. For example, if you're going to be away on vacation but want posts to publish automatically in your absence, this is where you can schedule them to go live at a later date. Just enter the date and time when you want your post to go live, and click **OK**. Notice the **Publish** button changes to **Schedule**. Click the **Schedule** button, and the status of your post shown at the top of the Publish module changes to **Scheduled**. The post will go live automatically on the date and time you entered. It's that easy to schedule a post to publish at any time in the future!

PROCEED WITH CAUTION

Don't click the **Move to Trash** link at the bottom of the Publish module unless you want to delete the blog post you're working on.

Once your post is published, you can go to your live blog and see how it looks. Congratulations, you're now officially a blogger!

The Least You Need to Know

- You can publish a blog post with WordPress.com in minutes—literally!
- The visual blog post editor in WordPress.com is similar to word processing software, making it easy for you to work with.

- You can change settings for specific blog posts so they're different from the global settings you used to configure your overall blog functionality.
- You don't have to use all the features available to you when you create and publish a new blog post.

Enhancing Blog Posts

In This Chapter

- Working with the post editor toolbars
- Adding links and text enhancements
- Inserting images and video
- Editing blog posts

Publishing a basic blog post is very easy, as you saw in Chapter 9, but you can do so much more with your blog than simply publish plain old text. You can add images, videos, links, and more to make your posts really eye-catching! This chapter shows you how.

Once you publish your blog post, you can easily edit it if you realize you made a mistake or need to add or delete something in it. Get ready because it's time to make your blog posts look fantastic!

Using the Post Editor Toolbar

Depending on your knowledge of HTML, you can write and enhance your blog posts using the visual post editor, which uses functionality and a toolbar similar to word processing software, or the HTML editor, which uses a toolbar that offers shortcuts to apply commonly used HTML tags to your content.

If you know some HTML, you might find yourself switching back and forth between the visual and HTML post editors for maximum customization and formatting of your content. However, if you don't know HTML, you might never use the HTML editor at all.

Regardless of which post editor you use, the five Upload/Insert icons located above the post editor are always accessible. With these options, you can upload and insert images, video, audio, media, or polls into your blog posts. (I explain each of these features in more detail later in this chapter and in Chapter 12.)

Working with the Post Editor

You can spice up your blog posts with text enhancements, links, images, and video content in minutes when you use WordPress.com—and you don't have to know any HTML or special programming language to do it! All you need is the toolbar in your visual blog post editor to make the magic happen.

To begin, log in to your WordPress.com account and navigate to your dashboard. Click the **Add New** link in the Posts section of the left menu to open the **Add New Post** page, shown in Figure 10-1.

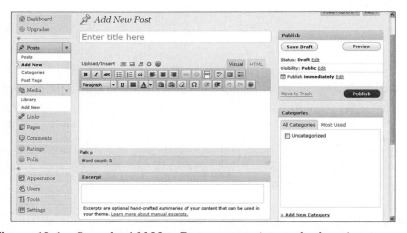

Figure 10-1 *Open the **Add New Post** page to write—and enhance!—a new post on your blog.*

Be sure you're viewing the visual post editor and the entire kitchen sink toolbar is visible in the post editor, as discussed in Chapter 9. Type some text into the post editor, highlight it with your mouse, and click on some of the icons in the toolbar to see how each affects the text you typed.

The following toolbar icons, as shown in Figure 10-1, should be available to you:

Bold Click to make the highlighted text bold.

Italic   Click to make the highlighted text italic.

Strikethrough   Click to make a line appear over the highlighted text so it looks like the text has been crossed out.

Bullet   Click to format the highlighted text as a bulleted list.

Number   Click to format the highlighted text as a numbered list.

Block quotes   Click to format the highlighted text as quoted text. The format for text set in block quotes varies depending on the WordPress theme you're using.

Left align   Click to left align the text.

Center align   Click to center align the text.

Right align   Click to right align the text.

Add link   Click to turn the highlighted text into a link.

Remove link   Click to remove a link from the highlighted text.

More   Click to insert the *HTML More tag* where your cursor is placed in the text of your post.

DEFINITION

The **HTML More tag** is a piece of HTML code that truncates a blog post where the tag is inserted, so only part of the post appears on the home page of most recent blog posts. To read the entire post, a visitor needs to click a link that's automatically inserted into the post where the More tag is used. The wording of that link depends on the WordPress theme you're using, but it usually says something similar to "read more."

Proofread   Click to run the WordPress proofreader function and check your blog post for spelling and grammatical errors.

Toggle full screen mode   If you want to make your post editor the size of your computer monitor screen, click this icon. Click it again to return to regular screen mode.

Kitchen sink   Click to show or hide additional toolbar menu items in the visual post editor.

Paragraph formatting   Click the drop-down menu to apply a paragraph formatting option to specific paragraphs in your blog post. The appearance of these options changes depending on the WordPress theme you're using.

Underline Click to make the highlighted text underlined.

Full align Click to full justify your text, so both the left and right sides are aligned.

Text color Click the drop-down arrow to change the color of the highlighted text.

Paste as plain text Click to paste text copied from another source into your post with no formatting applied to it.

Paste from Word Click to paste text copied from Microsoft Word into your blog post. Note that copying and pasting text from Word to your blog post editor can cause problems in the HTML coding of your post, which can affect the display of the post live on your blog. Read Appendix B for more information about avoiding this problem.

Remove formatting Click to remove any special formatting applied to the highlighted text.

Insert custom character Click to insert a custom character, such as a copyright symbol, into your blog post.

Outdent Click to remove the indent from text that's been indented.

Indent Click to indent paragraphs of text.

Undo Click to undo the last action performed in the visual post editor.

Redo Click to redo the last action performed in the visual post editor.

Help Click to launch a pop-up window with basic help information about the post editor.

QUICK TIP

With most of the icons in the visual post editor, all the text you type after you click the icon will appear with the chosen formatting until you click the icon again to return to standard text formatting. You can also highlight specific text with your mouse and then click the desired formatting icon to apply that formatting to just the chosen text.

The more you use WordPress, the more familiar you'll get with the visual editor toolbar.

Working with the HTML Editor

The HTML editor, shown in Figure 10-2, enables you to input blog post content in HTML format if you know HTML. The HTML editor gives you complete flexibility in terms of formatting your blog post content. And you can save time using the HTML editor toolbar by simply clicking on a button to apply commonly used formatting to text in your post.

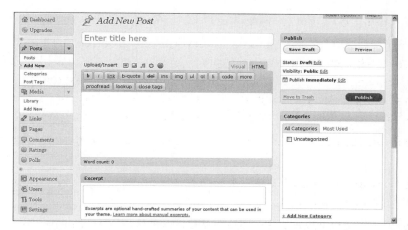

Figure 10-2   *The HTML editor toolbar provides quick access to common HTML tags.*

The following buttons are available in the HTML editor toolbar:

Bold   Click this button to apply the bold tag to highlighted text.

Italics   Click this button to apply the italics tag to highlighted text.

Link   Click this button to turn the highlighted text into an active hyperlink to the URL of your choice.

B-quote   Click this button to turn the highlighted text into a quotation using the formatting coded into your WordPress theme.

Delete   Click this button to show where text has been changed or deleted in your post. When you apply this tag to text, it typically appears crossed out in your live post.

Insert   Click this button to show where text has been inserted into your post. When you apply this tag to text, it appears shaded in a colored box, underlined, or in another format, depending on your browser and WordPress theme.

Image   Click this button and enter the URL of an image you want to display in your post.

Unordered List   Click this button to create a bulleted list.

Ordered List   Click this button to create a numbered list.

List Item   Click this button to create line items in a bulleted or numbered list.

Code   Click this button to insert programming code into your post.

More   Click this button to insert the HTML More tag into your post.

Proofread   Click this button to use the WordPress proofreading function to check your post for spelling or grammar errors.

Lookup   Click this button to look up HTML tags you can't remember.

Close Tags   Click this button to automatically close any HTML tags you might have left open in your post.

 INSIDER SECRET

You can highlight text in your post and then click the HTML formatting buttons from the toolbar to apply that code to the selected text, or you can use the HTML formatting buttons while you type your post. For example, click on the bold button to start the HTML tag, type the text you want to format as bold in your post, and click on the bold button again to end the HTML tag. The text within the tag will be bold on your live post.

Using the buttons in the HTML editor is up to you. Some people find the buttons help them save time because they don't have to type all the HTML tags, but other people find it easier to actually type the coding themselves. Only you can decide how to make the features of WordPress work best for you, and that includes the HTML editor.

Making Your Posts Shine

Now that you understand what all those icons on your post editor toolbar mean, it's time to put them into action. Adding text enhancements, images, video, and more to your blog posts can make your blog more visually appealing and even add inter-activity to your posts. This section teaches you how to do it using the free features available to you from WordPress.com.

Adding Links

Links are an essential part of blogs because they help bloggers cite sources and offer a way for readers to find more information both on your blog and on other sites. As you learned in Chapter 9, using links can also help you increase traffic to your blog through WordPress's trackback function.

To add a text link to your blog post, simply highlight the text you want to serve as the link and click the **Insert/edit link** icon (it looks like a closed chain link) in your visual post editor toolbar. This opens the **Insert/edit link** dialogue box, shown in Figure 10-3.

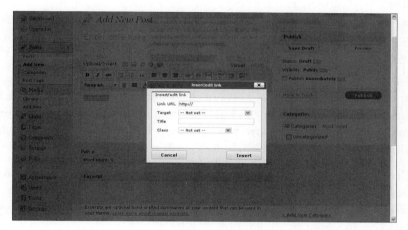

Figure 10-3 *You can use the Insert/edit link dialogue box to add a link in your blog posts.*

In the **Link URL** text box, enter the exact URL of the page you want people to go to when they click on the linked text in your blog post.

QUICK TIP

If the page you want to link to has a very long URL, don't try to retype the whole URL into the Link URL box. Instead, open the page in a new browser window or tab and copy and paste the URL into the Link URL box.

Next, click the drop-down menu next to **Target** and select **Open link in the same window** if you want the linked page to open in the active window, so visitors will have to hit the **Back** button in their browser to return to your blog post. If you prefer, you can select **Open link in a new window**. This causes a new browser window to open when a visitor clicks on the link, taking them to that URL. To return to your blog, the visitor simply needs to return to the original browser window. If you don't select an option from this drop-down menu, it remains **-- Not set --** and the linked page opens in the same browser window as your post.

If you want to add a title to the HTML coding of your link, which might help with your search engine optimization efforts, you can do so by typing the text into the **Title** box.

Finally, the **Class** drop-down menu allows you to apply unique formatting to your links, which are defined in the CSS of your WordPress theme. Some people never use this drop-down menu, while others find it very useful. Your best bet is to test out how each of the items in this drop-down list affects your linked text when applied to see which ones you'd like to use.

Once your link settings are configured, click **Insert**. The text in your visual editor now appears as a live hyperlink. You can make additional edits to the link by placing your cursor somewhere within the linked text and clicking the **Insert/edit link** icon again to reopen the dialogue box. You can delete the link by clicking the **Unlink** icon, which looks like a broken chain link, in the visual editor toolbar.

Click **Preview** to see how your link will appear in your post when it's live on your blog. Depending on your WordPress theme, your link formatting can vary, but typically, links are set in a different color from other text in your posts, or they might be underlined or displayed in a bold font.

Inserting Images

One of the easiest ways to make your blog posts look better is to add images. Photos, for example, give your blog a boost of color and give visitors' eyes relief from otherwise text-heavy pages. The first step to adding images into your blog posts is finding images you're legally allowed to republish, preferably for free. See Chapter 4 to learn more about what kinds of images you can legally use on your blog. You certainly don't want to be accused of violating copyright laws!

In Appendix C, I give you several websites where you can find free images you can legally use on your blog. See the "Free Images Sites" section there. Just be sure to read the requirements for using each image individually to ensure you provide appropriate notification and attribution as determined by the image's owner.

PROCEED WITH CAUTION

If you upload a lot of very large files, you might run out of space to store your blog and associated files in your WordPress account quickly. Save images into a web-friendly size and format before you upload them to your blog.

When you find an image you want to use in your blog post, save it to your computer's hard drive. Save it again at the actual size you want it to appear in your blog and in either .jpg, .gif, or .png format. The size you should save images in for your posts depends partly on the WordPress theme you're using.

For example, if you want an image to be the same width as your blog's post column, you need to know how wide your post column is. The best way to determine the size you like images to appear in your blog posts is to insert an image into a post and play around with it, as described later in this section, to find the size you like. Then you can save images to that size for future posts.

If you don't have an image-editing software program like Adobe Photoshop loaded on your computer, a number of free programs are available you can download and use on your computer or use online. See the "Image-Editing Tools" section in Appendix C for several great options.

When your image is the size and format you need, you can upload it to your WordPress account and insert it into your blog post. Place your cursor where you want to insert an image into your blog post, and click the **Add an Image** icon next to **Upload/Insert** above the visual post editor. This opens the **Add an Image** dialogue box, shown in Figure 10-4.

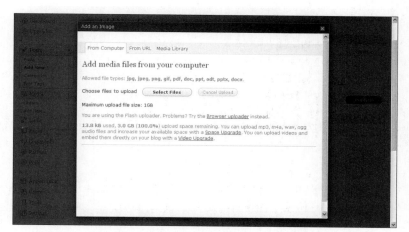

Figure 10-4   *Insert an image into your blog post using the **Add an Image** option.*

Notice the tab links in the top navigation bar of the Add an Image dialogue box. You can upload an image from your computer, insert an image you link to from another website, or insert an image you've already uploaded that's available in your WordPress.com media gallery.

To insert an image from your computer, be sure the **From Computer** tab is selected, and click the **Select Files** button, shown in Figure 10-4, to open a new dialogue box where you can navigate your hard drive folders and select the file you want to insert. When you find the file, select it and click **Open**. Your image is automatically uploaded to your WordPress account, and a new portion of the dialogue box is revealed where you can add information to your image file and insert it into your post, as shown in Figure 10-5.

The first text box in Figure 10-5 shows the title of your image, which was generated from the filename you uploaded. The second text box, **Alternate Text,** is where you can add text that appears on a visitor's screen when the image won't load.

INSIDER SECRET

Alternate text also appears in the HTML code for your image, so it can help with search engine optimization efforts. You might want to consider using keywords when you complete this box.

Figure 10-5 *Add information to your image, and insert it into your post.*

If you want, you can also add an image caption in the **Caption** text box and a description in the **Description** box.

The **Link URL** box is an important one, because this is the URL for the uploaded image. By editing this text box, you can change where the image shown in your live blog post links to, or you can delete the link entirely. Just enter the URL into the text box where you want visitors to go when they click on it in your post, or click **None** to remove the link from the image.

In the **Alignment** section, select the radio button next to the alignment you want for your image. You can choose **None** so the image appears on its own line with no word wrapping around it, or you can choose **Left**, **Center**, or **Right**. Play around with these settings to see how they look on your blog.

Finally, you can change the size of the image by selecting the appropriate radio button in the **Size** section. Depending on the image you uploaded, some or all of these size options will be available.

When you've completed configuring your image settings, click **Insert into Post**, and the image is instantly inserted into your post editor. You can click **Preview** to see how your post will look on your blog when it's live.

If you want to make any changes to your image after you've inserted it into your post, you can do so by clicking on the image in the post editor. Two icons appear in the upper-left corner of the image, as shown in Figure 10-6. These icons allow you to edit or delete the image. Click the **Edit Image** icon to open the **Edit Image** dialogue box, where you can make changes to the image within your post.

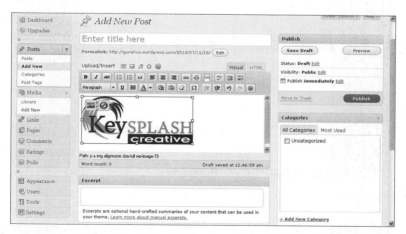

Figure 10-6   *Edit an image by selecting it and then clicking the* **Edit Image** *icon.*

When you open the **Edit Image** dialogue box, you are presented with the Edit Image page, shown in Figure 10-7, where you can modify the alignment, title, alternate text, caption, and link URL for the image.

Figure 10-7 *Change settings for your image by entering information into the Edit Image dialogue box.*

You can make more edits and enhancements to the image in your post by clicking the **Advanced Settings** tab at the top of the dialogue box. Many more options are available to you in the Advanced Image Settings dialogue box, as shown in Figure 10-8.

Figure 10-8 *WordPress's advanced settings help you make your images look even better.*

The first option available to you in the Advanced Settings page is the resizing function. With this, you can choose a new size for your image based on percentages. Next, you can view the source of the image file you uploaded and make further size changes using the text boxes in the **Size** section.

> **QUICK TIP**
>
> You can resize images directly from the visual post editor by clicking on an image to select it and then clicking and dragging from any corner of that image.

If you know CSS, you can add CSS class coding into the **CSS Class** text box and the **Styles** text box. Even if you don't know CSS, you can enter numbers into the **Image properties** text boxes to place a border around your image (the CSS of your WordPress theme determines the color of the border) and add vertical space or horizontal space between the image and the text that wraps around it.

In the Advanced Link Settings section, you can make changes to your image link, such as the link title or opening the page the image links to in a new window (select the check box in the **Target** section).

When you're satisfied with your configurations, click **Update** to apply your settings to the image in your post. You can click **Preview** in your WordPress Add New Post page to view how your changes will look on your live blog.

Don't be overwhelmed by the amount of options available to you. Test them out and see what they do so you can determine if they're useful to you and help you meet your blogging goals or not. Remember, there's no wrong or right way to use WordPress. As long as you're doing what you need to do to meet your personal blogging goals, you're doing great.

Adding Video

If you want to be able to upload videos from your computer directly to your WordPress.com account and publish them in your blog posts, you need to pay for the WordPress.com VideoPress Upgrade, which I discuss in Chapter 13. Fortunately, several websites allow you to upload your video content and embed the code to play that video content in your blog posts. A few popular examples are YouTube (www.youtube.com), Dailymotion (www.dailymotion.com), and Google Video (video.google.com).

INSIDER SECRET

You can embed any video into your blog post that has embed code available (even if you didn't create it), so visitors can play it without leaving your blog.

YouTube is by far the most popular video upload and sharing site. You can create a free account and upload a video in minutes. Once that video is uploaded, you can embed it into your WordPress.com blog posts with a few clicks of your mouse.

To embed a YouTube video into a WordPress.com blog post, copy the URL for the YouTube.com video to your clipboard. Next, return to your visual post editor and insert your cursor where you want the video to appear in your post. Click the **Add Video** icon above the post editor, and select the **From URL** link at the top of the **Add Video** dialogue box to open the **Add media file from URL** page, shown in Figure 10-9. Paste the link into the **URL** text box, and click **Insert into Post**.

The appropriate embed code is automatically inserted into your post. When you publish your post, the embedded video will display in your post where visitors can watch it without leaving your blog, as shown in Figure 10-10.

Figure 10-9   *Paste the URL for the YouTube video you want to play in your blog post into the **URL** text box.*

Figure 10-10   *Visitors can watch embedded YouTube videos without leaving your blog.*

Adding Audio

To upload audio content to your blog using the Add Audio icon and make it playable on your blog, you need to purchase the WordPress.com Space Upgrade, which I discuss in Chapter 13.

If you don't need to upload audio but simply want to play audio available from other sites, some sites like Google, Odeo, and Yahoo! offer players while others, like Playlist.com, allow you to play your own playlist on your blog. Just be sure any audio you play on your blog is not copyright protected.

Adding Media

The Add Media icon allows you to upload and modify the settings for any media you want to insert into your blog post. You can also add media to upload and later insert into blog posts, pages, and sidebars using the **Add New** link in the Media section of the left menu in your WordPress account.

To see all images in your Media library at any time, click the **Library** link in the Media section of your left menu.

Adding Polls

You can easily add polls to your blog posts by clicking the **Add Polls** icon and opening a free account with Polldaddy (polldaddy.com) or importing information from your existing Polldaddy account into WordPress.

The process of creating polls takes just a few minutes. Simply enter your poll question and answers and select your customization settings. (See Chapter 12 for more on polls.)

Applying Text Enhancements

You can make text in your blog posts bold, italicized, underlined, bulleted, numbered, indented, aligned, and more using the icons in your visual post editor toolbar. Depending on the WordPress theme you're using, formatting such as bullets, numbers, and block quotes can vary. The same is true of the paragraph formatting options you can access from the drop-down menu in your visual editor toolbar.

Take a look at Figure 10-11 to see how the various paragraph attributes make your text look on a live blog using the default WordPress.com Twenty Ten theme.

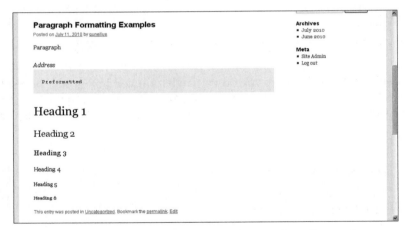

Figure 10-11 *Paragraph attribute appearances vary depending on the WordPress theme you're using on your blog.*

Editing Posts

What happens if you publish your blog post and later realize there's something wrong you need to change or something missing you need to add? No need to worry! WordPress makes it easy to edit your blog posts after you've published them.

Click the **Posts** link in the Posts section of your WordPress dashboard left menu to open the Posts page of your WordPress account, as shown in Figure 10-12.

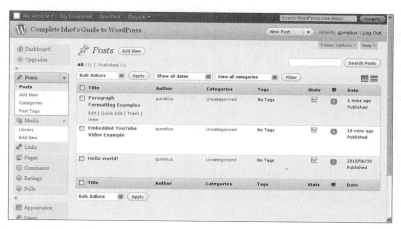

Figure 10-12   *All your blog posts are listed in the Posts section.*

You can filter your list of posts using the links under the Posts title, depending on whether you want to view all posts, scheduled posts only, published posts only, or drafts only. You can also use the drop-down menus to filter posts by date and categories.

PROCEED WITH CAUTION

These link options only appear if you have posts saved in each of the aforementioned states of publication.

Scroll through your list of links to find the post you want to edit. Hover your mouse over the post to be edited, and several links will appear beneath the post title: edit the post, do a quick edit (this allows you to make minor changes to elements like categories and tags, as shown in Figure 10-13), send the post to the trash, or preview it.

Click **Edit** to open the post and make your changes. When you're finished, click **Update** in the Publish module to make your changes go live on your blog. That's all there is to it!

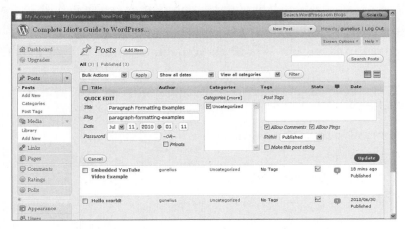

Figure 10-13 *Make minor edits to posts using the Quick Edit feature.*

As always, your blog is your own space on the web, and you can publish, edit, and delete posts on your own blog whenever you want. Just be sure to follow the rules of the law and the blogosphere described in Chapter 4 to ensure you don't get yourself into any trouble with your blog post content.

The Least You Need to Know

- You can write blog posts using an editor that simulates word processing software or using HTML.

- WordPress.com offers many functions and options to enhance your blog posts. It's not necessary to use every option available to you. Experiment to see which ones are worth your time.

- Some features to enhance posts are only available if you pay for a WordPress.com account upgrade.

- The published style of many enhancements varies depending on the WordPress theme you use on your blog.

Adding Pages to Your Blog

In This Chapter

- Comparing posts and pages
- Creating new pages
- Configuring page settings
- Changing or removing pages

Beyond blog posts, WordPress.com allows you to add another layer to your blog to make it resemble a "real" website—pages. Of particular interest to many bloggers is the flexibility in terms of page navigation WordPress.com offers.

After you learn about page navigation, page configuration, and page creation in this chapter, you'll be able to take your blog to the next level of web publishing.

Pages Versus Posts

One of the biggest areas of confusion for new WordPress.com users is the difference between pages and posts. In simplest terms, pages are typically used for static content, meaning content that doesn't change often. For example, you can create an About Me page, a Contact page, a Products and Services page if you own a business, and so on. Pages are usually accessible through your blog's top navigation bar and can be accessed through the Pages widget links, if you include that widget in your blog's sidebar.

Additionally, pages do not offer categorizing or tagging. Page formatting might also differ from post formatting, depending on the WordPress theme you're using. In fact, some WordPress themes allow you to have different sidebars for pages versus posts.

On the other hand, posts are published in reverse-chronological order and are usually accessible through archives that list posts by date or category. Sometimes, bloggers include links to tags in their blog sidebars, which is another way visitors can access archived posts. You can control how many posts are displayed on a single archive page—including your blog's home page—by modifying the Reading settings for your blog (as discussed in Chapter 7).

Furthermore, your blog posts are included in your blog's RSS feed, while pages are not. (Learn more about feeds and subscriptions in Chapter 19.)

Publishing a Page on Your Blog

Publishing pages on your blog is not that different from publishing posts. Some configuration options differ from post creation to page creation, but the post editor is the same as the page editor. If you can create posts, you can create pages.

Creating a New Page

The first step to publishing a new page on your blog is to click on the drop-down arrow next to **Pages** in the left menu of your WordPress dashboard to reveal the links in that section. Next, click the **Add New** link to open the **Add New Page** screen, shown in Figure 11-1.

Figure 11-1 *You can enter your page information in the **Add New Page** screen.*

Start your page by entering a title for it in the **Title** text box, which is the text box located directly beneath the Add New Page heading. Next, enter the body text for your page into the page editor. All the icons available to you through the page editor toolbar are the same as those described in Chapter 10 for the post editor toolbar. As you enter text and images, you can see how your page will look on your live blog by clicking **Preview** in the Publish module located on the right side of your screen.

QUICK TIP

Be sure to click the **Save Draft** button occasionally so you don't lose your work if your power goes out or your Internet connection goes down. WordPress. com does autosave your page, but it might not do it often enough for you, especially if you're making lots of changes. It's better to be safe than sorry.

In fact, all features in the Publish module work the same way for pages as they do for posts. You can modify the **Status**, **Visibility**, and scheduling settings for your page, just as you can modify them for posts (as discussed in Chapter 10).

Configuring Page Attributes

The Page Attributes module located on the right side of the Add New Page window offers you several options to configure the formatting and navigation of your page. If you want your new page to be a primary page on your blog (typically, primary pages appear in your navigation bar and other subpages can be published hierarchically beneath primary, parent pages), be sure the **(no parent)** option is selected. If you want your new page to be a child of an existing page, click on the drop-down menu and select the desired parent page from the list. Note that the parent page needs to be created first before you can make a new page a child of that parent page. Also, keep in mind that not all WordPress themes offer all these page attribute features.

For example, if you write a blog about making money online, you might want to offer a resources section made up of static pages. The parent page could be called "Resources" and include an explanation of the types of resources available to readers. Child pages could be called "Online Resources," "Books," "Seminars," and "Organizations," where you can provide specific links and details for different types of resources.

In the **Template** section of the Page Attributes module, you can select the drop-down menu to see if your WordPress theme offers more than one type of page template for you to choose from. For example, some themes offer specific Contact page templates or page templates with and without sidebars. Select the template you want to apply to your page from the drop-down menu.

The final section of the Page Attributes module is where you can set the order of your pages, which affects how they appear in your blog's navigation bar. Typically, pages are listed in your navigation bar from left to right in the order they were published. If you want to change that order, you can do so by numbering your pages in your preferred order and entering the number of each specific page in the **Order** text box for that page.

INSIDER SECRET

You can also configure navigation settings for pages using the **Menus** link located in the Appearance section of your WordPress dashboard left menu. (See Chapter 8 for more.)

Choosing Discussion Settings

You can set up your pages to accept comments, trackbacks, and pings in the same way you configure those settings for your posts (as discussed in Chapter 10). Most blogs allow comments, trackbacks, and pings on posts to encourage discussion and interactivity—thereby growing their blogs—but allowing them on pages is a different story entirely.

If your blog pages are truly static content, you might not want to allow comments, trackbacks, and pings. For example, do you want people to leave comments on your Contact page? That might not be an appropriate place for conversations.

QUICK TIP

Many comments and trackbacks published on pages are spam. If you notice a lot of spam comments and trackbacks on your pages, you might want to disable discussion on some or all of your blog pages.

Depending on which WordPress theme you're using on your blog, you may have additional modules available to you on the Add Page window of your WordPress dashboard. Click the **Screen Options** drop-down arrow in the upper right of the Add New Page screen to see all available modules. Check the box next to any modules that aren't active to add them to your screen and experiment with them.

Remember, you can't break your blog by testing out features. If additional options are available to you, try them out and see what they do. You can always remove them if you don't like them.

Editing or Deleting Pages

You can edit and delete pages in your blog similarly to how you edit and delete posts. Simply click on the **Pages** link located in the Pages section of the left menu of your WordPress dashboard. A directory of all of your published, draft, scheduled, and deleted pages is available through this screen, as shown in Figure 11-2.

Figure 11-2   *You can access all your pages through the Pages directory.*

Note that you'll only be able to view links to pages identified as **Published**, **Drafts**, and **Trash** under the Pages heading if you have pages saved in those states of publication. If you have a lot of pages and have trouble finding a specific page, you can filter pages by status of publication or by date if you use the drop-down menu provided.

When you locate the page you want to edit, simply hover over the title to reveal links to **Edit**, **Quick Edit**, **Trash**, or **View** the page. When you click the **Edit** link, the Edit Page window opens, which looks just like the Add Page window. You can make changes to your post and click the **Update** link in the Publish module to update your page on your live blog.

If you click on the **Quick Edit** link, your page directory screen expands to reveal several editing functions to make simple modifications to your post, as shown in

Figure 11-3. Just make your edits and click the **Update** button to instantly update your page on your blog.

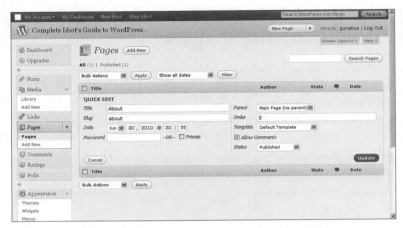

Figure 11-3 *Make simple changes to a page with the Quick Edit function.*

You can view your page live on your blog at any time by clicking the **View** link or delete it by clicking on the **Trash** link. Note your page isn't completely deleted from your WordPress account until you click the **Trash** link at the top of the page directory screen (under the Pages heading) and click the **Delete Permanently** link for that page.

The Least You Need to Know

- Pages live outside the post chronology and archives on WordPress blogs.
- Creating a new page is very similar to creating a new post.
- You can change the navigation and hierarchy of your pages easily with WordPress.
- You can allow comments, trackbacks, and pings on pages or disable the function on specific pages to suit your needs.

Using Popular WordPress Features

In This Chapter

- Links, comments, ratings, polls, and more
- Adding users and setting permissions
- Importing and exporting blogs to WordPress.com
- When it's time to delete your blog

The WordPress.com dashboard is your one-stop shop for everything you need to manage and maintain your blog. The longer you use WordPress, the more you'll find that there are certain tools you couldn't live without and other tools you never use at all. No matter what you do with WordPress, everything you need is available to you through the left menu of your WordPress dashboard. It couldn't be easier!

This chapter teaches you how to manage links, comments, ratings, and polls through your WordPress dashboard, as well as extra tools that allow you to accomplish tasks like publishing blog posts via e-mail. You also learn how to add users to your WordPress.com account. Finally, if you need to import a blog from another blogging application to WordPress.com (or vice versa), or if you want to delete your blog entirely, you find out how to do it in these pages.

Links

WordPress.com's Links feature makes it easy for you to create lists of links you want to remember and even share on your blog. To view your Links directory, click the drop-down arrow to expand the **Links** section of your WordPress dashboard left menu, and click the **Links** hyperlink. This opens the Links directory page, shown in Figure 12-1.

Figure 12-1 *The Links page shows all the links you've saved.*

A new WordPress blog automatically includes a number of links saved to the Blogroll link category. These handy links, visible in Figure 12-1, help you access help and other information from WordPress. Most people delete these links or create a new link category and move these links to that new category so they can use the blogroll category for those links they truly want to share in their blogrolls (as discussed in Chapter 6).

> **QUICK TIP**
>
> You can add a list of links in any category you've created (such as a blogroll) by visiting the **Appearance, Widgets** section of your WordPress dashboard and dragging a Links widget into your blog's sidebar module. Simply click on the drop-down arrow to expand the Links widget and choose the category of links you want to publish.

You can edit existing links by hovering over the link title in the Links directory. This reveals two hyperlinks beneath it that allow you to edit or delete the link. Click the **Edit** link to open the Edit Link page, shown in Figure 12-2, where you can make changes to the link name, URL, or description. If you have multiple link categories, you'll also be able to select which category you want the link to be in by checking the appropriate box in the Categories section of the Edit Link page. Finally, you can hide a link so only you can see it by checking the box next to **Keep this link private** in the Save module. For example, you might want to include a link to the login page for your WordPress dashboard so you can easily log in to your account directly from your blog. However, that's not a link that adds value to the user experience on your blog, so it makes sense to hide it from visitors. When you're satisfied with your changes, click **Update Link** to save your edited link.

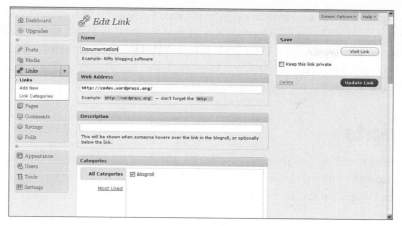

Figure 12-2   *You can make changes to an existing link in the Edit Link page.*

You can add a brand-new link to your Links directory by clicking the **Add New** link in the Links section of your WordPress dashboard left menu. This opens the Add New Link page, which is almost identical to the Edit Link page, but you'll need to enter the name, link, and optional description from scratch.

Finally, you can manage your link categories by selecting the **Link Categories** link in the Links section of your WordPress dashboard left menu to open the Link Categories page, shown in Figure 12-3.

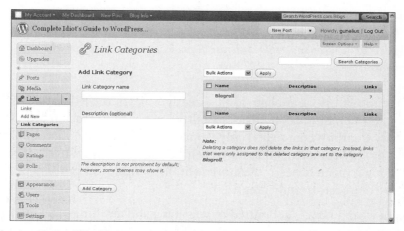

Figure 12-3   *WordPress.com makes it easy for you to add, edit, and delete categories from the Link Categories page.*

Enter a title for your new category in the **Link Category Name** text box as well as a description in the **Description** text box, if you want. Click the **Add Category** button to add your new category to your link categories directory, which is visible in the module on the right side of the Link Categories page, shown in Figure 12-3. You can also edit and delete link categories from the right module.

Comments

You can moderate and manage comments submitted on your blog posts by clicking the **Comments** link in the left menu of your WordPress dashboard to open the Comments page, shown in Figure 12-4.

Figure 12-4 *You can easily moderate discussions on your blog from the Comments page.*

Across the top of the Comments page, directly beneath the title, are five links. These allow you to filter all the comments submitted to your blog so you can view **All** comments, only **Pending** comments, only **Approved** comments, only comments identified as **Spam**, or only comments that have been deleted and moved to the **Trash**. Using the drop-down menu beneath the aforementioned links, you can also filter your list to show only comments or only pings.

When a new comment is submitted to your blog and awaiting your moderation before it's published (if you configured your blog Discussion settings to require comment moderation, as discussed in Chapter 7), it will appear in the comment list set off in a different background color than approved comments. When you hover over the comment text, six links appear beneath it, as shown in Figure 12-4. These allow you to **Approve** the comment, **Reply** to the comment without leaving the page, perform a **Quick Edit** to the comment, perform a full **Edit** on the comment, mark the comment as **Spam**, or move the comment to **Trash**.

INSIDER SECRET

It's important to mark spam comments as such so Akismet, discussed in Chapter 6, can learn to better identify spam and automatically send similar comments to your comment spam rather than to your moderation queue.

When you click **Approve**, the comment immediately appears on your live blog post. When you click **Reply**, the page expands and reveals a text editor, shown in Figure 12-5, where you can enter your reply and click the **Submit Reply** button to instantly publish your reply to that comment on your live blog post.

Figure 12-5 *It's easy to reply to comments without leaving the Comments page of your WordPress dashboard.*

When you click the **Quick Edit** or **Edit** links, your page expands to reveal text boxes and text editors where you can make changes to the comment. Just make your edits and click the **Update Comment** button to save the revised comment. Note that you'll still have to approve the comment, if you haven't already done so, before it publishes on your blog.

QUICK TIP

Be sure you publish a comment policy (see Chapter 4) before you edit or delete comments so visitors know what they can and can't publish on your blog and expectations are set correctly.

Remember, the comments you identify as spam or trash are not published on your blog, but they remain in your comments directory until you delete them permanently. To do so, hover your mouse over the comment you want to delete forever in your trash or spam list and click on the **Delete Permanently** link that appears beneath it.

To quickly approve, unapprove, mark as spam, or delete to multiple comments at the same time, check the box to the left of each comment you want to perform the action on and then click the **Bulk Actions** drop-down menu at the top of your screen. Choose the action you want to perform on all the comments you selected from the list, and click the **Apply** button to carry out the action for all selected comments at the same time. This is a great time-saver!

Ratings

WordPress.com offers a fun feature through Polldaddy (polldaddy.com) where your blog visitors can rate your blog posts. To access the feature, click the drop-down menu next to **Ratings** in the left menu of your WordPress dashboard and then click the **Settings** link to open the Rating Settings page, shown in Figure 12-6.

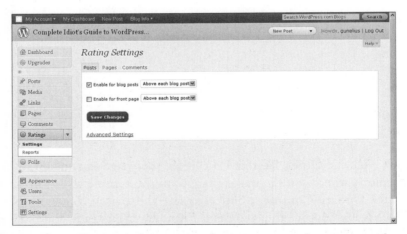

Figure 12-6 *You can configure ratings for posts, pages, and comments on the Rating Settings page.*

Three link tabs are located in the navigation bar at the top of the Rating Settings page. These enable you to configure ratings settings for **Posts**, **Pages**, or **Comments**. In the Posts settings page, shown in Figure 12-6, you have two configuration settings. You can allow ratings on individual post pages, which can appear above or below each post, or you can allow ratings on posts that appear on your blog's home page above or below each post. Check the boxes next to the settings you want to enable, and choose your preferred rating placement from the drop-down menus.

Similarly, you can configure whether or not you want comments to appear above or below each page on your blog and each comment on your blog by clicking on the **Pages** and **Comments** tabs and choosing your preferred settings. Be sure to click **Save Changes** on each page of the Rating Settings configuration screens or your settings won't go into effect.

When you enable a rating function on posts, pages, or comments and click **Save Changes**, a new **Advanced Settings** link appears beneath that button. Click that link to reveal a variety of additional settings you can configure for that ratings selection, as shown in Figure 12-7 for post ratings.

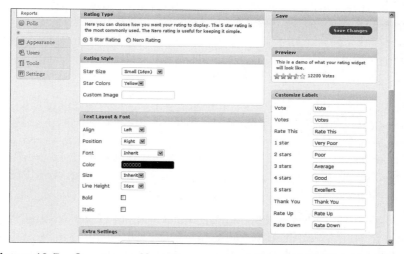

Figure 12-7   *Once you enable ratings, you can configure advanced settings for them.*

The first module lets you choose the **Rating Type**, which can be a 5-star rating or a Nero rating system (a simple thumbs-up or thumbs-down rating). Click on the radio button next to the type of rating system you want to use. You can see what the rating system will look like on your blog in the Preview module on the right side of your screen.

Next, in the **Rating Style** module, you can choose the styles you want to use for your ratings and make any changes to the layout, colors, and fonts used in your rating system appearance through the options available in the **Text Layout & Font** module.

You can also change the labels used in your ratings by typing in new titles in the text boxes found in the **Customize Labels** module on the right side of your screen.

Finally, if you publish any posts you don't want visitors to be able to rate, you can enter the Post IDs for those posts in the **Exclude Posts** text box in the Extra Settings module. Once all your settings are configured, click **Save Changes** in the Save module to put your changes into effect on your blog.

> **QUICK TIP**
>
> You can find a Post ID by clicking on the **Posts** link within the Posts section of the WordPress dashboard left menu to open the posts directory. Hover your mouse over the title of any post to reveal the **Edit** link. Click on that link to open the **Edit Post** page. The Post ID can be found within the URL displayed in your web browser as "post=#" where # is replaced by the numeric Post ID.

Polls

WordPress.com makes it easy for you to add polls using Polldaddy (polldaddy.com) to your blog posts without even leaving the blog post editor (as discussed in Chapter 10). You can also add, edit, and customize polls by clicking the drop-down arrow next to **Polls** in the left menu of your WordPress dashboard to reveal the available options. Get started by clicking the **Edit** link to open the Polls in your WordPress page, shown in Figure 12-8.

The first step is to create a Polldaddy account or import your existing Polldaddy account into your WordPress account. Select the radio button to create a new account with Polldaddy if you don't already have one, or select the radio button to import your existing Polldaddy account information into your WordPress.com account. Notice that when you choose the radio button to import your existing Polldaddy account, a new section of the page is revealed where you can enter your Polldaddy account e-mail address and password, as shown in Figure 12-9. After you make your choice, click on the **Do it: I want some polls!** button to configure your new account or instantly import your existing polls to your WordPress dashboard.

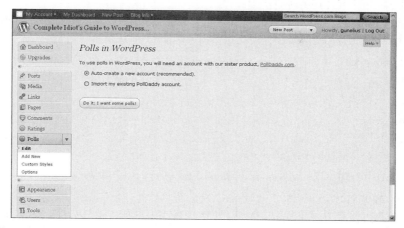

Figure 12-8   *Connect your Polldaddy account to your WordPress.com account.*

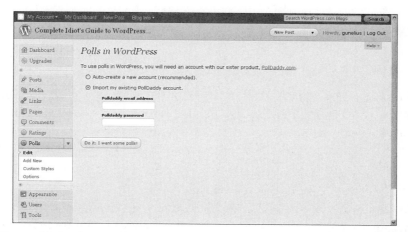

Figure 12-9   *It just takes a click of the mouse to import a Polldaddy account or start a new one without leaving your WordPress dashboard.*

With your existing Polldaddy account imported or your new account set up, you're automatically taken to the Polls list page in your WordPress dashboard, shown in Figure 12-10. Here you can create polls or edit existing polls directly from your WordPress dashboard.

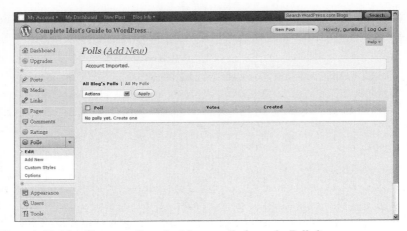

Figure 12-10 *You can edit and add new polls from the Polls list page.*

To create a new poll, click the **Add New** link at the top of the Polls list page or select the **Add New** link in the Polls section of your WordPress dashboard left menu to open the Create Poll page, shown in Figure 12-11.

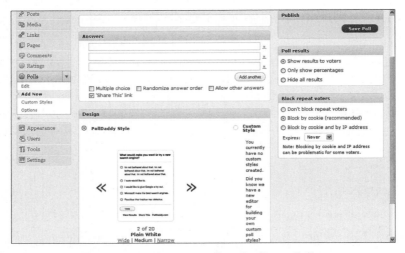

Figure 12-11 *You can customize your poll on the Create Poll page.*

In the top text box, enter your poll question. Next, enter the possible responses to your question you want people to choose from in the **Answers** text boxes. Notice the **X** to the right of each answer text box. Click the **X** to delete that answer text box if your question has fewer answers than provided text boxes. To add more possible answer text boxes, click the **Add another** button beneath the answer text boxes to create more responses.

You can also select the check boxes next to **Multiple choice, Randomize answer order, Allow other answers**, and **'Share This' link**. These options allow your visitors to select more than one answer to your poll, change the order answers are displayed in the poll so it's random for each visitor, allow visitors to add their own custom answers, and include a 'Share This' link, which makes it easy for visitors to share the poll on Twitter, Facebook, and other social media sites.

In the Design module, choose the style you want for your poll. You can click on the double arrows to the left and right of the displayed poll design to see the available choices. You can also choose the size of your poll by selecting the **Wide, Medium,** or **Narrow** links beneath the design you choose. Be sure you choose a width that will fit in your blog theme layout. If you want to take your poll design a step further, you can create a fully customized design by clicking the **Custom Style** radio button and using a design you created previously through the **Custom Styles** link in the **Polls** section of your WordPress left menu.

You can configure the amount of information you want your blog visitors to see related to your poll in the **Poll results** module on the right side of the Create Poll page. By choosing the appropriate radio button, you can display numeric and percentage results to all voters, show percentages only, or hide all results from visitors.

The final customizations you should make to your poll before you save it allow you to block repeat voters so they can't skew the results of your poll by voting again and again. If it doesn't matter to you if visitors vote repeatedly, you can select the **Don't block repeat voters** radio button. However, if you want to try to eliminate repeat voting, select the **Block by** *cookie* **(recommended)** or **Block by cookie and by** *IP address* radio buttons.

DEFINITION

A **cookie** is a text file stored in a web browser when you visit a specific web page. The server that sends that page data uses cookies to identify visitors to that page. An **IP address,** or Internet Protocol address, is a unique identifier number assigned to each connection to the Internet.

You can also set an expiration date for your poll by selecting when you want to close voting on your poll using the **Expires** drop-down menu.

When your poll is set up the way you want it, click **Save Poll** to save it to your polls list.

To add your poll to a blog post, simply write your blog post and place your cursor within the post editor exactly where you want the poll to appear. Click the **Add Poll** icon in the Upload/Insert area above the post editor (the icon looks like a circle), shown in Figure 12-12.

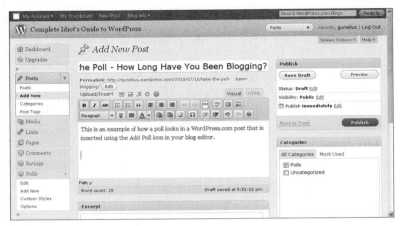

Figure 12-12   *Click the **Add Poll** icon to insert a poll into your blog post.*

The Add Poll dialogue box opens. Here you can hover your mouse over the poll you want to insert into your blog post to reveal a list of action links beneath the poll title, as shown in Figure 12-13.

Figure 12-13   *In the Add Poll box, you can choose the poll you want to insert into your blog post.*

Click the **Send to editor** link, and you're automatically returned to your blog post editor where the necessary code for your poll has already been inserted into your live blog post within brackets, as shown in Figure 12-14.

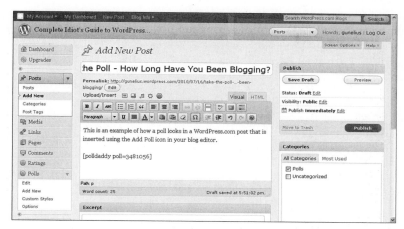

Figure 12-14   *In the blog post editor, an inserted poll displays as a snippet of code.*

Click the **Publish** button, and your new blog post goes live with your poll in it, as shown in Figure 12-15.

Figure 12-15   *A poll adds interactivity to your blog posts.*

You can also configure the general settings for your polls by selecting the **Options** link in the Polls section of your WordPress dashboard left menu to open the Options page, shown in Figure 12-16.

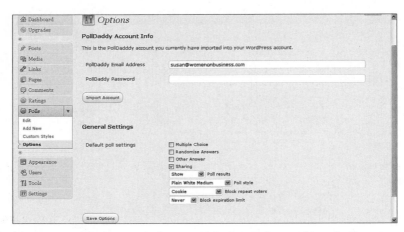

Figure 12-16 *You can configure your default poll settings from the Options page.*

In the General Settings section of the Options page, you can set defaults for most of your poll functions, which can save you time when you create polls in the future if you always use the same settings for your polls.

Adding Users

WordPress.com blogs can have multiple administrators, authors, and contributors. As long as your blog settings are not configured so your blog is private (as discussed in Chapter 7), you can add an unlimited number of users to your blog. However, if your blog is set to private, you can only add 35 users before you have to pay for an upgrade to your account.

Note that users are different from visitors to and readers of your blog. Users can access all or part of your WordPress account dashboard to add content to your blog, edit content, publish content, and even maintain your blog. Their access depends on what role you assign to them when you add them as users to your WordPress blog.

To view a list of the users who have been given access to some or all of your WordPress dashboard, click the drop-down arrow next to **Users** in the left menu of your WordPress dashboard and then click the **Users** link revealed in that section. This opens the Users directory list for your blog, as shown in Figure 12-17.

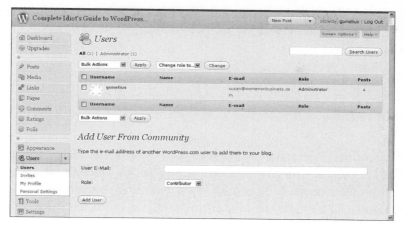

Figure 12-17 *View a list of users who have access to your WordPress dashboard in the Users directory.*

Each user is listed along with the name associated with their account, e-mail address, their role, and the number of posts they've published on your blog. Hovering over any username in the list reveals an **Edit** link beneath that username. Click the **Edit** link to open that user's profile and make any changes.

You can also add new users to your blog by completing the information requested in the **Add User from Community** section beneath the User directory list, as shown in Figure 12-17. Note that you can only add new users through this form if they already have WordPress.com accounts. Simply enter the new user's e-mail address (which is associated with his or her own WordPress.com account) and select the new user's desired role from the **Role** drop-down menu.

Defining User Roles and Permissions

You can set roles for your blog users depending on what level of access to your WordPress account you want to give them and what tasks you want them to perform on your blog. Changing a user's role at any time is easy. Just navigate to the **Users** directory page, shown in Figure 12-17, check the box next to the username whose role you want to change, and click the **Change role to...** drop-down box beneath the page title. Click on the new role you want to assign to that user from the drop-down list, and click the **Change** button to instantly change that user's role within your WordPress.com account for your blog.

You can choose from four roles for your users:

- Administrator

- Editor

- Author

- Contributor

An administrator has access to all parts of your WordPress dashboard associated with your blog. In essence, administrators are equivalent to owners of the blog because they have complete control. Be careful when assigning this role because an administrator can go so far as to delete your entire blog!

An editor can access a lot of your blog's settings and maintenance tasks. For example, she can publish, edit, or delete pages and posts. She can also moderate comments; upload images and media; and manage tags, links, and categories. An editor also has access to any blog statistics available through your WordPress dashboard.

An author can edit, publish, and delete the posts she creates, as well as upload images and media.

A contributor can create posts, but she can't publish them. Instead, she submits them to an administrator of the blog for review and publishing. Once the administrator publishes a contributor's post, the contributor can no longer edit it. A contributor cannot upload images or media to her posts.

Sending Invitations

You can also add users to your blog who do not have WordPress.com accounts yet. To do so, just click the **Invites** link in the Users section of your WordPress dashboard left menu to open the Invites page, shown in Figure 12-18.

Type the first and last name of the user you wish to invite to your blog into the **First Name** and **Last Name** fields in the **Send Invite To** form. Next, enter the new user's e-mail address where you want the invitation sent into the **Email** text box. If you'd like to add a message to go with your invitation, you can type it in the **Personal Message** text box. Finally, check the box next to **Add user to my blog as a contributor**, and click **Send Invite** to e-mail your invitation to the address you entered in the form.

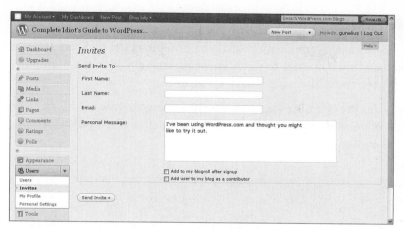

Figure 12-18   *You can invite users without WordPress.com accounts to access your blog using the Invites form.*

The new user receives an e-mail that invites her to sign up for a WordPress.com account. When she creates her WordPress.com account, she'll automatically appear in your Users directory list. Once she appears in your list of users, you can change her role on your blog if you need to.

Deleting Users

When the time comes to remove a user's access to your WordPress account, you can do so easily by clicking on the **Users** link in the Users section of your WordPress dashboard left menu to open the Users directory list page, shown in Figure 12-17. Check the box next to the username you want to delete, click the **Bulk Actions** drop-down menu located beneath the page title, and select **Remove** from the list. Click **Apply** to delete that user from your blog entirely.

Tools

Several additional tools are available through your WordPress.com dashboard that can make your life easier or speed up tasks. It's quite possible you'll never use these extra tools, but you should know they exist just in case you need them one day.

Press This

Press This is a handy application (called a bookmarklet) you can access at any time while you surf the Internet to open up a rudimentary blog post window and publish a new blog post about the page you're viewing.

To access the Press This tool, click the drop-down arrow to the right of **Tools** in the left menu of your WordPress dashboard. Next, click the **Tools** link to open the Tools page, as shown in Figure 12-19.

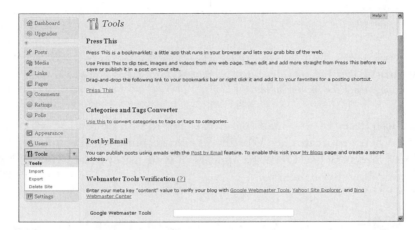

Figure 12-19 *You can configure Press This, Categories and Tags Converter, Post by Email, and Webmaster Tools Verification from the Tools page.*

Just drag and drop the **Press This** link to your browser's toolbar, so you can click on it at any time and write a new blog post faster than ever!

Categories and Tags Converter

You can selectively convert existing categories in your blog to tags or tags to categories by clicking the **Use This** link under the Categories and Tags Converter heading in the Tools page, shown in Figure 12-19. This opens the Import window, shown in Figure 12-20. Click the **Categories and Tags Converter** link in the Import window to do the conversion.

The Categories and Tags Converter is helpful if you import a blog to WordPress from another application and need to rearrange imported posts.

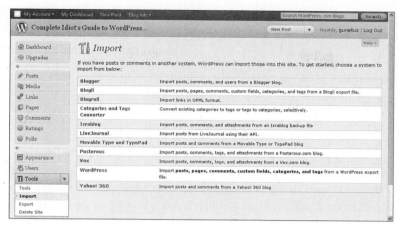

Figure 12-20 *You can convert tags and categories from the Import page.*

Post by Email

To be able to publish posts to your blog via e-mail, you need to first click on the **My Blogs** link in the Dashboard section of your WordPress dashboard left menu to open the **Blogs You're a Member Of** page, as shown in Figure 12-21.

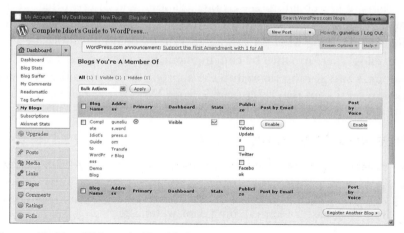

Figure 12-21 *Click on the **Enable** button to post to your blog by e-mail.*

Just click on the **Enable** button in the Post by Email column for the blog you want to be able to publish posts to via e-mail, and WordPress will send you a secret e-mail address you can use to send blog posts via e-mail for publishing on your blog.

When you create a post via e-mail, the subject of your e-mail message is used as your published post title, and the body of your e-mail is your post content. You can also include images as attachments to your e-mailed post, and they will be published with your post.

After you e-mail your post, you should receive a response e-mail within a few minutes that confirms your post's publication. It's a good idea to publish some test posts via e-mail to see how formatting is retained on your blog and how images appear before you use the Post by Email tool to publish a critical post to your blog.

INSIDER SECRET

You can include special codes to apply tags, categories, and more to your posts via e-mail. Visit en.support.wordpress.com/post-by-email for the current list of supported code.

Webmaster Tools Verification

The three major search engines—Google, Yahoo!, and Bing—offer special tools to help website owners track performance statistics and make the most of their sites. You can associate your blog with your Google, Yahoo!, or Bing webmaster accounts to track your blog's performance by copying your meta key content value from each of these accounts and pasting them into the appropriate fields in the **Webmaster Tools Verification** section of the Tools page in your WordPress dashboard, as shown in Figure 12-19.

You can sign up for each of these tools by visiting the following URLs:

- Google Webmaster Tools: google.com/webmasters/tools
- Yahoo! Site Explorer: siteexplorer.search.yahoo.com
- Bing Webmaster Central: bing.com/webmaster

QUICK TIP

For help in finding the necessary meta key content values, click the question mark link after the **Webmaster Tools Verification** heading on the Tools page to access additional information from the WordPress.com Support site.

Importing and Exporting Blogs

What if you started a blog using a different blogging application but now you want to use WordPress.com? What if you're using WordPress.com but want to export some or all of your content to another blog or application? Fortunately, it's relatively easy to do using the import and export functions accessible through your WordPress dashboard.

Importing Content to WordPress.com

WordPress.com makes it easy for you to import content from other blogging applications through the **Import** link located in the Tools section of the WordPress dashboard left menu. Click the **Import** link to open the Import page, shown in Figure 12-20. Choose from the menu the blogging application you want to import content from into WordPress, and follow the simple instructions for your specified application.

PROCEED WITH CAUTION

The content imported into WordPress.com might vary depending on the application you're importing from. Be sure to read the current information on the Import page in your WordPress dashboard so you fully understand what data will be imported before you begin the process.

Some blogging applications might require you to create an export file before you import into WordPress.com. Others might require you to log in to that account and authorize WordPress to access it before you can import content into WordPress. These types of requests are normal. Be sure to read the exporting directions from the other blogging application before you begin the import process to ensure your data is ready for the move.

Exporting Your WordPress.com Blog Content

You can also export your blog content by clicking the **Export** link in the Tools section of your WordPress dashboard left menu to open the **Export** page, shown in Figure 12-22.

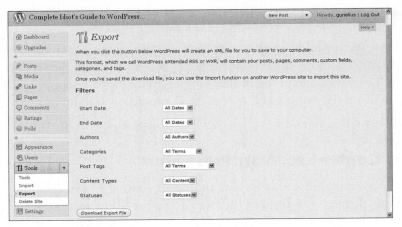

Figure 12-22 *Here you can configure the settings to export your blog.*

Using the drop-down menus on the Export page, select the data you want to export from your blog to an *XML* file that can be used to move your blog posts, pages, comments, *custom fields* (used in some WordPress themes), categories, and tags to another blogging application. For example, you can export all data or limit the exported data to a specific user's posts only or posts published in specific categories only.

DEFINITION

XML, or extensible markup language, is a generic formatting code that makes it easy to provide information to a wide variety of applications. **Custom fields** are used in WordPress themes to allow bloggers to add extra content or information to their blog posts, most often to enhance appearance. For example, a custom field might enable a blogger to attach a thumbnail image to a blog post.

Follow the instructions from your new blogging application to import the content from your WordPress.com blog to that account.

Deleting Your Blog

When the time comes that you want to delete your blog, you should take a moment and be sure you're completely certain because once you do it, your blog is gone forever.

Before you delete your blog entirely, you might want to set it to **Private** and remove it from search engines and WordPress.com indexing (as discussed in Chapter 7). This way, no one can see it, but you know it's still available if you need it.

To delete your blog permanently, click the **Delete Site** link in the Tools section of your WordPress dashboard left menu. Then read the various warnings one more time! If you're certain you want to delete your blog forever, check the box next to **I'm sure I want to permanently disable my blog, and I am aware I can never get it back or use** *myaccountname*.**wordpress.com** again (note that *myaccountname* will be replaced with your actual account information). Next, click **Delete My Blog Permanently.** You'll receive an e-mail to the address associated with your WordPress.com account asking you to click on a link if you're sure you really want to delete your blog forever. Once you click the link in that e-mail, your blog will be completely gone.

> **PROCEED WITH CAUTION**
>
> Don't delete your blog so you can free up your account name and URL address. Even after your blog is deleted, your WordPress account name and URL address won't become available because there's no way to delete a WordPress.com account. If you want to create a new WordPress account using the e-mail address associated with your original account, you'll first need to change your e-mail address in your original account.

The Least You Need to Know

- You can approve, edit, delete, or mark comments as spam, so you're in complete control of the conversations on your blogs—if you want to be.
- You cannot use the Ratings and Polls features in WordPress.com unless you register for a free account with Polldaddy.
- Only people with WordPress.com accounts can be given access to your WordPress.com dashboard as administrators, editors, authors, or contributors, depending on the roles you assign them.
- You can easily import content from a variety of applications to WordPress.com and export WordPress.com content to other applications.

Paying for Upgrades

In This Chapter

- Paying for your own domain
- Getting rid of the ads
- Upgrading to more storage space
- Working with CSS
- Adding video

The free features of WordPress.com are varied and flexible. They allow many people to create blogs and own a piece of space online without paying a dime. However, bloggers who really want to flex their publishing muscles might need more than what the free WordPress.com offers. If you're one of those people, but you're not ready to move to WordPress.org (which I highly suggest you consider before you start paying for WordPress.com upgrades), this chapter is for you.

Whether you want to drop the *.wordpress.com* from your blog's URL by getting your own domain name, remove ads from your blog, get more storage space, edit your blog's theme's CSS, add video, or invite more than 35 users to a private blog, you learn how to do it in this chapter. I also give you some ideas on what all these upgrades cost. (Be sure to check the Upgrades section of your WordPress dashboard for current offerings and prices before you buy because they may have changed since I wrote this.)

Getting Your Own Domain

WordPress.com offers an Add a Domain upgrade, so you don't have to use the .wordpress.com extension for your blog. For example, instead of using a domain like

MyBlog.wordpress.com, you could register a domain and just use *MyBlog.com* instead (assuming, of course, *MyBlog.com* is available).

WordPress.com's Add a Domain upgrade costs $14.97 per year for both domain name registration and mapping that domain to your existing blog. If you already obtained a domain from another domain registrar, you can map that domain to your WordPress.com blog for $9.97 per year.

Add a Domain Through WordPress.com

To obtain a new domain through WordPress.com and map it to your blog, click the drop-down arrow to the right of **Upgrades** in the left menu of your WordPress dashboard to reveal the links in that section. Next, click the **Upgrades** link you just revealed to open the Upgrades page, as shown in Figure 13-1.

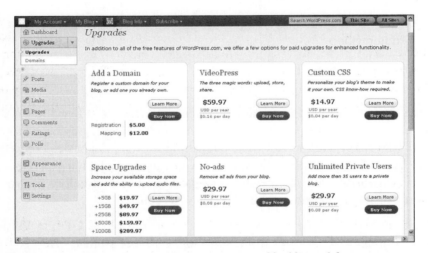

Figure 13-1 *From the Upgrades page, you can add additional features to your blog for a fee.*

Click the **Buy Now** link in the Add a Domain section to open the Domains page, shown in Figure 13-2. You can also access the Domains page by clicking on the **Domains** link in the Upgrades section of your WordPress dashboard left menu.

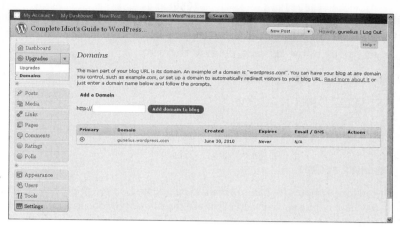

Figure 13-2 *Manage and add new domains to your account from the Domains page.*

To add a new domain to your blog, type in the domain name you want to use in the **Add a Domain** text box and click the **Add domain to blog** button near the top of the Domains page. If the domain name isn't available, you'll get an error page telling you there is a problem with that domain (most likely, someone else already owns it). Try again by entering a different domain name until you find one that is available.

QUICK TIP

Enter your desired domain name into the **Add domain to blog** text box in the format of domain + extension—for example, *MyBlog.com* or *MyBlog.net*.

Once you select a domain name that is available, you can simply follow the prompts to pay for it via PayPal or credit card. Once the domain is purchased, simply return to the Domains page shown in Figure 13-2, and the new domain will be shown in your list of domains. Under the **Primary** heading, click the radio button next to your new domain to make it the primary domain for your blog.

Map a Domain You Already Own to Your WordPress.com Blog

If you already own a domain and want to map it to your WordPress.com blog, you can do that, too. It's a bit more complicated because you need to change the name servers for your domain through your registrar before you can purchase the Domain Mapping upgrade from WordPress.com.

Different registrars have different procedures for updating name servers, so you'll have to check with your registrar to learn how to change yours. Once you find out how to change your name servers, change them to:

NS1.WORDPRESS.COM

NS2.WORDPRESS.COM

NS3.WORDPRESS.COM

INSIDER SECRET

It can take 72 hours for name servers to be updated, so you might have to wait a few days before you can actually make the domain change in your WordPress account.

When your name server changes take effect, you can return to the Domains page of your WordPress dashboard, shown in Figure 13-2, and enter your new domain into the **Add a Domain** text box. Next, click the **Add domain to blog** button. If the name servers are successfully verified, you'll be prompted to complete the upgrade and mapping process by paying via PayPal or credit card. Then you can simply go back to the Domains page and click the radio button under the **Primary** heading to select your new domain as the primary domain for your blog.

Mapping domains can get confusing, but a lot of help is available from WordPress.com, and domain registrars are very used to fielding questions about domain name registration and mapping. Don't be afraid to ask for help if you need it. You can also get help from the WordPress.com support site at en.support.wordpress.com/topic/upgrades and from the WordPress.com user forum at en.forums.wordpress.com.

Go Ad Free

WordPress displays Google AdSense ads on all WordPress.com blogs in an effort to make money so most features can be offered for free. If you don't want those ads to display on your blog, you need to pay for the No-ads upgrade, which costs $29.97 per year.

To purchase the No-ads upgrade, click the **Upgrades** link in the Upgrades section of the WordPress dashboard left menu to open the Upgrades page. In the No-ads section, click **Buy Now** to open the My Shopping Cart page shown in Figure 13-3.

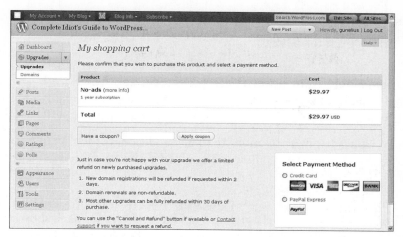

Figure 13-3 *You can pay for your No-ads upgrade via PayPal or credit card.*

Click the radio button next to your chosen payment method—credit card or PayPal. Doing so reveals additional text boxes where you can submit your personal payment information. Once you've provided your account details for payment, click **Purchase** to complete your transaction.

That's all there is to it! Ads will no longer appear on your blog.

INSIDER SECRET

The No-ads upgrade allows you to omit ads served on your blog to generate money for WordPress, but there's no upgrade that allows you to display ads on your blog to make money for yourself. Displaying ads of any kind on a WordPress.com blog is a violation of WordPress.com terms of service.

Buying More Storage

WordPress.com users get 3 gigabytes (GB) of space to upload and store images and files, but if you need more than that, you can purchase Space Upgrades. Five Space Upgrade options are available:

- Add 5GB for $19.97
- Add 15GB for $49.97
- Add 25GB for $89.97

- Add 50GB for $159.97

- Add 100GB for $298.97

Space Upgrades are cumulative. When you pay for another Space Upgrade, that additional amount of space is added to the amount of space you already have. In other words, if you pay for a 5GB upgrade, you'll have your original 3GB + 5GB = 8GB.

The Space Upgrade gives you more than just additional space. When you purchase a Space Upgrade, you will be allowed to upload audio files to your WordPress.com account.

To purchase a Space Upgrade, click the **Upgrades** link in the Upgrades section of your WordPress dashboard left menu to open the Upgrades page shown in Figure 13-1. Select the **Buy Now** link in the Space Upgrades section to open the Space Upgrades dialogue box, shown in Figure 13-4.

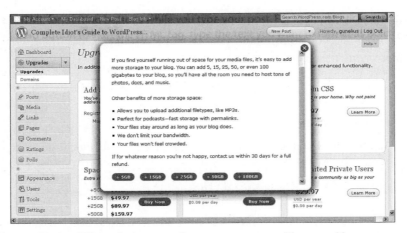

Figure 13-4 *Choose the amount of space you want to add to your blog.*

Scroll to the bottom of the dialogue box and click the button for the amount of space you want to add to your blog. The My Shopping Cart page opens, where you can select your payment method, add your personal payment information, and click **Purchase** to complete your transaction.

PROCEED WITH CAUTION

You must renew all your WordPress.com upgrades annually or you'll lose them. Furthermore, all WordPress.com upgrade purchases apply only to the blog for which they're purchased. If you have multiple blogs and want upgrades to work on more than one of your blogs, you must purchase separate upgrades for each blog and renew each annually to continue using them.

Customizing CSS

If you want to customize the design of your blog beyond what any of the WordPress themes available to you from your WordPress dashboard provide, you can purchase the Custom CSS upgrade for $14.97 per year. (As with all other upgrades, if you don't renew your Custom CSS upgrade before it expires, all the custom CSS edits you made to your blog will be lost.)

It's important to understand that the Custom CSS upgrade only allows you to modify the coding that determines the presentation layout for your blog. You cannot upload custom themes or premium themes purchased from WordPress theme designers, and you can't make changes to functionality built into WordPress theme *PHP* (hypertext preprocessor) files. However, you can use the Sandbox theme to create your own design, or you can make edits to any of the free themes that come with WordPress. com when you purchase the Custom CSS upgrade.

DEFINITION

PHP is a scripting language web developers use to create dynamic web pages. WordPress themes include PHP files.

I recommend you select the **Edit CSS** link in the Appearance section of your WordPress dashboard left menu to test out the Custom CSS upgrade feature before you pay for it. You can use the feature for free, but your edits can't be saved or applied to your live blog until you pay for the upgrade (as discussed in Chapter 8).

When you're ready to purchase the Custom CSS upgrade, select the **Upgrades** link in the Upgrades section of your WordPress dashboard left menu to open the Upgrades page, shown in Figure 13-1. There, click **Learn More** in the Custom CSS section to open the Custom CSS dialogue box.

Next, click **Buy Now** in the Custom CSS dialogue box to open the My Shopping Cart page, where you can confirm your order details, select your payment method, and enter your payment information. Click **Purchase** when you're ready to complete your transaction.

Keep in mind, CSS is a unique coding language you need to know to be able to effectively get your money's worth out of the Custom CSS upgrade.

QUICK TIP

A great resource to learn CSS online—for free—is w3schools.com at www.w3schools.com/css/default.asp.

Using VideoPress

Many sites allow you to upload and share video content for free, such as YouTube, but if you want to be able to upload video content directly to your WordPress.com account, you cannot do so unless you purchase the VideoPress upgrade for $59.97 per year.

The VideoPress upgrade allows you to upload files up to 1GB in size and in .mp4, .m4v, .mov, .wmv, .avi, .mpg, .ogv, .3gp, or .3g2 format. You'll also be able to track viewing statistics for your uploaded and published videos.

After you purchase the VideoPress upgrade, you can upload and insert videos directly from your blog post or page editor, or you can upload them from the Media section of your WordPress dashboard. When you publish a video in a blog post or page, it appears in a familiar viewer that looks similar to viewers used by video-sharing sites like YouTube. You even can choose to add a rating to your video and enable sharing by allowing visitors to download or embed your published video into their own blogs and websites.

To purchase the VideoPress upgrade, select the **Upgrades** link from the Upgrades section of your WordPress dashboard left menu to open the Upgrades page shown in Figure 13-1. Click **Buy Now** in the VideoPress section of the page to immediately add it to your My Shopping Cart page.

Click your preferred payment method, enter your personal payment details, and click **Purchase** to complete your transaction.

Inviting 36 or More Users

If you configured your blog to be private through the **Settings, Privacy** section of your WordPress dashboard (as discussed in Chapter 7), you're only able to add 35 users to your blog through the Users section of your WordPress dashboard. You can give users access to your WordPress dashboard by assigning them roles (as discussed in Chapter 12).

If you need to add more than 35 users to your WordPress.com blog, you have to pay $29.97 per year for the Unlimited Private Users upgrade.

 PROCEED WITH CAUTION

Even with the purchase of the Unlimited Private Users upgrade, a person cannot be given access to your WordPress.com blog as a user unless he has a WordPress.com account. You can use the **Users, Invite** option to invite people to get a free WordPress.com account and obtain access to your blog (as described in Chapter 12).

To purchase the Unlimited Private Users upgrade, select the **Upgrades** link from the Upgrades section of your WordPress dashboard left menu to open the Upgrades page, shown in Figure 13-1. Click the **Learn More** button in the Unlimited Private Users section of the page to open the Unlimited Private Users dialogue box.

Click **Buy Now** in the Unlimited Private Users dialogue box, and the upgrade is automatically added to the My Shopping Cart page, shown in Figure 13-5.

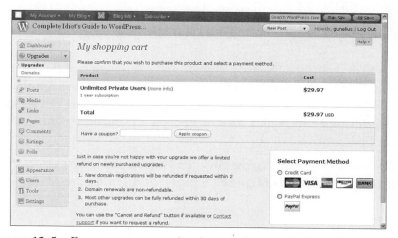

Figure 13-5   *Enter your payment details to purchase the Unlimited Private Users upgrade.*

Click the radio button next to your preferred payment method, enter your payment details into the boxes that appear, and click **Purchase** to complete the transaction.

Remember, WordPress.com upgrades must be renewed annually for each blog you use them on. If you don't renew your Unlimited Private Users upgrade before it expires, users added beyond the first 35 free users won't be able to access your private blog after the upgrade's expiration date.

Offsite Redirect

Scroll to the bottom of the Upgrades page, shown in Figure 13-1, to see additional upgrades available to you, as shown in Figure 13-6.

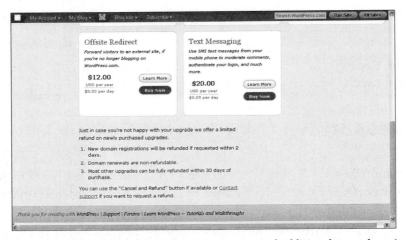

Figure 13-6 *Scroll down the Upgrades page to reveal additional upgrade options.*

If you purchase the Add a Domain upgrade and obtain your own domain for your blog, you could lose the search engine links you've built up through that original domain. To retain some of that traffic from search results, you can purchase the Offsite Redirect upgrade, which forwards people to your new domain from your old one. It's $12 per year.

To set up your offsite redirect, just click the **Buy** button from the Upgrades page to open the Offsite Redirect configuration page, shown in Figure 13-7.

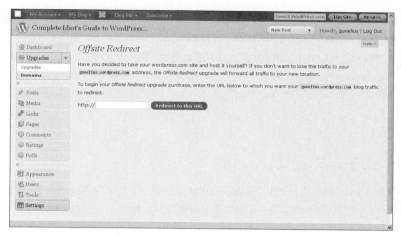

Figure 13-7   *Enter the URL where you want your blog to redirect to in the text box.*

Click the **Redirect to this URL** button and then click **Yes, redirect it!** in the confirmation page to purchase the upgrade and complete the redirect.

Text Messaging

If you want to publish posts, moderate comments, and more via text message, you might want to pay the $20 per year for the Text Messaging upgrade. Simply click the **Buy Now** button on the Upgrades page to open the shopping cart, where you can complete your purchase.

Currently, the Text Messaging upgrade is only available for users in the United States, and standard text and data rates charged by your mobile carrier apply.

The Least You Need to Know

- You can purchase your own domain through WordPress.com or through a separate domain name registrar and preserve search engine traffic by purchasing a separate redirect upgrade.
- You can purchase upgrades to remove ads from your WordPress.com blog, customize the presentation of your blog, increase your storage space, or invite more than 35 users to your private blog.

- Upgrades enable you to upload video directly to your WordPress.com account or update your blog via text message.

- A WordPress.com upgrade applies only to the blog for which you purchase it. If you have multiple blogs, you must purchase upgrades for each specific blog for which you need them. You must renew each upgrade annually.

Using WordPress.org

Part **4**

If you've made the decision to use the self-hosted version of WordPress at WordPress.org as your blogging application, this part is for you! In Part 4, you learn how to get a domain name and a host for your blog, as well as how and why you need to understand and use a little something called FTP when you blog with WordPress.org.

Part 4 also teaches you how to start your blog using WordPress.org, choose a theme, upload a theme, find and use plug-ins to extend the functionality of your blog, and make your WordPress site look less like a blog and more like a traditional website.

After you've read Parts 3 and 4 of this book, you'll be able to confidently use all the features the WordPress.org blogging application offers.

Domains, Hosting, and FTP

In This Chapter

- Choosing a domain
- Deciding on a blog host
- All about FTP

If you've chosen to use WordPress.org as your blogging application, let me be the first to welcome you to the active and satisfied community of self-hosted WordPress bloggers. Don't worry if you don't know exactly what that means yet. I explain it all in this chapter.

Before you can start a blog using WordPress.org, you have to do a few housekeeping things first. This chapter teaches you how to get a domain for your new WordPress. org blog (or website), how to choose a host for your new blog, and what "FTP" means and why it should matter to you.

Now, get ready to enter the world of blogging using the most powerful blogging tool—WordPress.org!

Getting Your Blog Domain Name

As discussed in earlier chapters, every website, blog, and page on the web has a specific address, called a URL (uniform resource locator), you can type into your web browser toolbar to access that site, blog, or page. The primary part of any web address is the domain. For example, one of my websites (which happens to be built on WordPress. org) has a domain of SusanGunelius.com. The URL for the home page is http://www. SusanGunelius.com. Subpages of the site are identified with extensions to the primary domain, which create a URL like http://www.SusanGunelius.com/about/ and leads you to the About page on that site.

The blog or website you build using WordPress.org needs to have a domain, and choosing a domain is explained in part in Chapter 5. Keep reading to learn more about choosing a domain and obtaining one for your WordPress.org blog.

Extensions Explained

As you travel across the web, you'll find domains with a variety of extensions. The most common domain extension is .com; .edu is used exclusively by schools; and .gov is used exclusively by government organizations. Some domain extensions are specific to individual countries, like .uk for sites originating in the United Kingdom.

When you choose the registrar site where you want to register a domain for your blog (discussed later in this chapter), you'll have a number of extension choices. The following table lists some of the most common generic extensions open for anyone to register.

Generic Domain Extensions Available to Bloggers

Extension	Registration Guidelines
.biz	Anyone can register, but registrations could be challenged if they aren't by commercial entities
.com	Anyone can register
.info	Anyone can register
.name	Anyone can register, but a registration could be challenged if it isn't by the individual or owner (for fictional characters) of that name
.net	Anyone can register
.org	Anyone can register

Some domain extensions were originally intended only to be used by certain types of entities—for example, the .org extension was originally only used by nonprofit organizations—but those restrictions have loosened. However, your domain could be challenged in the future if it does not fit the original restrictions placed on a domain extension in the domain's charter.

For example, even though the .biz extension is intended to be used by businesses, no legal restrictions are related to its use. You can register and use a domain with the

.biz extension, but if the site you build for that extension isn't a business site, the day might come when you'll no longer be allowed to use that domain. Most web professionals believe it's unlikely that day will ever come, but it's better to be safe than sorry.

QUICK TIP

Most bloggers try to obtain the .com or .net versions of their preferred domain name because those are the first two extensions people are likely to type into their web browser search bars to find a site they're looking for.

Don't feel like it's essential that you obtain a domain with a .com extension. Many of the most popular websites use .net or another extension. If the domain you want isn't available, you have a number of options available, as discussed in the next section.

Get Creative to Find an Available Domain

When you visit a domain registrar and search for a domain for your WordPress.org blog, be prepared to try several options because the one you want might not be available. Some people and businesses, called domain squatters, purchase popular domain names for the purpose of reselling them for a profit. Some even purchase popular domain names for the sole purpose of publishing ads on them in an effort to make money.

If the domain you want isn't available, you can attempt to contact the owner to learn if the domain is for sale and at what price.

Or you can pick another domain name. Most domain registrar sites offer suggestions if the domain name you searched for isn't available. These suggestions typically include different extensions or modified domain names.

Here are some more suggestions to help you find a domain name for your blog:

- *Add a word:* If you want a domain name like MyBlog.com but it's not available, try adding a word. For example, try MyCoolBlog.com or ThisIsMyBlog.com.

- *Add a prefix or suffix:* A site like Friendster.com is a perfect example of a domain name with a suffix added to it. The *-ster* makes it unique.

- *Choose a different extension:* If .com isn't available, try .net.

- *Make up a word:* A site like Squidoo.com is a great example of a made-up word (in this case also the site's brand name) being used in a domain name.

Put together a list of possible domain names and then conduct web searches to learn if any are available. Read through the alternate suggestions provided by the domain registrar, too. You might just find another name that will work perfectly if your first choice isn't available!

What's This Gonna Cost Me?

Domain registration varies by domain name registrar, the domain extension you choose, and how many domain names you register at one time. The length of time you register the domain for can affect the price, too.

QUICK TIP

Many web hosts offer domain name registration for free or at a discounted price as part of their hosting packages. Before you purchase a domain name separately, consider purchasing it *with* your hosting package for the best price and the easiest purchase and management process. (More on this later in the chapter.)

It's critical that you shop around and compare prices before you make your domain name purchase. You can use any domain registrar to search for domain availability, but be prepared to see registration prices run the gamut. Typically, a .com domain will cost you less than $10 per year when purchased alone, and it can be even cheaper when purchased as part of a hosting plan.

Where to Register

If you want to register a domain separate from your web hosting package, you can do that, too. Many companies offer registration sites that enable you to search domain names and purchase a domain in minutes.

Popular domain registrars include GoDaddy.com, NetworkSolutions.com, 1&1.com, and DreamHost.com. Each of these also offers web hosting services. (The following web hosting section offers more hosting options.)

Choosing a Host

WordPress.org is the application that allows you to create content for publishing on the web. However, you can't publish that content on the web if you don't have somewhere to upload and store it as well as a way to display it to people when they visit. That's where a web host comes in.

A web host provides the space for you to store your content and serves it to visitors on the web. Because you have to pay for and maintain a hosting account to use WordPress.org as your blogging application, you'll often hear WordPress.org referred to as *self-hosted WordPress*, while WordPress.com, which is hosted by WordPress, is referred to as *WordPress-hosted*.

Web hosting accounts come in a variety of shapes and sizes, so there's an option for everyone. Most bloggers are surprised to learn that annual web hosting fees are not as expensive as they expect.

Types of Hosting Accounts

Before you pay for a hosting account for your blog, be sure you're looking for the right type of host to meet your needs. Several types of hosts are available:

Shared host: The vast majority of bloggers can get by with a shared hosting account. With a shared host, multiple customers with their own websites share a server that's dedicated to storing the content for those sites and making them available online.

Reseller host: Some people and companies purchase server space from a host and resell it to customers.

Dedicated server host: If your website or blog is extremely popular, you might need to purchase a hosting account that gives you a dedicated server, so you're not sharing it with other users. This ensures that your site always loads quickly because space is dedicated to it at all times.

Features You Need from Your Hosting Account

The first step to choosing a hosting account is determining your needs for your blog. As you compare current offerings between web hosting providers, consider the following:

Cost: Compare what the host is offering at a specific price point to ensure it's a good deal. Use the other items in this list as your comparison criteria to ensure you're comparing apples to apples.

Storage space: Find out how much space you're given to store your blog content. Many hosting accounts offer unlimited space at competitive prices.

Bandwidth: Some web hosts set limits on how much data you can transfer through your blog each month. In other words, your transfer limit (or bandwidth) needs to be enough to allow your content to be viewed by every person who visits your blog. You can always upgrade your transfer limits as your blog grows, if necessary.

Domains and e-mails: Different hosting accounts offer different limits and pricing on domains and e-mails. Choose a plan that matches your needs and is competitive.

cPanel with Fantastico or SimpleScripts: cPanel is a control panel feature many web hosts offer that makes it extremely easy to work with your hosting account. Fantastico and SimpleScripts are tools that help you install WordPress.org to your hosting account and associate it with your blog's domain. If you're not tech savvy, this is an essential feature for you.

QUICK TIP

It's also important that the web host you choose reports a high uptime so your blog is available when people visit it. Also, look for a hosting provider that offers e-mail and telephone support (online chat support is another benefit), so you can get help when you need it.

A shared blog host is certainly the least expensive option, but because you'll be sharing space, it's possible that your site might not always load at top speed. Additionally, you might be limited in the amount of content, images, and media you can upload to your site if your shared hosting account places restrictions on your storage space.

If your blog grows to be popular and you attract huge amounts of traffic to it each day, or your content archives grow so big you need more space, you might want to get a dedicated blog host account. However, dedicated accounts are significantly more expensive than shared host accounts.

Reseller hosts are another story entirely. You should research the reseller host's offerings and compare them to the cost of purchasing a hosting account directly from a web host company to ensure the reseller is offering you something extra or a better deal than you can get by purchasing direct.

Bottom line: the vast majority of WordPress.org bloggers use shared hosting services. The space and speed of shared hosting accounts is typically more than adequate for most bloggers, particularly if your blog is new.

Costs

Web hosting costs can vary greatly, depending on the provider and the features included. That's why it's important to compare hosting plans among multiple providers (see the preceding section).

Most bloggers are satisfied with shared server hosting plans priced under $10 per month. Many reliable web hosting providers offer excellent hosting accounts in that price range.

> **QUICK TIP**
>
> If you need a dedicated server, be prepared to pay over $100 per month for your hosting account.

Most web hosts provide detailed lists of everything included in their hosting plans, so you can easily compare one package to another.

Popular Hosts

A Google search for "web hosts" will give you many options for hosting your blog. But how do you know which hosting providers are reliable, and where to begin?

It's always smart to ask other bloggers which hosting provider they're using and if they're satisfied with the service they receive. Check out the "Blog Host and Domain Registrar Sites" section in Appendix C for some of the more popular hosts for bloggers that continually get positive reviews.

Remember, if you're confused by all the technical jargon used on these sites and feel overwhelmed, focus on comparing the criteria in the earlier "Features You Need from Your Hosting Account" section so you can get a balanced comparison of some of the most important features for WordPress bloggers.

Understanding FTP

FTP is an acronym for file transfer protocol. FTP is used to transfer files from one host to another. You can also use FTP to transfer files from your computer to your web hosting account.

Why Do You Need FTP?

It's quite possible you'll never need to use an FTP account to transfer files to your blog. Recent WordPress.org upgrades have made it so you can add plug-ins to your WordPress blog and upgrade to newer versions of WordPress directly from your WordPress dashboard. In the past, these processes were not as simple and had to be done by uploading files to your hosting account. If they were large, the files had to be uploaded via FTP.

If you want to use a WordPress theme that does not come as a default with the WordPress.org application, an FTP service is perfect to use to upload it to your hosting account. Themes are made up of many files, which can be uploaded quickly and easily through an FTP account. In other words, FTP is still useful for uploading many files to your hosting account at the same time or uploading very large files. (Learn more about using FTP to upload WordPress theme files to your hosting account in Chapter 17.)

But what if you need more features than a free FTP service offers? Fortunately, a number of free FTP services offer enough capabilities to meet most beginner bloggers' needs, as well as paid services you can purchase at reasonable prices.

Popular FTP Tools

Many FTP tools are available. You have to download some to your computer hard drive, while others are web-based. It's a good idea to test a free FTP tool before you invest in a paid service.

Check out Appendix C's "FTP Tools" section for a few FTP tools bloggers often use, and any others you've received recommendations for, and find the one that works best for you.

PROCEED WITH CAUTION

When you select an FTP tool, be sure you choose one that offers secure file transfers so your data is always protected.

The Least You Need to Know

- You can register a domain name as part of most hosting plans and save money.
- A shared server hosting plan is plenty for most bloggers.
- If you're not tech savvy, choose a web host that offers a cPanel with Fantastico or SimpleScripts to make installing WordPress and other applications easy.
- You might never need to use an FTP service, but if you do, try a free service first.

Installing WordPress.org

In This Chapter

- Assigning your domain
- Using handy tools to make WordPress installation a snap
- Doing the install the right way
- Considering other installation options

The first steps to using the self-hosted version of WordPress available through WordPress.org are to assign your domain and install WordPress through your hosting account. That's exactly what you learn to do in this chapter.

The process of uploading WordPress to your hosting account takes just seconds, thanks to easy-to-use tools most web hosts offer. These tools provide a control panel (or cPanel) and instant access to various software tools that turn previously painstaking tasks into painless ones. This chapter introduces you to a few of the most popular WordPress installation options, so you can choose the one that best matches your skill level and needs.

Note that all screenshots and step-by-step processes described in this chapter use BlueHost.com as the hosting provider. If you use a different hosting provider, the screens and processes you'll use might vary from the ones in this chapter. However, the basic concepts are the same. Contact your hosting provider if you have questions or problems with your specific service or account.

Assign Your Domain to Your Web Host cPanel

If you acquired a web hosting account through a provider that offers a cPanel, and you registered your new blog's domain name through that provider (both are discussed in Chapter 14), you're ready to assign your domain to your hosting account cPanel and start the WordPress installation process.

You can register as many domains as you're willing to pay for, but until you assign a domain to your hosting account's cPanel, you won't be able to install WordPress to that domain using a one-click installation tool. And it's a lot easier to install WordPress through your hosting account cPanel using a one-click installation tool rather than trying to do it manually, as you'll learn later in this chapter.

Let's look at how to assign a domain to your cPanel. First, log in to your hosting account and navigate to the cPanel, as shown in Figure 15-1.

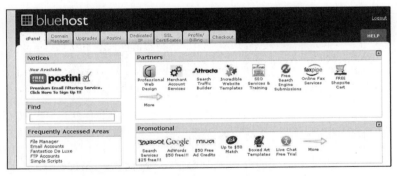

Figure 15-1 *The cPanel in a web hosting account.*

Scroll down to the Domains section, and click the **Domain Manager** icon, shown in Figure 15-2.

The Domain Management page opens, as shown in Figure 15-3. Here you can manage all the domains you registered through your hosting account.

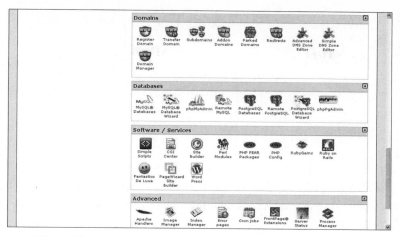

Figure 15-2 *The Domain Manager icon is accessible from the hosting account cPanel.*

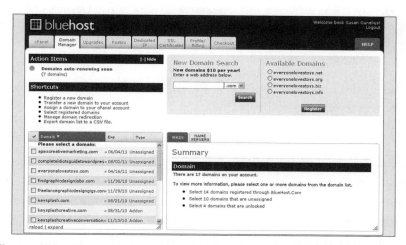

Figure 15-3 *You can manage your domains from your hosting account.*

Find the domain you already registered and want to use for your new WordPress blog. It will be listed in your list of domains as Unassigned. Click the **Unassigned** link next to that domain to open the Domain Assignment Page, shown in Figure 15-4.

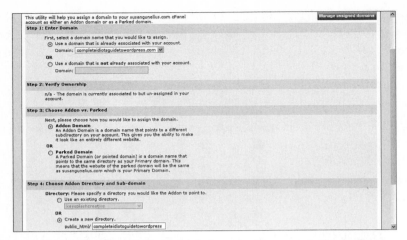

Figure 15-4 *Complete the Domain Assignment form to assign your chosen domain to your cPanel.*

In **Step 1: Enter Domain,** be sure the radio button next to **Use a domain that is *not* already associated with your account** is selected and confirm that the correct domain you want to use is entered into the **Domain:** text box. If not, you should change it to the correct domain.

You shouldn't have to do anything in **Step 2: Verify Ownership** if you registered the domain through the same web host. You should see a message in this section that reads, **n/a—The domain is currently associated to but un-assigned in your account**.

In **Step 3: Choose** *Addon* **vs.** *Parked,* be sure the radio button next to **Addon Domain** is selected.

DEFINITION

An **addon domain** is one that points to a different subdirectory in your main hosting account, which enables you to make it look like an entirely new web-site, different from any others you already created in your hosting account for different domains. A **parked domain** is one that points to the same directory as your account's primary domain, so the website for that domain is the same as the one for your primary domain.

In **Step 4: Choose Addon Directory and Sub-domain,** be sure the radio button next to **Create a new directory** is selected if you want this domain to act as its own separate site. If you want it to be a subdomain of another domain, you can choose the radio button next to **Use an existing directory** and choose the existing directory from the drop-down list. For our purposes, select the **Create a new directory** radio button.

Finally, click the **Add Domain** button at the bottom of the page. This returns to the Manage Domains page, as shown in Figure 15-5, where you can see a new message that says, "Successfully assigned *yourdomainname.com* as addon domain." You'll also see the link next to that domain in your list of domains has changed from Unassigned to Addon.

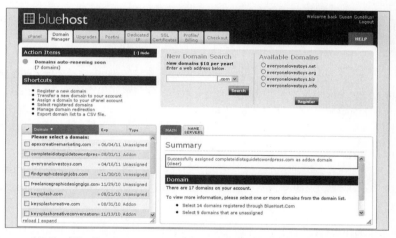

Figure 15-5   *The Summary section of the Domain Management page indicates the domain has been assigned.*

You're now ready to install WordPress to that domain!

Installing WordPress with SimpleScripts

In recent years, SimpleScripts has bypassed Fantastico (discussed later in this chapter) as the preferred method for one-click WordPress installs. That's because SimpleScripts allows users to upload newer versions of WordPress sooner than Fantastico has been able to offer those versions.

SimpleScripts guides you through the process of installing WordPress. You don't have to download the WordPress software and then upload it to your WordPress account, as you have to when you do a manual install (discussed later in this chapter). In fact, it's virtually unnecessary to do a manual WordPress installation, because tools like SimpleScripts can do it all for you!

The first step to using WordPress.org as your blogging application is to install the WordPress software to your web hosting account. You can begin the WordPress installation process by logging in to your hosting account and navigating to your cPanel, as shown in Figure 15-1.

Scroll to the Software/Services section, and double-click the **SimpleScripts** icon, as shown in Figure 15-2. SimpleScripts opens within your hosting account, as shown in Figure 15-6.

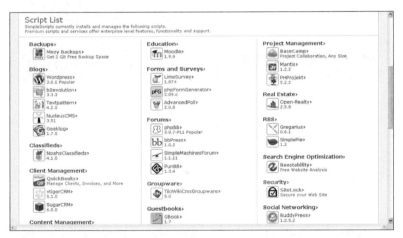

Figure 15-6   *The main SimpleScripts page offers access to a variety of applications.*

Click the **WordPress** link to open the main WordPress installation page, as shown in Figure 15-7.

Next, click the **Install** button to begin the installation process and open the Installation Setup Page, shown in Figure 15-8.

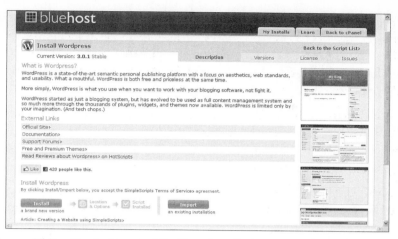

Figure 15-7   *Here's the main WordPress installation page in SimpleScripts.*

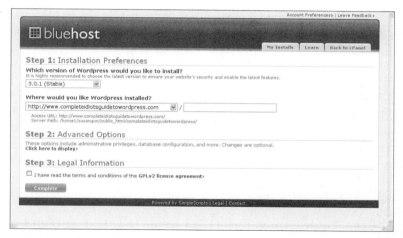

Figure 15-8   *Choose where you want to install WordPress on the WordPress Installation Setup Page.*

Click the **Click here to display** link under **Step 2: Advanced Options** to expand that section of the page, as shown in Figure 15-9.

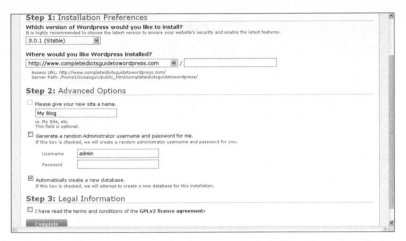

Figure 15-9 *Enter the requested information into the WordPress Installation Setup Page.*

In **Step 1: Installation Preferences**, choose the most recent stable version of WordPress from the drop-down menu and then, in the second drop-down menu, select the domain where you want WordPress installed.

In **Step 2: Advanced Options**, you can enter the name of your blog, which will display in your live blog. (If you prefer, you can create a title later or change it later through your WordPress dashboard, as described in Chapter 16.) You can also change your WordPress account login username (if you'd like to) and enter a password you'll use to log in to your WordPress account in the future. Or you can check the **Generate a random Administrator username and password for me** box. You can always change your password later and create a new user account at a later time through your WordPress dashboard.

In **Step 3: Legal Information**, check the **I have read the terms and conditions of the GPLv2 license agreement** box. You can click the link to read the agreement beforehand if you want.

Finally, click **Complete** to start the installation, as shown in Figure 15-10.

When the installation process is complete and WordPress is fully installed to the domain you chose, the installation In Progress page will update and provide you with links to access your new site live on the web, a link to access your new WordPress account login page, and a reminder of your username and password, as shown in Figure 15-11.

Figure 15-10   *You can watch the status of your WordPress installation on the In Progress page.*

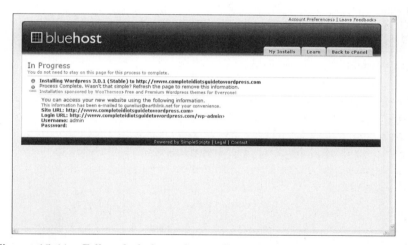

Figure 15-11   *Follow the links on the installation completion page to see your live WordPress blog or log in to your WordPress account.*

QUICK TIP

Be sure to copy and save the link to your new blog, the link to log in to your WordPress account, and your username and password so you don't forget them later. You'll also receive an automated e-mail with this information from SimpleScripts to the e-mail address you have on file in your web hosting account. It's also a good idea to bookmark the links in your browser.

You can click on the **Site URL** link to see your new WordPress blog in its default form live on the web, as shown in Figure 15-12.

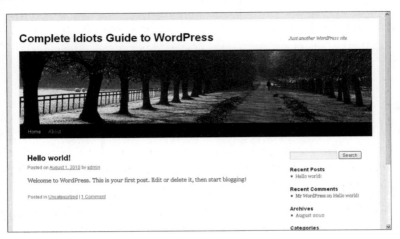

Figure 15-12   *Your new blog is instantly accessible online.*

You can click on the **Login URL** link to access your WordPress account login page online, as shown in Figure 15-13.

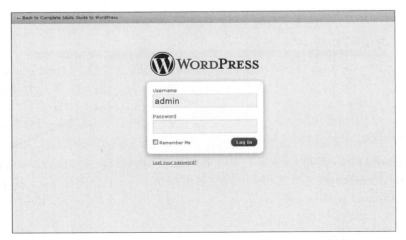

Figure 15-13   *You can log in to your new WordPress account immediately.*

Just type in your username and password to log in to your new WordPress account! It really is that easy!

Other Installation Options

There are other ways to install WordPress, but SimpleScripts has become the most popular option among most users because it's easy to use and up to date. However, if you're not comfortable with SimpleScripts, in this section, I offer two other popular options. Be warned, though: they are either not as easy to use or not as current as SimpleScripts tends to be.

Fantastico De Luxe

Fantastico De Luxe is available through many web host cPanels and offers easy and automated WordPress installation in a process very similar to SimpleScripts. In fact, you're likely to find the Fantastico icon located in the same section of your cPanel as the SimpleScripts icon, as shown in Figure 15-2.

To use, just click on the **Fantastico** icon in your cPanel and follow the step-by-step instructions to choose your domain and installation preferences. As with SimpleScripts, your new blog will be live online within minutes.

However, you might not be able to install the most current version of WordPress using Fantastico. The easiest process is to simply install the current version offered by Fantastico and then upgrade through your WordPress dashboard to the most current version.

Manual WordPress Installation

Installing WordPress manually takes a bit longer than using a one-click installation tool like SimpleScripts or Fantastico does. The process also requires more technical ability because you have to use an FTP service to upload the files (FTP is discussed in Chapter 14), and you need to set up MySQL databases (the databases WordPress runs on behind the scenes).

The vast majority of bloggers don't know how to do those things and don't have a reason or desire to learn. Unless you have goals to learn blog developing and designing, it's unlikely you'll need to learn how to install WordPress manually when far easier tools are available to get the job done.

However, if you decide you'd like to learn how to do a manual WordPress installation, you can access tutorials on the WordPress Codex site at codex.wordpress.org/Installing_WordPress. The instructions are offered in multiple languages and provide varied processes depending on your needs.

The Least You Need to Know

- Once you register a domain, you still have to assign it to your web hosting account cPanel before you can install WordPress to that domain.

- SimpleScripts is the most popular one-click WordPress installation tool. You can access it through your web hosting account cPanel and use it to install WordPress in minutes.

- Fantastico used to be the top one-click installation tool but updates to offer new versions of WordPress were slow, causing the tool to lose some users.

- Most bloggers use one-click installation tools to install WordPress.org software, but a manual installation process is available to developers, designers, and anyone else who understands or wants to learn the more technical aspects of the application.

Customizing
WordPress.org

In This Chapter

- Comparing WordPress.com and WordPress.org
- Getting to know the WordPress.org dashboard
- Configuring WordPress.org

The two versions of WordPress are extremely similar, but some features available through a WordPress.com blog account dashboard are not available in a WordPress.org blog account dashboard. Likewise, some features WordPress.org users can access and apply to their blogs, WordPress.com bloggers cannot.

This chapter clears up the confusion and introduces you to the new features you can find in a WordPress.org dashboard and any differences in features accessible through both WordPress dashboards. Note that all information included in this chapter is based on the most recent version of WordPress.org available at the time of writing.

WordPress.org Similarities to WordPress.com

As discussed earlier in this book, it's always a good idea to start a free blog with WordPress.com so you can play around, experiment, and get to know the features of WordPress before you dive into using WordPress.org. This makes the process of self-hosting a blog with WordPress.org far less overwhelming.

WordPress.org and WordPress.com are the same application. However, because WordPress.com is hosted by WordPress, Automattic (the company that owns Word-Press) includes features through the WordPress dashboard that enable users to readily access other Automattic-owned tools, test new tools, and create a sense of community among WordPress.com users.

On the other hand, WordPress.org enables users to take complete control of their sites because they're hosted through third-party web hosts. WordPress.org users have complete access to all the code that makes their blogs work, so the sky's the limit.

Reviewing the WordPress.org Dashboard

The easiest way to see the differences between WordPress.com and WordPress.org features is to look at the two default dashboards and compare them side by side. The biggest differences you'll find are in the left menus, as shown side by side in Figures 16-1 and 16-2. I discuss these differences in detail in just a bit.

Figure 16-1   *The top of the WordPress dashboard left menus.*

The first thing you're likely to notice as you compare the WordPress.com and WordPress.org dashboards is that the WordPress.com top navigation bar is not available in the WordPress.org dashboard.

Figure 16-2 *The bottom of the WordPress dashboard left menus.*

The layouts of the dashboards are the same. The left menu offers access to all areas of the WordPress configuration features and a variety of modules you can move by dragging and dropping them. You can also move, add, or remove modules by clicking the **Screen Options** button in the top right, as shown in Figure 16-3. (The dashboard layout is discussed in detail in Chapter 6.)

As mentioned earlier, the biggest differences between the WordPress.com and WordPress.org dashboards are in the left menus. If you click on the drop-down arrows to expand each section of the dashboard menus (as shown in Figures 16-1 and 16-2), you'll notice WordPress.com offers sections for Upgrades, Ratings, and Polls, which are not available in the WordPress.org dashboard.

WordPress.org users have complete control over their blogs and don't need to pay for any upgrades or domains through WordPress. They do all those tasks through their web hosts, if necessary. Furthermore, Ratings and Polls are options offered through Automattic's Polldaddy services. WordPress.org users aren't limited to those services and can insert polls and more from any provider that allows WordPress integration.

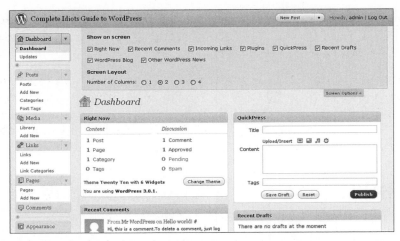

Figure 16-3 *Click the **Screen Options** button to change the modules visible on your dashboard.*

The left dashboard menus also contain some other differences. For example, the Posts, Media, Links, and Pages sections look the same, but some of the features within those areas of your WordPress dashboard might be a bit different from what they were in WordPres.org. (I discuss these differences more throughout this chapter.)

Configuring Your Options

You can use the links in the left menu of your WordPress.org dashboard to configure all the options and settings related to your site, create and publish new content, and much more. The remainder of this chapter shows you what parts of WordPress.org's left menu differ from those in WordPress.com and directs you to the appropriate chapter in this book to learn more about configuring specific settings.

Dashboard—Updates

Unlike the WordPress.com dashboard, which offers a variety of WordPress.com community tools, the Dashboard section of the WordPress.org left menu offers just one feature: Updates. That's because WordPress.com users are automatically upgraded to the newest application release, but WordPress.org users can wait and upgrade at their convenience.

If a newer version of WordPress is available, you'll see a message across the top of your WordPress dashboard's main page notifying you with a link to visit the WordPress Updates page to do the upgrade.

To update your WordPress installation to the newest version, click the **Updates** link in the Dashboard section of the left menu in your WordPress account, as shown in Figure 16-2. This opens the WordPress Updates window, shown in Figure 16-4. If a new version of WordPress is available, simply follow the instructions on this page to upgrade to that version with a click of the mouse!

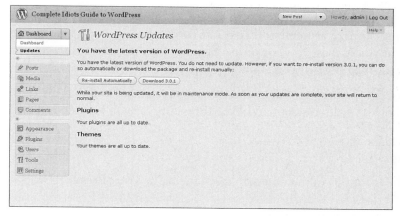

Figure 16-4 *Upgrade to the newest version of WordPress on the WordPress Updates page.*

Note that when you upgrade, a message appears on your screen suggesting that you back up your WordPress database and files before you start the WordPress upgrade. In Chapter 18, I cover WordPress plug-ins that can help you automate backups so you won't have to worry about it each time you upgrade WordPress.

You can also download the newest version of WordPress from the WordPress Updates page and manually upload and install it to your blog host, but most bloggers simply use the update links within WordPress to upgrade.

PROCEED WITH CAUTION

If you use plug-ins in your WordPress.org blog (discussed in more detail in Chapter 18), you might want to wait to upgrade to the newest version of WordPress until all the plug-ins you use are upgraded to work with that new version. This ensures that your blog will continue to work without any problems due to incompatible plug-ins.

Posts

The process of writing, publishing, editing, and deleting posts is almost identical between WordPress.com and WordPress.org. However, in WordPress.org, you have complete control over what you can publish on your blog. For example, while you can't simply copy and paste embed code from a YouTube.com video to a WordPress.com blog post, you can do so with WordPress.org. Just be sure to paste the embed code into the HTML blog post editor. (Embedding YouTube videos is discussed in more detail in Appendix B.)

Just as you can publish a post in WordPress.com, you can do it in WordPress.org. Chapters 9 and 10 teach you how to create, publish, and enhance blog posts. The important thing to remember is that in WordPress.org, you aren't limited by the type of content you include in your posts. You can even include ads in your self-hosted WordPress blog posts if you want!

The process of adding, editing, and deleting categories and tags also works the same way in both WordPress.com and WordPress.org, as you learned in Chapter 9.

Media

The process of uploading and managing media in WordPress.org works exactly the same as it does for WordPress.com users. However, WordPress.org users can upload any types of media they want.

The only file type and size upload limitations for your WordPress.org blog are those set by your web host. Even if a file is too big to upload directly from your WordPress dashboard (meaning it's over the 8MB upload threshold), you can still upload it to your hosting account using an FTP service, as discussed in Chapters 14 and 17.

Links

Creating links, categorizing them, and deleting them can be done using WordPress.org in the same way they're done in WordPress.com. There are no differences from what you learned in Chapter 12 about this section of your WordPress dashboard.

Pages

As with posts, pages work the same way in WordPress.org as they do in WordPress.com. You have more flexibility in creating content for your WordPress.org pages because you're not limited by the type of media or coding you can put in those pages.

However, the process of creating, editing, publishing, and deleting pages is the same as the process discussed in Chapter 11.

Comments

The process of publishing and moderating comments doesn't change from WordPress.com to WordPress.org. As long as you take the time to set up your preferences, as discussed in Chapter 7, you can publish, edit, or delete comments as described in Chapter 12.

However, there is one big difference you need to be aware of. The WordPress comment spam detection tool, Akismet, works automatically with WordPress.com, but for WordPress.org blogs, the Akismet plug-in must be activated before it begins to flag spam comments. Activate Akismet by clicking the **Plugins** link in the Plugins section of your WordPress dashboard left menu. This opens the Plugins page, where the plug-ins that come preinstalled with WordPress.org are listed, as shown in Figure 16-5. (Plug-ins are discussed in more detail in Chapter 18.)

Figure 16-5 *Activate Akismet from the Plugins page.*

Just click the **Activate** link under Akismet in the plug-ins list, and it will immediately begin scanning new comments for potential spam.

Appearance

The Appearance section of your WordPress.org dashboard is where you can really see what sets WordPress.org apart from WordPress.com in terms of customization.

When you click on the **Themes** link in the Appearance section of your Word-
Press dashboard left menu, as shown in Figure 16-6, you notice that unlike
WordPress.com, which gives you access to many free themes for use on your blog,
WordPress.org offers only the default WordPress theme.

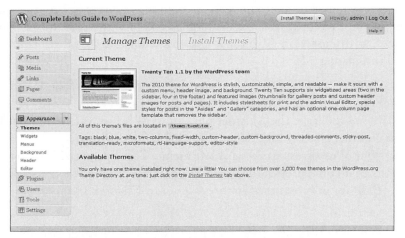

Figure 16-6 *Only the default WordPress theme is available in the Manage
Themes page.*

You can install other themes offered through WordPress by clicking the **Install
Themes** tab near the top of the page. This opens a new page with a search feature,
as shown in Figure 16-7.

Figure 16-7 *You can search for available themes from the WordPress library.*

You can search for themes in the WordPress theme library by keyword, author, or tab. Simply enter your search words in the text box, and click the **Search** button. Or you can click on theme elements using the check boxes and click the **Find Themes** button at the bottom of the page. A new page opens with matching themes displayed, as shown in Figure 16-8. You can click the **Install** button under any theme to install it to your account. To see what your blog will look like (including your content) with the new theme applied to it before you commit to using it, click the **Preview** button.

Figure 16-8 *Scroll through available themes to choose the one you want to use for your blog.*

You can also use the links under the navigation tabs to upload a new theme (as discussed in Chapter 17) or browse through featured, new, or recently updated themes.

In the Appearance features of your WordPress dashboard, the Widgets section also works similarly to WordPress.com. The widgets available depend on the theme you're using. However, WordPress.com users are limited by what they can put in their widgets. WordPress.org users are only limited by how far they can extend the technology.

PROCEED WITH CAUTION

When you use WordPress.org, you can put ads in your widgets, special coding such as JavaScript, and more. It's up to you!

The Menus, Background, and Header sections of the Appearance features also work the same in WordPress.org as they do in WordPress.com, which are discussed in detail in Chapter 8. Keep in mind, some of these functions depend on the theme you're using for your blog.

Aside from themes, the Editor section within the Appearance features of your WordPress.org left menu is where you find the biggest differences between WordPress.org and WordPress.com. WordPress.com users can only access the CSS files to edit their blog themes and functionality if they pay for an upgrade. Even with the upgrade, there are still limitations related to what WordPress.com users can do to their blogs.

WordPress.org users are not subject to those restrictions. They can access all parts of their WordPress installation, including CSS files, to change anything and everything about their blog's design. Clicking the **Editor** link within the Appearance section of the WordPress.org left dashboard menu opens the Edit Themes page, which is discussed in detail in Chapter 17.

Plug-Ins

Plug-ins are another area where WordPress.org and WordPress.com differ. By installing plug-ins, you can increase the functionality, efficiency, and features of your blog. Be sure to read Chapter 18 to learn all about plug-ins!

Users

The Users section of your WordPress.org dashboard is also quite different from the WordPress.com dashboard version. That's because you're not limited to "inviting" users to join your blog by first creating a WordPress.com account. Anyone can get access to your WordPress.org dashboard. You just need to click the **Add New** link in the Users section of the left menu to open the Add New User page, shown in Figure 16-9.

Enter a username for the person you want to give access to your WordPress account (this is the username they'll use to log in to WordPress) and an e-mail address (where their new account e-mail will be sent) into the **Username** and **E-mail** fields, respectively. Next, enter the user's first and last name and a URL for your blog—or the user's website, if you prefer. Follow the tips on screen to create a password for the new user, and be sure the box next to **Send Password?** is checked if you want the new user to receive an e-mail (sent to the address you entered into the E-mail field) with their new account information.

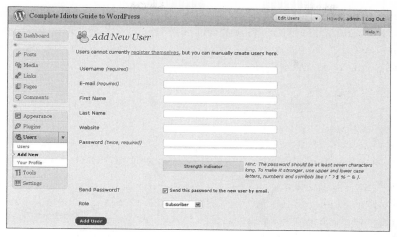

Figure 16-9   *It takes just seconds to add new users to your WordPress.org blog.*

PROCEED WITH CAUTION

Users can change any of the information you enter in this form when they log in to their new accounts. The only information they cannot change is their usernames and roles.

Finally, use the **Role** drop-down menu to determine what the new user will be allowed to do and access in your WordPress account (roles are discussed in Chapter 12). Click on the **Add User** button, and the new user is immediately added to your account and can perform the functions allowed based on the role you assigned him or her.

To edit users' roles or information, simply click the **Users** link in the Users section of your dashboard left menu to open the Users page, shown in Figure 16-10.

Hover your mouse over a user's name in the Users list, and an Edit link appears under that user's name. Click the **Edit** link to open the user's profile and make any necessary changes. You can also delete users from the Users page.

For quick user changes or to make the same change to multiple users at the same time, you can use the drop-down menus at the top of the Users list. Just select the boxes next to the users you want to modify, click the **Bulk Actions** drop-down menu, and click **Delete** to mark users for deletion from your WordPress account. Click the **Apply** button to make the deletions.

Figure 16-10 *Edit users from the Users page in your WordPress account.*

Similarly, you can select users using the checkboxes next to their names in the Users list, click the **Change Role to...** drop-down box, select a new role from the menu, and click the **Change** button to immediately change the selected users to a new role.

You can also modify your own WordPress profile from the Your Profile link in the Users section of your dashboard left menu. The process is the same as the one used to modify your profile in WordPress.com, which you can read about in Chapter 7.

Tools

The tools available to you through the Tools section in your WordPress left menu work the same way in WordPress.org as they do in WordPress.com. You do have fewer options through this menu in WordPress.org than you do in WordPress.com. For example, when you click the **Tools** link in the Tools menu, the Tools page opens, as shown in Figure 16-11. Here you can access the Press This bookmarklet and the Categories and Tags Converter, discussed in Chapter 12.

If you click the **Import** link in the Tools menu, the Import page opens, as shown in Figure 16-12. This works the same as the WordPress.com import function, discussed in Chapter 12.

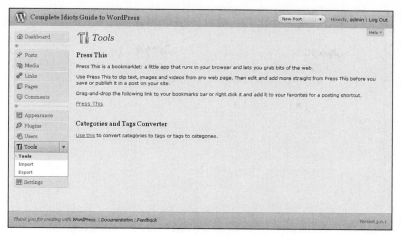

Figure 16-11   *Access handy features on the Tools page.*

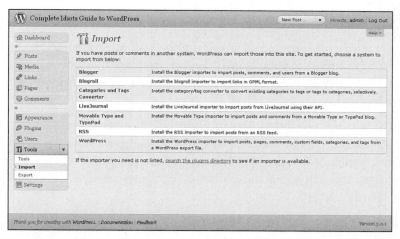

Figure 16-12   *WordPress makes it easy to import data from another site into WordPress.org.*

Finally, if you click the **Export** link in the Tools menu, the Exports page opens, as shown in Figure 16-13. Here you can export your WordPress.org site data for use elsewhere. This is discussed in detail in Chapter 12, where the function works the same in WordPress.com.

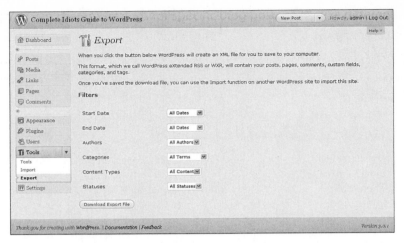

Figure 16-13   *Prepare your blog for exporting by choosing your export settings.*

Settings

The vast majority of features and configuration options available through the links in the Settings section of your WordPress.org dashboard left menu are the same as those you find in WordPress.com. However, there are some nuances, as discussed in the following sections.

Read about Settings configurations in Chapter 7 (note that some options available in WordPress.com are not available in WordPress.org, so don't be surprised if some options aren't included in the WordPress.org Settings pages on your screen). Return to this chapter to learn about the additional options accessible through these settings pages in WordPress.org.

General   The General Settings page for your WordPress.org dashboard, shown in Figure 16-14, includes four sections that are not available through WordPress.com:

WordPress address (URL): This is the URL of the site associated with your WordPress installation. It's unlikely you'll ever need to change this unless you move your core WordPress files in your hosting account.

Site address (URL): This is the URL of your site's home page. If you want it to be different from the directory where you installed WordPress, you can enter the new address here, but you'll need to create a subdirectory in your hosting account to do so. This is not common for most bloggers, but help is available if you want to try it: codex.wordpress.org/Giving_WordPress_Its_Own_Directory.

Membership: You can check this box if you want anyone to be able to register an account on your site. This is not common for most bloggers.

New User Default Role: Click the drop-down arrow and choose the role you want all new users to default to if you forget to assign a role to them when you add them to your WordPress account.

PROCEED WITH CAUTION

You don't want users to have too much access to your WordPress account unless you're absolutely certain you want to give them that kind of power. Therefore, it's a good idea to keep the New User Default Role setting set to Subscriber, so new users default to the role that gives them the least amount of access to your WordPress account.

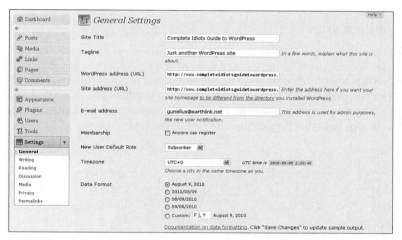

Figure 16-14 *Configure the general settings for your WordPress site.*

Be sure to click the **Save Changes** button to save all your changes before you leave the General Settings page.

Writing   The Writing Settings page of a WordPress.org account, shown in Figure 16-15, has three configuration options the WordPress.com version discussed in Chapter 7 does not:

Post via e-mail: The process to post via e-mail in WordPress.org is a bit different from WordPress.com. To set this up, you need to know your e-mail server URL address and port. (You can get this from your e-mail account or e-mail provider.) Next, enter a login name (the part of the e-mail address you want to use to post via e-mail that comes before the @ symbol) and password. Finally, choose the category you want e-mailed posts to publish in. That's it!

Remote Publishing: This option allows you to post to your blog from a desktop blogging application or remote website that uses Atom or XML-RPC publishing interfaces. Just click on the appropriate check box to select it and enable the function. This is not common for most bloggers.

Update Services: When you publish blog posts, WordPress automatically notifies a variety of services through Ping-O-Matic (pingomatic.com) that you have updated your blog. This automated service helps quickly index your new content on search engines and other directory sites that use ping services for updates. The default setting is adequate for most bloggers.

 INSIDER SECRET

There was a time when bloggers had to manually enter a long list of ping services to ensure as many search engines and similar sites as possible were automatically notified of new posts on their blogs. Now, Ping-O-Matic automatically notifies the major ping services, so before you spend time adding new ones to the Update Services section of your WordPress.org account, double-check that Ping-O-Matic isn't already notifying them.

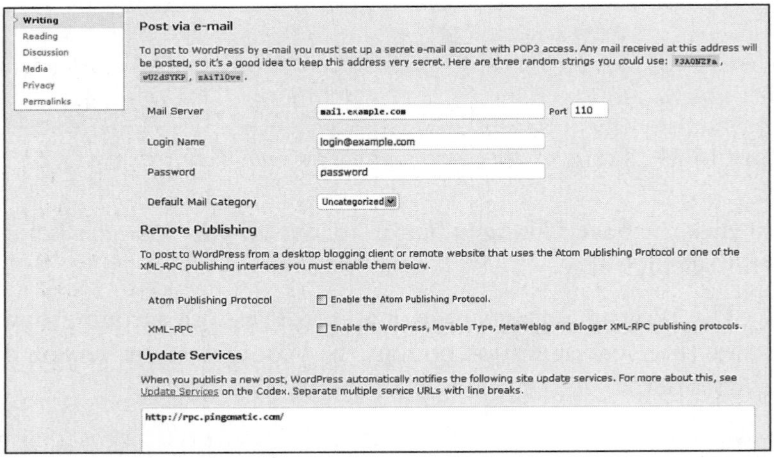

Figure 16-15 *Modify settings related to writing your blog on the Writing Settings page.*

Don't forget to click the **Save Changes** button before you navigate away from the Writing Settings page.

Reading   The Reading Settings page of a WordPress.org account, shown in Figure 16-16, is the same as the WordPress.com Reading Settings page, minus a few elements that don't apply to WordPress.org readers. So follow the directions in Chapter 7 to configure your blog's reading settings, and simply skip the sections of that chapter that don't apply to your own WordPress.org account.

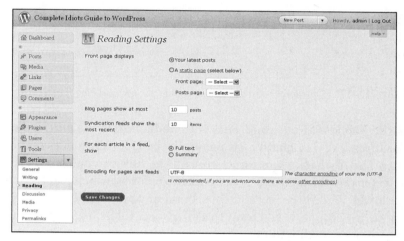

Figure 16-16   *Set up the reading options for your WordPress site on the Reading Settings page.*

Discussion   The Discussion Settings page of your WordPress.org account, shown in Figure 16-17, is extremely similar to the Discussion Settings page for a WordPress.com account, as discussed in Chapter 7. A few options are not available in WordPress.org, but simply follow the steps in Chapter 7 to configure your discussion options, and your blog will be ready for comments and conversation in seconds!

Media   The big difference in the Media Settings page for a WordPress.org account is the inclusion of the Uploading Files section, shown in Figure 16-18. This is not available in WordPress.com. Read the configuration steps for the Media Settings page in Chapter 7, and return here to learn how to configure the Uploading Files section for WordPress.org.

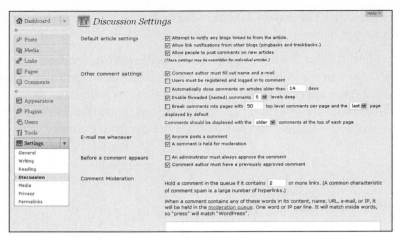

Figure 16-17 *Configure your discussion settings for optimal blog commenting.*

To open the Media Settings page, click the **Media** link in the Settings section of your WordPress.org dashboard's left menu. In the Uploading Files section, you can enter a new folder where you want to store all the files you upload to your WordPress account. Typically, this defaults to wp-content/uploads, which identifies a folder called "uploads" within the wp-content section of your WordPress installation files in your hosting account. If you want to change that folder, enter the new directory in the **Store uploads in this folder** text box.

If you want to change the URL to your uploaded files, you can enter a new URL in the **Full URL path to files** text box, but this is not common. Most bloggers leave this field blank and use the default configuration.

If you want to organize all your uploads by month and year to make it easier to find them later, be sure to check the **Organize my uploads into month- and year-based folders** box. Most bloggers leave this box checked.

Click the **Save Changes** button to ensure your edits go into effect.

Privacy   The Privacy Settings page of your WordPress.org account, shown in Figure 16-19, includes just two options.

If you want your blog to grow, everyone needs to be able to find it, including search engines. Therefore, be sure the radio button next to **I would like my site to be visible to everyone, including search engines (like Google, Bing, Technorati) and archivers** is selected.

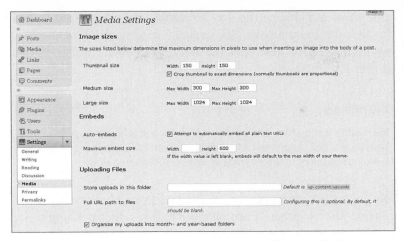

Figure 16-18   *Determine how you want images and files to upload to your WordPress site on the Media Settings page.*

Alternately, if you want people to be able to find your blog but you're not interested in growth from search engines, you can select the radio button next to **I would like to block search engines, but allow normal visitors.**

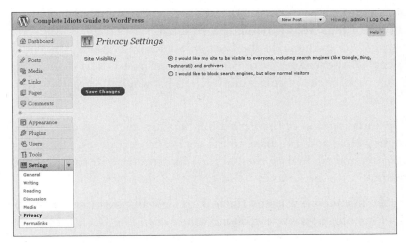

Figure 16-19   *Configure your site's privacy settings.*

Click the **Save Changes** button after you make your selection.

Permalinks You can change the way *permalinks* are configured for your published content through the **Permalinks** link in the Settings section of the left menu of your WordPress.org dashboard. Just click on that link to open the Permalinks Settings page, shown in Figure 16-20.

> **DEFINITION**
>
> **Permalink** is the fusion of *permanent* and *link* and refers to the URL to a specific web page that's permanent. Even when content is archived, the permalink remains the same, so links to that content from other sites are not broken.

The default permalink structure for WordPress posts includes the number of the post as the extension after your site's primary URL. This does nothing to help readers or you. In other words, by changing your permalink structure, you can help readers understand when the content was originally published and what the content is about. You can also help your site gain search traffic by structuring your permalinks to include post names or category names in an attempt to add keywords to your URLs.

To configure your permalink structure, click the radio button next to the structure you prefer in the **Common settings** list. The most common choices are **Day and name** or **Month and name**.

To create a custom structure, you can use any of the available tags accessible through the **Number of tags are available** link in the top paragraph on the Permalink Settings page. For example, in the Custom Structure text box, you could enter **/%category%/%postname%/** to configure your post URLs to include the category and post name after the primary site URL. This would be great for search engine optimization!

In the **Optional** section of the Permalink Settings page, you can enter a new name for **Category base** and **Tag base** in the applicable text boxes. If you leave these fields blank, *category* and *tag* will be used in the link structure for category and tag links, respectively.

For example, if someone selected the link to view all posts in the Career Development category of my blog at www.womenonbusiness.com, the URL for that page with the list of posts in the Career Development category is http://www.womenonbusiness.com/category/career-development/. However, if I entered the word *topics* into the Category base field on the Permalink Settings page, that URL would change to http://www.womenonbusiness.com/topics/career-development/. It's entirely up to you if you want to change these names.

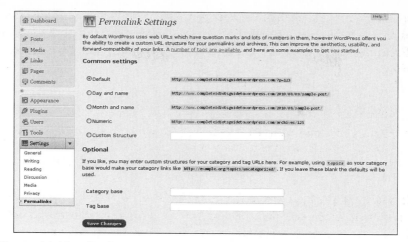

Figure 16-20 *Configure the structure for your site's permalinks.*

As always, be sure to click the **Save Changes** button before you navigate away from the Permalink Settings page, or your changes won't go into effect.

The Least You Need to Know

- It's a good idea to start a free test blog with WordPress.com before you tackle WordPress.org.

- The majority of settings in WordPress.org are identical to or at least very similar to WordPress.com.

- WordPress.org is installed to your hosting account as a series of files and folders, just as files and folders in your computer hard drive store your data. You have complete control over them and the content in them.

- The biggest functionality differences most users notice between WordPress.com and WordPress.org are that WordPress.org gives you total access to your blog's CSS files, the ability to upload themes, and the use of plug-ins.

WordPress Themes Galore

In This Chapter

- A look at the WordPress Theme Editor
- Choosing a WordPress theme
- Working with a third-party theme
- Getting help from a blog designer
- Building a website with WordPress

One of the biggest benefits of choosing WordPress.org as your blogging application is the level of customization available to you. Because you can access all the code that makes your self-hosted WordPress blog run, you can tweak even the tiniest aspects of your blog's design and functionality. But you don't have to be a programmer to make your WordPress blog look amazing!

Thanks to the many free, premium, and custom WordPress theme options, you can make your blog look unique and professional with no programming knowledge at all. This chapter teaches you how to do it!

Introducing the WordPress Theme Editor

When you create a new blog or website using the self-hosted version of WordPress from WordPress.org, you have complete access to the theme files your blog's design is based upon. A new WordPress site uses the default WordPress theme, Twenty Ten, which you can see on a new blog in Figure 17-1.

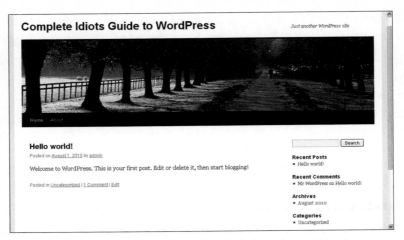

Figure 17-1 *Here's a WordPress site with the default Twenty Ten theme.*

As a WordPress.org user, you have complete control over your blog's design through the Appearance section of your WordPress dashboard's left menu. You can install a new theme (discussed later in this chapter) or edit the theme you're already using on your site by clicking on the **Editor** link in the Appearance section of your WordPress dashboard left menu. This opens the Edit Themes page, shown in Figure 17-2.

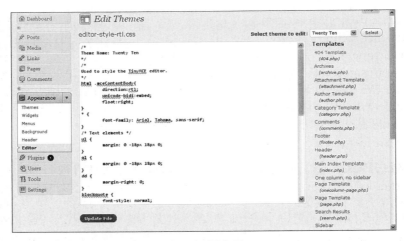

Figure 17-2 *You can edit your theme's CSS files.*

Your WordPress site design is built using Cascading Style Sheets (CSS), a programming language used to create the design of web pages. The content of your web pages published with WordPress are created using HTML, but the presentation of those pages is determined by the CSS coding working behind the scenes.

The editor box in the middle of the Edit Themes page includes the code that determines your WordPress site's design. On the right side of the page is a list of links to the various files that include the CSS code for different sections of your site. The Stylesheet file includes the main code for your site design such as heading fonts, block quote font, margins, and so on. The individual page, post, footer, and other files accessible through the links on the right side of the Edit Themes page add specific information for those individual sections of your site.

PROCEED WITH CAUTION

Don't make changes to your WordPress site's CSS files through the Edit Themes text box without first copying and pasting all the content in that text box into another file. If you make a mistake, you can always revert to the original code and start again.

You can edit any part of your theme files through the Edit Themes page. Just be sure to click the **Update File** button to save your changes and make them go live on your site.

The Benefits of Learning CSS

CSS is not a difficult programming language to learn, and many WordPress users with minimal technical knowledge and abilities are able to learn CSS in a short amount of time. The benefits of learning even simple tasks in CSS can deliver big results. For example, if you don't like the color or formatting of links in your blog posts, you can make a universal change to all the hyperlinks on your WordPress site in seconds through your theme's Stylesheet file. You just need to know where to look for the code that formats links within the Stylesheet file and how to enter coding to change that formatting.

Many WordPress users are perfectly happy to never learn CSS. Fortunately, well-coded themes that look and perform the way WordPress users want them to are available for little or no cost. However, if you want to take your blog to the next level of uniqueness, you either need to know some CSS or you need to hire a blog designer to help you. Both choices are good ones, and it's up to you to decide which route you prefer.

If you do take the time to learn some CSS, you'll save time and money in the long run because you won't have to struggle to figure out how to make changes to your WordPress site design. You won't have to pay someone to help you either.

Where to Learn CSS

Many online and printed resources can help you learn CSS. Whether your goal is to learn just enough to make small changes to your WordPress site design or you want to learn enough to become a WordPress designer, you can do it without spending a fortune.

Appendix C's "CSS and HTML Help Sites" section offers a few good websites to check out if you want to learn CSS. *CSS: The Definitive Guide* by Eric A. Meyer and *CSS: The Missing Manual* by David Sawyer McFarland are also good resources.

Types of WordPress Themes

In addition to the themes you can access through the WordPress themes library, themes are also available from many third-party WordPress theme designers. As you search the web for themes, you'll find three primary types:

Free themes are easy to find through a simple web search for "free WordPress themes." Anyone can download and use these themes without paying a penny.

Premium WordPress themes are typically available with a price tag, although the price is usually reasonable. For example, the majority of premium themes are priced anywhere from $49 to $99 for a single-site use license.

Custom WordPress themes are created by designers and are used only by the site they were specifically designed for. The price tag for a custom WordPress theme built from the ground up can cost thousands of dollars.

QUICK TIP

Custom themes are available directly through WordPress designers and are typically negotiated individually in terms of functionality, layout, and price.

If you're thinking free and premium themes are more what you're looking for, check out the "WordPress Theme Sites" section of Appendix C for several sites where you can find them.

Selecting the Best Theme for Your Blog

All three types of WordPress themes come with their own pros and cons, and you should understand them before you choose the theme for your blog or website. You don't want to spend time installing a theme and setting up your header, footer, side-bars, and so on, only to learn that the theme doesn't function well or lacks specific elements you need for your site.

It's important to choose a theme that offers the number of columns you want in the positions you want, but you also need to be sure the theme allows you to customize the header and other elements with ease, if those customization options are important to you. Well-coded themes make it easy to do all this customization in minutes.

Here are some other considerations to keep in mind as you choose your WordPress theme:

Branding and individuality: Is it important that your site looks like no other site online? Do you need it to adhere to your brand standards and reflect a specific message to visitors? If you answered yes to these questions, you should choose a custom or premium theme.

Price: How much are you willing and able to invest in the unique design and functionality of your site? Your budget has a big impact on the type of theme you choose.

Support: If you don't know CSS or HTML and are likely to need help installing and modifying your site once you choose a theme, be sure you choose a premium theme that comes with some form of support (a forum or e-mail contact), or work with a designer on a custom theme or on tweaking a premium theme who can give you support (for a fee) in the future.

Reputation: Not all WordPress theme designers are equal. Be sure the designer you work with has a reputation for creating well-coded themes.

Reviews: Read reviews of themes, and contact other bloggers who have used the theme you're interested in to be sure it's well coded and easy to use.

Gallery: Look through the gallery of sites using the theme you're interested in to see what others have done with it. This is a great way to get new ideas and truly see how well a theme performs. Not all theme designers offer galleries, but if you can find one, do check it out.

Spam-free: Beware of free themes that are not offered by recognized sources. Some free themes can include viruses, spyware, or hidden code you don't want!

When you select the **Themes** link in the Appearance section of your WordPress dashboard's left menu, the Manage Themes page opens, as shown in Figure 17-3 (and discussed more in Chapter 16). Here you can see all the themes you've installed to your WordPress account and which theme is currently active on your site.

You can also install themes available in the WordPress theme library by clicking on the **Install Themes** tab at the top of the Manage Themes page. Turn to Chapter 16 to learn how to install themes from the WordPress theme library.

Figure 17-3 *You can see your active theme on the Manage Themes page.*

Installing a Third-Party Theme

If you choose a third-party theme to use for your WordPress site, you need to install it to your WordPress account and activate it. Once it's activated, you'll need to go through your site (if you already have content published on it) to make sure your sidebars, header, footer, and other content look good. Often when you install a new theme, you'll need to adjust some of your existing content and site setup to work well and look good with the new theme. For example, the width of your sidebar might change, which means you might need to resize images in your sidebar.

INSIDER SECRET

Don't be surprised if you need to make a number of tweaks to your site after you change your theme.

To install a WordPress theme from a third party, you first need to download that theme to your computer hard drive. Most designers and theme providers offer a one-click download button. Just click on the download link or button for the theme you like and save it to your computer hard drive in a location where you can easily find it again. Note that the theme files will download in a single zipped file. That's because a WordPress theme consists of many different folders and files, which you need to upload to your hosting account in order to use them on your blog or website. Make sure you remember where you saved the zip folder with your theme files in it.

Installing a Third-Party Theme from the WordPress Dashboard

Since WordPress 3.0 was introduced, the process of installing a new theme to use on your blog is easier than ever. In the past, WordPress.org users had to upload theme files using an FTP server and save the files in specific folders within their hosting accounts before they could activate that theme on their WordPress blogs. Of course, you can still manually upload a theme that way, but with WordPress 3.0, you can upload a new theme directly from your WordPress dashboard.

PROCEED WITH CAUTION

Not all themes upload correctly using the one-click upload function available through your WordPress dashboard. If you encounter an error, you can upload your theme via FTP, as described later in this chapter.

To upload a third-party theme through your WordPress dashboard, click the **Themes** link in the Appearance section of your WordPress dashboard's left menu. This opens the Manage Themes page, shown in Figure 17-3. Click the **Install Themes** tab at the top of the page to open the Install Themes page, shown in Figure 17-4.

Figure 17-4 *You can install third-party themes from your WordPress dashboard.*

Click the **Upload** link near the top of the page and then click the **Browse...** button to locate the zip file for the theme you want to upload from your hard drive. (This is the zip file you downloaded to your computer when you downloaded the theme.) When you locate the zip file on your hard drive, select it (which could be a zip file included within the zip folder you downloaded), and click the **Install Now** button to begin the upload process.

If the theme uploads successfully, you'll see a window like the one shown in Figure 17-5. This tells you the theme installed successfully and gives you the option to preview the theme, activate it immediately on your live site, or return to the Manage Themes page in your WordPress dashboard.

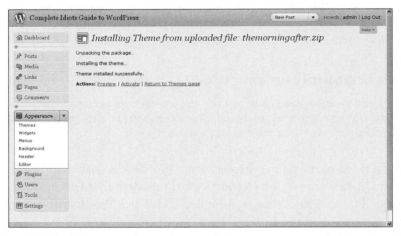

Figure 17-5 *If your theme installs successfully, you can activate it immediately.*

Click the **Return to Themes page** link to return to the Manage Themes page, as shown in Figure 17-6. Here you can see your newly uploaded theme in the Available Themes section. As you can see, The Morning After theme (a free theme from WooThemes) has been added to the list of available themes.

When you click the **Activate** link under your newly installed theme, that theme is instantly active on your live site. Note that some themes offer special point-and-click and click-and-drag configuration panels to make customizing your site with the new theme easier. The Morning After theme offers a special section in your WordPress dashboard left menu you can use to navigate through the various customization settings for your blog's new theme, as shown in Figure 17-7.

Figure 17-6 *Uploaded themes are added to your list of available themes.*

Figure 17-7 *You can customize some third-party themes through special dashboard menus.*

After you activate your newly installed theme, you can view it live on your blog and see how it looks to the world, as shown in Figure 17-8.

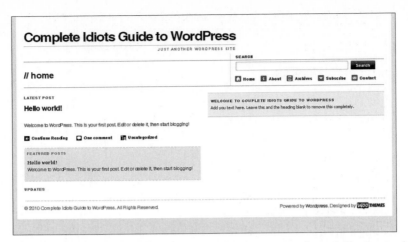

Figure 17-8 *When you click the **Activate** link, your new theme is live instantly.*

Installing a Third-Party WordPress Theme via FTP

Many third-party WordPress themes are very complex and include not just theme files but also plug-in files. (See Chapter 18 for more on plug-ins.) If a third-party theme is too complex to upload through your WordPress dashboard, you can use an FTP client (introduced in Chapter 14), such as the free Core FTP tool (www.coreftp.com), to upload a theme to your hosting account and WordPress site.

The first step to uploading a theme via FTP is to locate on your hard drive where you saved the theme's zip file when you downloaded it from the theme provider. When you find it, right click on it and select **Extract All...** from the menu that opens, as shown in Figure 17-9. This will extract all the zipped files into individual files and folders.

When the files are extracted from the theme's zip folder, you'll see several folders and files that were used to create the theme. You need to upload the contents of the **Theme** folder and the **Plugins** folder if the theme you're uploading comes with any plug-ins preinstalled, as shown in Figure 17-10. If the theme doesn't include any plug-ins, this folder won't be available, and you only need to upload the contents of the Theme folder.

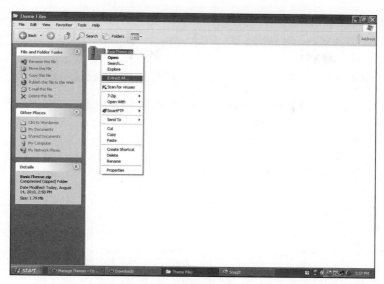

Figure 17-9 *To upload a theme via FTP, first extract the files from the zipped theme folder.*

Figure 17-10 *You must upload the contents of the **Theme** and **Plugins** folders to your hosting account.*

  INSIDER SECRET

It's a good idea to open, print, and keep a copy of the ReadMe file that comes in your Theme files. It usually includes helpful installation and configuration instructions and tips that can make it easier to use and customize the theme.

Once you've extracted your theme files, you're ready to upload them to your hosting account. The fastest way to do this is by using an FTP client. You must download and install the FTP client of your choice on your computer before you can upload a third-party theme to your WordPress account. In the following steps, I used the free version of Core FTP (www.coreftp.com) to upload the premium theme called "Basic" from ElegantThemes.

First, open Core FTP on your computer. Click **File** and then **Connect** to open the Site Manager window, shown in Figure 17-11.

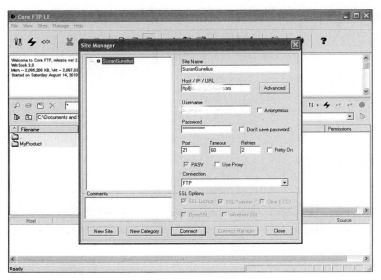

Figure 17-11 *Open Core FTP and connect to your hosting account.*

In the **Host/IP/URL** text box, enter your primary hosting account domain name, such as mydomainname.com. Next, enter your hosting account username and password in the applicable text boxes, and click the **Connect** button. This connects your computer hard drive to your hosting account file manager.

QUICK TIP

If mydomainname.com doesn't work, try ftp@domainname.com or ftp.domainname.com. If those don't work, contact your web host to find out your FTP login details.

When you're connected through your FTP client, you can see a window that's split into two panes. The left side shows all the files in your computer hard drive. The right side shows all the files in your hosting account. Work on the right side first.

In the right-side panel, find the root directory, which is usually called **public_html**, as shown in Figure 17-12. If you can't find this folder, contact your hosting company and ask what your root directory is called and where to find it. Once you find your root directory folder, double-click it to open it.

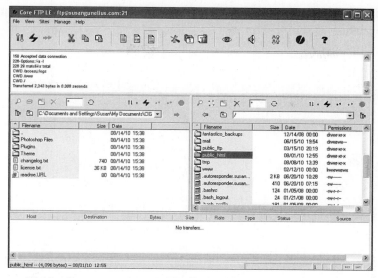

Figure 17-12   *Locate your root **public_html** directory.*

Next, find the **wp-content** folder, located in the folder where you installed WordPress, as shown in Figure 17-13.

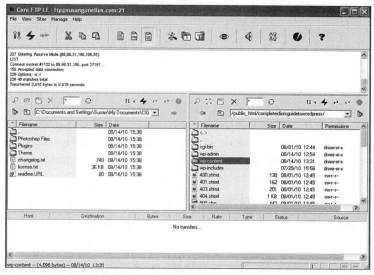

Figure 17-13   *Find the **wp-content** folder.*

Double-click the **wp-content** folder to display its contents. You're looking for the **themes** folder, as shown in Figure 17-14. This is where you want to install your new theme files.

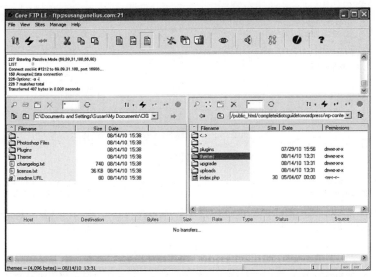

Figure 17-14   *Locate the **themes** folder in your hosting account.*

Double-click the **themes** folder to view its contents. You should see the default Twenty Ten theme folder and any other theme folders you've already uploaded.

When the themes folder is open in the right panel of the FTP window, it's time to focus on the left panel and find the theme files on your hard drive for the new theme you want to upload. In the left panel, navigate through the folders and files on your hard drive until you find the folder for your chosen theme, as shown in Figure 17-15. In this example, we'll upload the Basic theme from ElegantThemes. This is a premium theme and includes theme files and plug-in files you need to upload. Open the **Basic** folder on the left-side panel and select the **Theme** folder within it to upload the theme files.

Click the **Theme** folder to select it, and click the **Upload** button (the blue arrow to the right of the location bar on the left panel) to transfer it to the themes folder you already opened in your hosting account on the right panel. You'll see the files being transferred in the panel at the bottom of the FTP window, as shown in Figure 17-16.

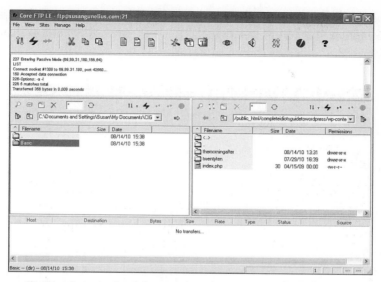

Figure 17-15   *On your hard drive (left panel), locate the theme folder you want to upload. In this example, it should be in the self-titled Basic folder.*

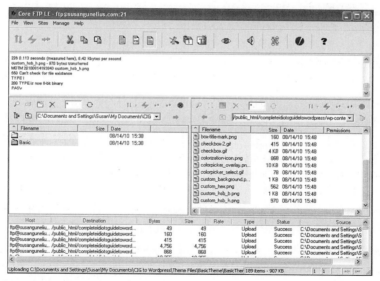

Figure 17-16   *You can watch the files being uploaded in the bottom of the FTP window.*

When the upload is complete, you'll see a new Basic folder in the right panel within the themes folder. This indicates that the Basic theme has been uploaded successfully to the appropriate folder, as shown in Figure 17-17.

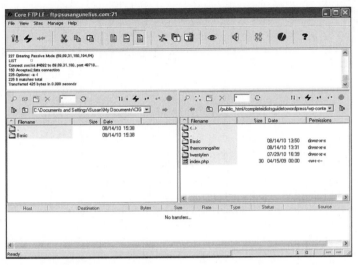

Figure 17-17 *The uploaded Basic theme appears in the Themes folder in the right panel of the FTP window.*

Now you need to upload the plug-ins that are preinstalled with your third-party theme.

QUICK TIP

Not all themes include preinstalled plug-ins. If the theme you want to use doesn't have a plug-ins folder, your theme doesn't have plug-ins for you to upload and you can skip that step.

The Basic theme comes with one plug-in preinstalled. To upload the plug-in files, select the **plugins** folder within the wp-content folder in the right panel of your FTP window, as shown in Figure 17-18. Double-click the folder to open it.

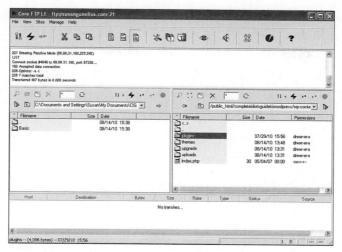

Figure 17-18 *Select the **plugins** folder in your hosting account.*

Next, return to the left panel of your FTP window (the files on your hard drive) and navigate back to the main directory of the theme you're uploading to reveal the **Plugins** folder, as shown in Figure 17-19.

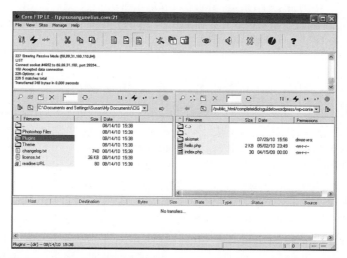

Figure 17-19 *Find the **Plugins** folder on your hard drive for the theme you just uploaded.*

Double-click the **Plugins** folder in the left panel to reveal its contents, as shown in Figure 17-20. Holding down the **Shift** key, select all the contents of the Plugins folder (in this example, there's only one item to select). You need to transfer all the files to your hosting account.

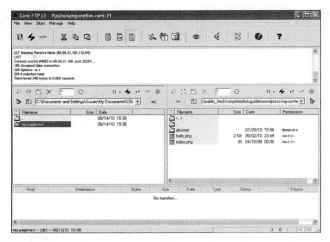

Figure 17-20 *Select all contents of the Plugins folder from your hard drive.*

Once all the contents of the Plugins folder in the left panel are selected, click the **Upload** button to transfer those files to your hosting account. You can watch the files being transferred in the bottom panel of your FTP client window, as shown in Figure 17-21.

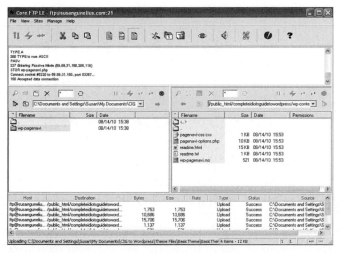

Figure 17-21 *You can see files being transferred from your hard drive to your hosting account.*

When the upload is complete, you can see the successfully transferred files in the right panel of your FTP window, as shown in Figure 17-22.

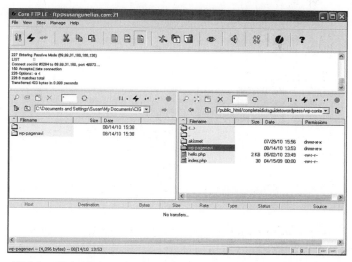

Figure 17-22 *Uploaded plug-in files appear in your hosting account file directory.*

After you have the theme and plug-in files uploaded, you can open the **Manage Themes** page in your WordPress dashboard again. You should see the newly uploaded theme immediately available, as shown in Figure 17-23.

Figure 17-23 *You can see uploaded themes in your Manage Themes page instantly.*

Click the **Activate** link under the newly installed theme on the Manage Themes page to move it up to the Current Theme section of the Manage Themes page, as shown in Figure 17-24.

Figure 17-24 *Once activated, a theme appears in the Current Theme section of the Manage Themes page.*

PROCEED WITH CAUTION

If your uploaded theme included preinstalled plug-ins, you need to activate those plug-ins from your WordPress dashboard or they won't work.

To activate the plug-ins installed with your theme, click the **Plugins** link in your WordPress dashboard's left menu to open the Plugins page, shown in Figure 17-25.

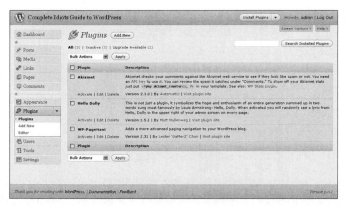

Figure 17-25 *You need to activate theme plug-ins or your theme might not work correctly.*

Locate the plug-ins you uploaded with your theme, and click the **Activate** link under each one to make them functional immediately.

Your new theme is now live on your blog, as shown in Figure 17-26, and ready for tweaking and content!

Figure 17-26 *An activated theme is immediately available on your live blog.*

At any time, you can change your theme by visiting the Manage Themes section of your WordPress dashboard.

Hiring a Designer to Help You

If uploading themes, using FTP, learning CSS, and designing your own blog isn't your idea of fun, you don't have to concern yourself with those tasks. Fortunately, many WordPress designers can help you upload new themes, tweak your theme's design, and completely customize your WordPress site. You can concentrate on creating content and pay someone else to take care of design and development.

WordPress design isn't that difficult to learn, and tweaking designs doesn't usually take very long, so after you start poking around, you'll find many people to help you—without you needing to invest huge amounts of money.

Where to Find WordPress Designers

You can find WordPress designers through freelance websites like Ifreelance.com, Elance.com, Odesk.com, Freelancer.com, and more. You can even publish a call for design help on Craigslist!

There are also blogs and websites that put designers and WordPress users in touch with each other. Check out Bloggingpro.com and Problogger.net, both of which offer job boards where you can post your design job.

Another great way to find blog designers is to search through galleries on premium theme provider websites. Find blogs and websites built on WordPress through those galleries or through your own trip across the web. Contact designers or site owners, and ask who did the design work for their blogs.

Or follow designers and WordPress gurus on Twitter. It's highly likely that these people will follow WordPress designers. I know I do! If you check out the people I follow on Twitter (www.twitter.com/susangunelius), you'll find a number of WordPress designers!

QUICK TIP

Use a Twitter application like WeFollow (wefollow.com) or Listorious (listorious.com) to find Twitter users by keyword tag such as *wordpress* or *wordpressdesigner.*

How Much Should I Expect to Pay?

How much does it cost to get help with WordPress design? That depends on what you want to have done to your site's design. If you're looking for minimal tweaks to an existing WordPress theme, such as a color or font change, a header file uploaded, or another change that can be done in under an hour, you should be able to find a qualified designer to help you for under $100.

If you're looking for more comprehensive tweaking of an existing WordPress theme to make your site more unique, you should expect to spend several hundred dollars.

If you want to get a highly customized site that looks like no other site, includes functionality and design elements unique to your site, and is a comprehensive project that will take weeks to complete, you can expect to pay several thousand dollars.

Of course, the more additional functionality and parts and pieces you need tweaked on your WordPress site, the more the design work will cost. Designers are likely to charge either by the project, for large-scale design work, or by the hour, for smaller tweaks and changes.

The investment you make in WordPress design is entirely up to you, your objectives, and your budget.

Choosing a Designer

Before you commit to working with a WordPress designer, get several estimates for your project as well as recommendations for a designer's work before you commit to anything. Not all designers' skill levels are equal. It's important that you take the time to visit sites they've designed and ensure that those sites work well and meet your standards.

> **PROCEED WITH CAUTION**
>
> Keep in mind, one WordPress designer's definition of a "custom" design might mean nothing more than tweaking a free WordPress theme with graphics and changing fonts. A custom WordPress theme is one that is coded from nothing. Therefore, the price for a truly custom WordPress design is much higher than the price of replacing a header graphic and changing font colors.

Be explicit with what you're looking for. Find examples of other sites you like that you want to emulate with your own site design, and ask for estimates to complete your specific project, along with any other recommendations from the designer. This way, you can compare apples to apples and be sure you're choosing the right designer to meet your needs.

When You Need a WordPress Developer

A WordPress designer is not the same thing as a WordPress developer. While many blog designers can do some development work, a designer works primarily with the CSS coding related to the presentation of content on your WordPress site. A developer, on the other hand, uses the databases and configures the functionality that make your WordPress site work. Think of it this way: an interior decorator makes a house look nice, but an architect puts together the parts and pieces that make the house stand and accommodate the design and other functionality inherent in that house.

So if you want to change something about the way your WordPress site works or functions, you probably need a WordPress developer rather than a designer. For example, a designer makes the front end of your WordPress site look good, while a developer makes the back end of your WordPress site work well.

WordPress for Websites

WordPress is so easy to use and customize that many large and small companies are using it for their business websites rather than simply for blogs. No longer do companies have to rely on programmers and web developers to make changes to their websites. Instead, they can log in to WordPress and allow employees with little technical knowledge to make edits to their websites within minutes. WordPress has moved from a simple blogging application to a powerful content management system.

You'd be amazed at how many of the websites you visit every day are built on Word-Press. In fact, there's a section on the WordPress.org website that showcases sites built on WordPress, including those owned by well-known companies, nonprofit organizations, government agencies, universities, celebrities, and more. Visit wordpress.org/showcase to take a look at some of the sites built using WordPress.

Want more examples? The following sites are also built on WordPress:

- *Ford:* The Ford Story at www.thefordstory.com
- *Boston University:* Boston University Admissions at www.bu.edu/admissions
- *Nokia:* Now Playing by Nokia at nowplaying.nokia.com
- *Wall Street Journal: Wall Street Journal* magazine at magazine.wsj.com
- *L.A. Marathon:* The L.A. Marathon at www.lamarathon.com

Even celebrities like Kobe Bryant, Jay-Z, Katy Perry, and Lance Armstrong (through his Livestrong project) use WordPress to power their branded online destinations. There's something for everyone when it comes to WordPress. For example, check out the U.S. Navy's Military Sealift Command website, shown in Figure 17-27, at www.sealiftcommand.com. It's built on WordPress!

Defining a Static Home Page

The easiest way to make a site built on WordPress look more like a traditional website than a blog is to choose a *static home page* to act as the main entry point to your site. Rather than displaying your blog posts on your site's home page, a static page that doesn't change is used as the welcome page, and blog posts are accessible through a link in your site's navigation bar or sidebar.

Figure 17-27   *You can find all kinds of websites that are built on WordPress.*

The specific layout of your site depends on the theme you're using, but there's almost always the option to choose a single page to act as your WordPress site's static home page. Simply choose the **Reading** link in the Settings section of your WordPress dashboard left menu to open the Reading Settings page, shown in Figure 17-28.

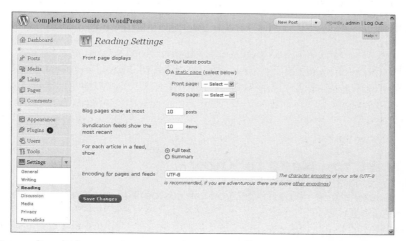

Figure 17-28   *Select a static home page from the Reading Settings page of your WordPress dashboard.*

Near the top of the Reading Settings page is the Front page displays section. Here you'll see two radio buttons for **Your latest posts** or **A static page**. To set your site's home page to a static page, select the radio button next to **A static page** and use the drop-down menus to select the page you want to use as your site's home page.

QUICK TIP

Note that the page must already be created for it to appear in the drop-down list in the Reading Settings page.

Click the **Save Changes** button, and your new static home page immediately appears as your site's home page on your live site.

Choosing a Theme for Your Website

Another option is to choose a WordPress theme that looks like a traditional website. Both free and premium theme providers offer WordPress themes that look nothing like traditional blogs. In fact, many WordPress themes give you the option to include a traditional blog with your WordPress site or omit blog content entirely.

Check out the "WordPress Theme Sites" section of Appendix C for several premium WordPress theme providers that offer well-coded themes for businesses that can give your website a unique look without looking like a blog at all.

Remember, WordPress is an open source application, so you can take it as far as your creativity and technical ability (or budget to hire technical experts) can stretch. You're not limited to a traditional blog with WordPress, so don't be afraid to see what you can do with it!

The Least You Need to Know

- By learning some basic CSS, you can customize your WordPress site design yourself.
- You can upload a new WordPress theme to your blog and give it a completely new look in minutes.
- Finding technical help for WordPress design or development at a reasonable price isn't difficult. Just be sure to get recommendations and compare prices and services.

A WordPress Plug-In for Everything

In This Chapter

- Understanding what WordPress plug-ins can do
- Where to find WordPress plug-ins
- Installing plug-ins
- Managing your plug-ins

WordPress.org is an open source application, so the code behind it is available for anyone to edit. That means developers around the world work with that code to create enhanced functionality and features. That, in turn, enables WordPress.org users to do amazing things with their self-hosted WordPress sites.

Plug-ins are just one of the things developers create so WordPress users can get added functionality from their sites. This chapter teaches you what plug-ins are, how they can help you, where you can find them, and what some of the most popular free WordPress plug-ins are. In a few pages, you'll be able to start using plug-ins and take your WordPress site to a new level!

What Are WordPress Plug-Ins?

WordPress plug-ins are functions written in php (a scripting language) that can extend the capabilities of your WordPress blog or website. Developers create both free and paid WordPress plug-ins, and you can access a huge variety of WordPress plug-ins in the WordPress Plugin Directory at wordpress.org/extend/plugins.

Some WordPress plug-ins come preinstalled with WordPress, but most must be uploaded individually to your WordPress plug-ins folder. Some might be included as part of a theme upload, as discussed in Chapter 17.

Plug-ins are what set WordPress apart from other blogging applications because they add so much more functionality above and beyond traditional blogging features, other blogging applications can't compete. In short, no other blogging application lets users do so much without the need for advanced technical knowledge and skills as WordPress.

Preinstalled WordPress Plug-Ins

When you upload WordPress to your hosting account and log in to your WordPress dashboard, the default Twenty Ten theme discussed in Chapter 17 is automatically activated for you. Log in to your WordPress dashboard and select the **Plugins** link from the left menu to open the Plugins page, shown in Figure 18-1.

Figure 18-1 *Some plug-ins come preinstalled with your new WordPress blog.*

Here you'll see two plug-ins already listed:

- Akismet, a comment spam detector and filter

- Hello Dolly, a just-for-fun plug-in that displays a random lyric from Louis Armstrong's famous song by the same name at the top of every page of your WordPress dashboard

I highly recommend you activate the Akismet plug-in to help catch spam comments before they're published on your blog and damage the user experience. It's entirely up to you if you want to activate the Hello Dolly plug-in. Visitors to your blog are not affected by this plug-in. Only you see it.

To activate the Akismet plug-in, click the **Activate** link under the Akismet listing on the Plugins page, shown in Figure 18-1. The plug-in is instantly activated on your blog, and a new option appears in the Plugins section of your WordPress dashboard left menu called Akismet Configuration. Click the **Akismet Configuration** link to open the Akismet Configuration page, shown in Figure 18-2. Here you can finish setting up Akismet to work on your blog.

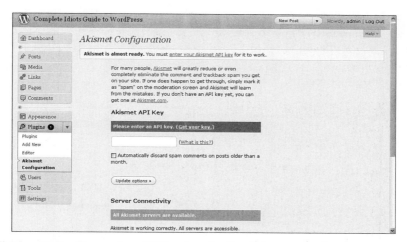

Figure 18-2 *You need an API key in order for Akismet to work on your WordPress blog.*

First, you need to enter your API key. You can get it by clicking on the **Get Your Key** link, which takes you to the Akismet website. Here you can enter your e-mail address to create a free Akismet subscription (if you make less than $500 per month from your blog; otherwise, you need to pay for an Akismet API key). Once you provide your e-mail address, your API key is e-mailed to you. Just copy and paste it into the **Please enter an API key** text box on the Akismet Configuration page.

 INSIDER SECRET

If you have a WordPress.com account, you can log in to your WordPress.com dashboard and copy and paste the API key from that account to use in your self-hosted WordPress.org blog.

Next, check the box next to **Automatically discard spam comments on posts older than a month** if you want to automate the process of cleaning out your comment spam folder.

Finally, click the **Update Options** button to complete the Akismet configuration process and start redirecting comments flagged as spam to the spam queue in the Comment Moderation section of your WordPress dashboard.

Where to Find WordPress Plug-Ins

The first place most WordPress users go to find plug-ins is the WordPress Plugin Directory, accessible at wordpress.org/extend/plugins and shown in Figure 18-3.

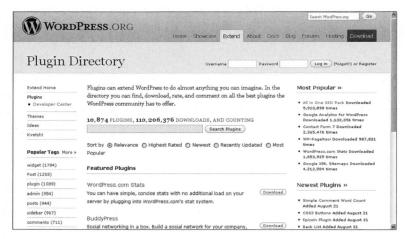

Figure 18-3 *More than 10,000 plug-ins are available for free download in the WordPress Plugin Directory.*

WordPress plug-in developers who want to make it easy for people to find and download their free plug-ins allow WordPress to host their plug-ins in the Plugin Directory. These plug-ins are also accessible directly through the search features found on the Install Plugins page of your WordPress dashboard (shown in Figure 18-4), which you can access by selecting the **Add New** link within the Plugins section of your WordPress dashboard's left menu.

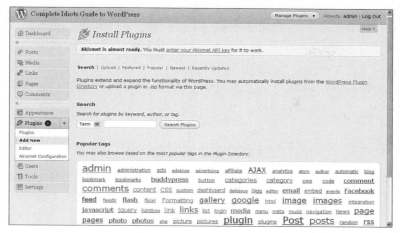

Figure 18-4 *You can search for and install plug-ins from your WordPress dashboard.*

You can search the WordPress Plugin Directory on the WordPress website by entering keywords into the search text box in the left sidebar; scrolling through the featured plug-ins listed on the main page of the Plugin Directory; or clicking through the Most Popular Plugins, Newest Plugins, and Recently Updated Plugins lists in the right sidebar. Similar search features are offered through the Install Plugins page within your WordPress dashboard.

The WordPress Plugin Directory offers additional information about each plug-in. For example, Figure 18-5 shows the listing for one of the most popular WordPress plug-ins, All in One SEO Pack (discussed in more detail later in this chapter).

PROCEED WITH CAUTION

Most of the details in the WordPress Plugin Directory are submitted by the developers, so it's not always as detailed as a user might like. But it can still be helpful in determining whether or not a plug-in will meet your needs.

Across the top of the listing is a navigation bar with several links. Each link offers more information about the listed plug-in, including a description, installation information, answers to frequently asked questions, screenshots, and statistics. Note that all plug-ins don't offer information in each of these sections.

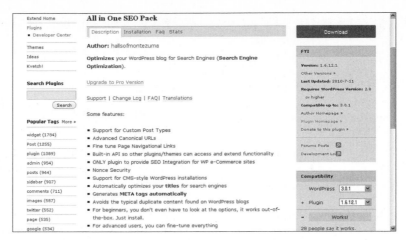

Figure 18-5 *Listings in the WordPress Plugins Directory can be very detailed.*

Along the right sidebar of the plug-in listing is even more information, including the most recent version of WordPress that the plug-in is compatible with, update information, links to the author's web page and the plug-in's home page, user reviews, and more.

You'll also see a **Download** button on the top right. Click this to download the plug-in to your hard drive so you can then upload it to your hosting account. (I discuss this in more detail later in this chapter.)

WordPress plug-ins are also available outside the WordPress Plugin Directory. A quick Google search for "WordPress plug-ins" delivers hundreds of thousands of results. Many bloggers and online publishers write about and review WordPress plug-ins, which makes it easier to find the most useful plug-ins for your blog.

The "WordPress Plug-Ins and Reviews" section in Appendix C offers a few resources to find and learn about WordPress plug-ins.

Free Versus Paid Plug-Ins

The vast majority of WordPress plug-ins are offered for free. Some developers ask for donations, but most simply want to share their work with other WordPress users. However, some WordPress plug-ins are available for a fee. It takes time to create plug-ins, keep them up-to-date, continue to improve them, offer support to users, and more.

> **QUICK TIP**
>
> Some developers offer a free version and also more advanced versions for a fee, while other developers offer a single option with a price tag.

It takes a lot for me to pay for a plug-in. With so many free options, a plug-in with a price tag has to be truly amazing, useful, or time-saving for me to pay for it. I have been very happy to pay for some, including these:

- *Gravity Forms* (www.gravityforms.com): This is more than just a contact form, and you have to see what it can do to truly understand that it's well worth the money.

- *OIOpublisher* (www.oiopublisher.com): If you want to sell ad space directly on your blog, this plug-in is worth the investment.

- *BackupBuddy* (pluginbuddy.com/purchase/backupbuddy): If the process of backing up your WordPress blog confuses you, this plug-in can make it easier and give you peace of mind that you won't lose your data.

It's always a good idea to do your research before you pay for a plug-in to ensure it offers the features you need, as well as support if you need help. Furthermore, be sure there's not a free plug-in available that does the same thing as a plug-in you're considering paying for. Visit some of the sites listed earlier in this chapter and leave a comment asking about plug-ins you have questions about. Alternately, post your question on your Twitter, Facebook, or other social media profile. You'd be surprised how many people will jump in to offer their opinions!

Installing WordPress Plug-Ins

Since WordPress 2.7 was released, the process of installing plug-ins to your blog from the WordPress Plugin Directory is easier than ever. With a few clicks of the mouse in your WordPress dashboard, you can have a new plug-in installed and activated within minutes. However, you must still manually upload plug-ins not available through the WordPress Plugin Directory. But don't worry—the process is easy.

In Chapter 17, you learned how to upload plug-ins via FTP when we covered themes. In this chapter, you learn how to install plug-ins through your WordPress dashboard and how to manually upload plug-ins to your WordPress account without using an FTP service.

There are two ways to install plug-ins to your blog through your WordPress dashboard. You can automatically install plug-ins available in the WordPress Plugin Directory, or you can manually upload plug-ins not in the directory, as long as you have the original zipped plug-in folder saved on your computer hard drive. This section shows you how to do both installation methods.

Automatically Installing Plug-Ins from the WordPress Plugin Directory

If the plug-in you want to install to your WordPress account is available through the WordPress Plugin Directory, you can find it by searching for it on the Install Plugins page of your WordPress dashboard, shown in Figure 18-4. You can search by keyword term, tag, or plug-in author.

INSIDER SECRET

If you have trouble finding a plug-in through the Install Plugins page of your WordPress dashboard, visit the WordPress Plugin Directory at wordpress.org/extend/plugins to conduct your search, learn who the plug-in author is, and get more information about it.

For example, a popular plug-in I use on my blogs is Subscribe to Comments, which allows people who leave comments on your blog posts to subscribe to those posts. By clicking on a button in the post comment form, they can sign up to receive e-mails whenever another comment is published on that post.

Type "subscribe to comments" into the text box in the Install Plugins page of your WordPress dashboard, and click the **Search Plugins** button to get the results shown in Figure 18-6.

Figure 18-6   *Scroll through plug-in search results to get more information.*

The Subscribe to Comments plug-in is first in the list of search results shown in Figure 18-6. You can install it to your blog by clicking the **Install Now** link beneath the plug-in title in the Name column. This opens a dialogue box, shown in Figure 18-7, that asks if you're sure you want to install this plug-in.

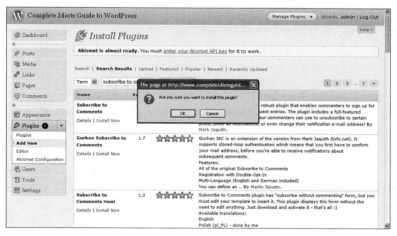

Figure 18-7   *Click **OK** to install your chosen plug-in.*

Click **OK** to start the installation process. When the plug-in is installed, you'll see a page like the one shown in Figure 18-8, confirming that the plug-in installed successfully.

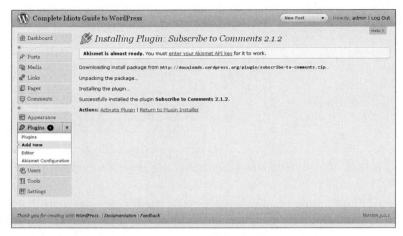

Figure 18-8 *Once your plug-in is installed, you still have to activate it.*

The final step is to click the **Activate Plugin** link to turn on the plug-in. Once you click on the activate link, you're returned to the Plugins page of your WordPress dashboard, shown in Figure 18-9, where you can see the new plug-in included in your list of installed plug-ins. You'll also see a Deactivate link beneath your new plug-in. That means it's currently active on your blog.

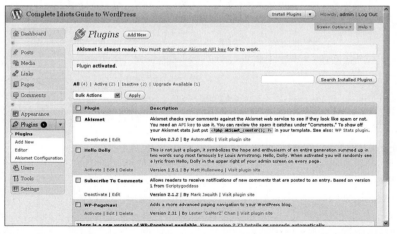

Figure 18-9 *Your newly installed plug-in now appears as an active plug-in.*

With the Subscribe to Comments plug-in active, you can visit any post in your live blog and see a **Notify me of followup comments via e-mail** check box at the bottom of the comment form section of your blog, as shown in Figure 18-10.

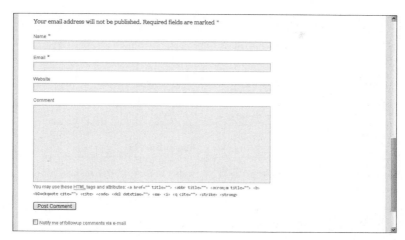

Figure 18-10   *The Subscribe to Comments plug-in is live on your blog as soon as you upload and activate it.*

Manually Uploading Plug-Ins Through the WordPress Dashboard

If the plug-in you want to install to your WordPress blog is not included in the WordPress Plugin Directory, you need to upload it manually to your WordPress account. You can do that through your WordPress dashboard.

PROCEED WITH CAUTION

If you try to manually upload a plug-in through your WordPress dashboard and get an error message telling you the plug-in did not install correctly, you'll have to delete it and manually install it to your hosting account. (I explain how to do this later in this chapter.)

First, you need to find the plug-in you want to upload and download its zip file to your hard drive. For example, if you want to manually upload the Subscribe to Comments plug-in and install it through your WordPress dashboard, you can do so by searching for the plug-in in the WordPress Plugin Directory at wordpress.org/extend/plugins, as shown in Figure 18-11.

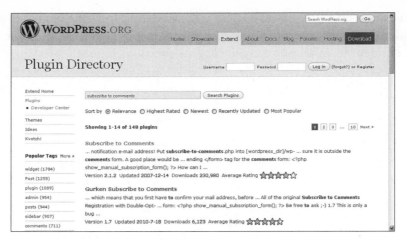

Figure 18-11 *Search for the plug-in you want to upload and install.*

Click on the plug-in to visit its page in the WordPress Plugin Directory. The Subscribe to Comments page is shown in Figure 18-12.

Figure 18-12 *Visit the main page of the plug-in you want to use in your WordPress blog.*

Click the **Download** button shown in Figure 18-12 (or on the plug-in web page if it's not part of the WordPress Plugin Directory). This opens a dialogue box asking you if you want to open or save the file, as shown in Figure 18-13. Be sure the **Save File** radio button is selected, and click **OK**. Choose the location on your hard drive where you want to save the downloaded zip file so you can easily find it later.

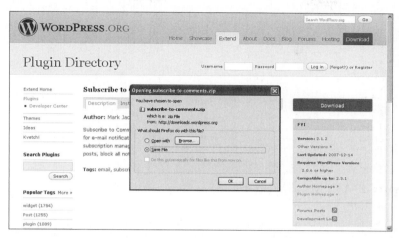

Figure 18-13 *Save the downloaded zip file to your hard drive.*

 QUICK TIP

Take note of the name of the zip folder you're downloading. It'll be easier to locate the folder later, when it's time to upload it to your WordPress account.

After the zip file has downloaded, you can upload it to your WordPress account by returning to the Install Plugins page, shown in Figure 18-4. Click the **Upload** link near the top of the page to open the Install Plugins page, shown in Figure 18-14, where you can upload your zip file.

Click the **Browse...** button and locate the zip file for the plug-in you want to upload from your hard drive. (It will be in the location where you saved it during the previous download process.) Select the file, and click the **Install Now** button. A new page opens, telling you the plug-in installed successfully (if not, you'll need to do a manual install through your hosting account, which is discussed in the next section), as shown in Figure 18-15.

Figure 18-14 *Upload the zip file of your chosen plug-in.*

Figure 18-15 *After the plug-in has uploaded, you still need to activate it.*

Finally, click the **Activate Plugin** link to turn on the plug-in. When the plug-in is activated, you are returned to your list of installed plug-ins where you can see the Subscribe to Comments plug-in has been added and is active, as shown in Figure 18-16.

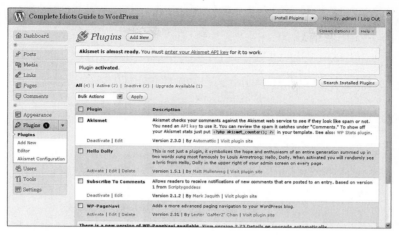

Figure 18-16 *Your uploaded plug-in is now active.*

Manually Installing Plug-Ins Through Your Hosting Account

If you can't install the plug-in you want to use through the automated or manual processes available in your WordPress dashboard, you need to upload the plug-in to your hosting account and then return to your WordPress account to activate it.

In Chapter 17, you learned how to upload plug-ins via FTP (the process is discussed as part of the steps to upload a third-party theme to your WordPress account). This section teaches you how to upload a plug-in to your hosting account without using an FTP service.

INSIDER SECRET

The steps in this section use BlueHost.com, a hosting service that offers one-click extraction of uploaded zipped folders. If your hosting account does not allow you to extract zipped folders, you'll need to manually upload individual files. In this case, using an FTP service might be faster and easier. Furthermore, your hosting account screenshots and uploading steps might differ from those used with BlueHost, but the basic process is the same.

First, log in to your hosting account and navigate to your control panel (cPanel). In the Files section, double-click **File Manager**, as shown in Figure 18-17.

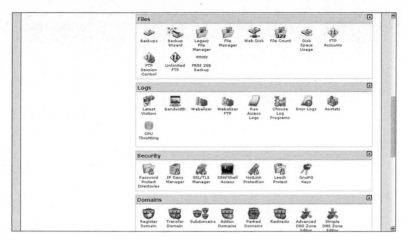

Figure 18-17 *You use File Manager to access the files in your hosting account.*

Navigate to your blog's WordPress installation files and find the **plugins** folder, as shown in Figure 18-18.

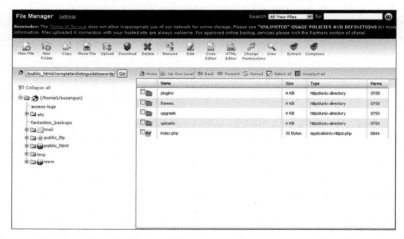

Figure 18-18 *Find the plugins folder in your hosting account WordPress installation files.*

Double-click the **plugins** folder to reveal its contents, as shown in Figure 18-19.

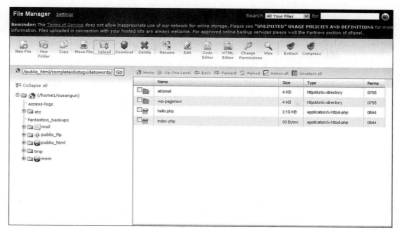

Figure 18-19 *Upload your zipped plug-in to the plugins folder in your hosting account.*

Click the **Upload** button to open the Upload File window, shown in Figure 18-20.

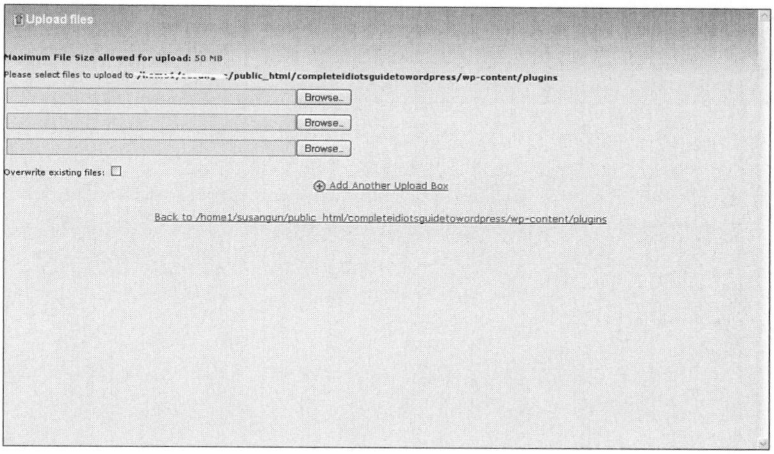

Figure 18-20 *Choose the zipped folder you want to upload.*

Click the **Browse…** button and locate the zipped folder for the plug-in you want to upload where you saved it on your hard drive during the download process. Select the file to begin the upload process. When the file is uploaded, you'll see a message telling you it has been uploaded successfully, as shown in Figure 18-21.

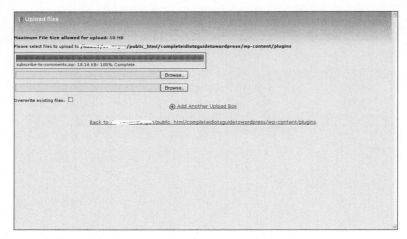

Figure 18-21 *When the zipped file is uploaded, you can return to File Manager.*

Click on the link to go back to File Manager or simply close the window to return. The zipped folder is now listed in the contents of the plugins folder in your hosting account, as shown in Figure 18-22.

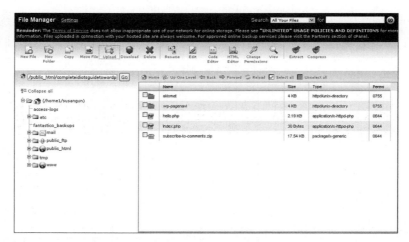

Figure 18-22 *After the zipped folder is uploaded, you have to extract the contents.*

Click on the zipped folder to select it and then click the **Extract** button to extract the contents from the zipped folder into individual files. When you click on the **Extract** button, a dialogue box opens, shown in Figure 18-23, asking you to confirm the path where you want the files to be saved. Be sure your plugins folder is the extract location.

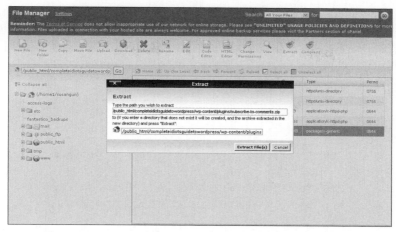

Figure 18-23 *You want to extract the files to your plugins folder.*

Finally, click the **Extract File(s)** button to extract the files. When the extraction is complete, you're returned to the File Manager page, as shown in Figure 18-24, where you can now see that the Subscribe to Comments folder has been added.

> **QUICK TIP**
>
> After you extract the files, the zipped folder is still visible. You can delete that if you want to.

Figure 18-24 *The extracted plugins folder is visible in your hosting account file manager.*

Now that the plug-in has been uploaded to your hosting account, you can log in to your WordPress dashboard and navigate to your Plugins page. You should see the uploaded Subscribe to Comments plug-in added to your list of plug-ins, as shown in Figure 18-25.

Figure 18-25   *The manually uploaded plug-in still needs to be activated.*

You still need to activate the plug-in in order for it to work on your blog. Just click the **Activate** link under the plug-in's name to immediately activate it on your blog. That's all there is to it!

Managing Your WordPress Plug-Ins

One of the best things about plug-ins is the fact that they're so flexible. You can turn them on or off with the click of a mouse, and many plug-ins offer a wide variety of configuration options.

In this section, I show you how to manage the basic functions of WordPress plug-ins so you can truly enjoy their flexibility.

Special Configuration Menus and Links

Some plug-ins offer advanced configuration options, which you can access in several different ways, depending on the plug-in. For example, some plug-ins offer a Settings link, visible next to the Activate or Deactivate link in the Plugins list in your

WordPress dashboard. Others add a Configuration link (although it might not be named "configuration") in the Tools section of your WordPress dashboard left menu. There is no standard name. You just have to look for a new link that wasn't there before. Highly advanced plug-ins add a completely new section to your WordPress dashboard left menu where you can access multiple configuration links.

 INSIDER SECRET

When you activate a new plug-in, look around your WordPress dashboard, particularly in the left sidebar menus, to see if any configuration options were added.

Updates

Plug-in developers often update their WordPress plug-ins to add new features, fix problems, or be compatible with a newer version of WordPress. If an update is available for one of your installed plug-ins, you'll likely see a message in one or more places.

First, plug-in update notices can be found by clicking the **Updates** link in the Dashboard section of your WordPress dashboard's left menu, as shown in Figure 18-26.

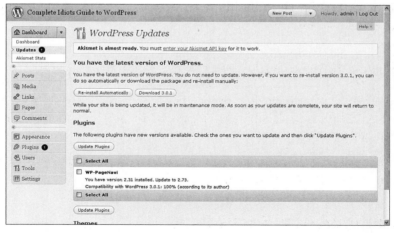

Figure 18-26   *WordPress application, plug-in, and theme updates are shown on the WordPress Updates page.*

Second, you can see plug-in update notices across the top of most pages of your WordPress dashboard as well as beneath the specific plug-in's listing in the Plugins page of your WordPress dashboard, as shown in Figure 18-27.

Figure 18-27   *Plug-in update notices are visible on the Plugins page.*

To update a plug-in when you find an update notice, just click the **Update** (or **Upgrade**) link. The plug-in updates immediately, and you're taken to the Upgrade Plugin page, shown in Figure 18-28.

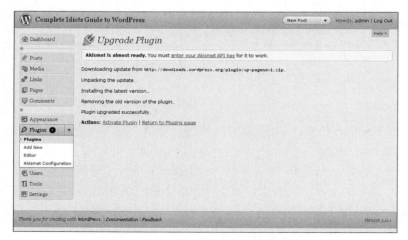

Figure 18-28   *Once a plug-in is updated, you have to activate it again.*

After a plug-in upgrade is completed, you have to reactivate the plug-in by clicking the **Activate Plugin** link.

Deactivating Plug-Ins

The time might come when you no longer want to use a plug-in. All it takes to deactivate a plug-in is one mouse click to turn it off.

Visit the Plugins page in your WordPress dashboard, and click the **Deactivate** link beneath the plug-in you want to turn off. The Subscribe to Comments plug-in, shown in Figure 18-29, can easily be deactivated by clicking the **Deactivate** link.

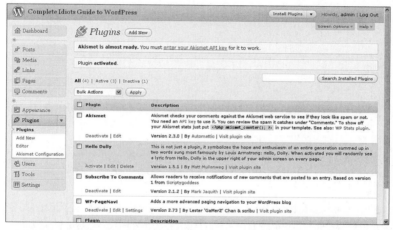

Figure 18-29   *Click the **Deactivate** link to turn off a plug-in.*

When the plug-in is deactivated, the Deactivate link disappears and an Activate link appears in its place. To turn the plug-in back on again, just click the **Activate** link.

INSIDER SECRET

If your blog is acting strangely or your theme looks odd, deactivate your plug-ins one by one and visit your blog between each deactivation to see if that fixes the problem. Sometimes plug-ins that have been working just fine suddenly cause problems. You can try to delete, reinstall, and reactivate them.

Deleting Plug-Ins

When you want to completely remove a plug-in from your WordPress installation, you can do it from your WordPress dashboard with a couple mouse clicks. Visit your Plugins page, shown in Figure 18-30, and click the **Delete** link under the name of the plug-in you want to delete. In this example, the Subscribe to Comments plug-in will be deleted.

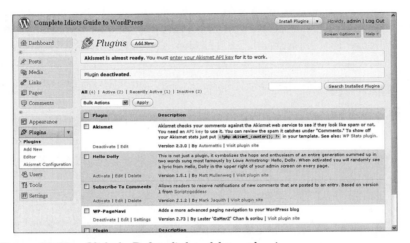

Figure 18-30 *Click the **Delete** link to delete a plug-in.*

When you click the **Delete** link, a new page opens, shown in Figure 18-31, asking if you're sure you want to delete the files associated with the selected plug-in. (You can view the files by clicking **Click to view entire list of files which will be deleted**.) Click the **Yes, Delete these files** button to complete the deletion.

When you click the **Yes** button, you're returned to your Plugins list where the selected plug-in (in this case, the Subscribe to Comments plug-in) is no longer listed, as shown in Figure 18-32.

Don't worry if you change your mind. You can always reinstall a plug-in you deleted and reactivate it. Keep in mind that some plug-ins might require you to reconfigure your personal settings after you reinstall it.

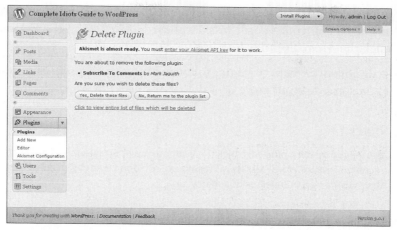

Figure 18-31 *Confirm that you want to delete the selected plug-in.*

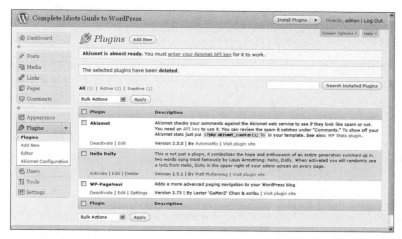

Figure 18-32 *A deleted plug-in is removed from your list of installed plug-ins.*

Popular Free WordPress Plug-Ins

Now that you know where to find plug-ins and how to install them, you're probably itching to get moving. But where do you start? Thousands of plug-ins are out there!

You can browse through lists of popular WordPress plug-ins by visiting the **Add New Plugins** page in your WordPress dashboard and clicking the **Popular** link, or you can click the **Most Popular** link in the WordPress Plugins Directory.

If you're still not sure where to begin, following are several useful and popular plug-ins to get you started. (Find more useful plug-ins listed in Appendix B.)

> **QUICK TIP**
>
> Before you install a plug-in, check the last time it was updated and the most recent version of WordPress it was tested on. You don't want to install a plug-in that hasn't been updated or tested in years.

All in One SEO Pack

All in One SEO Pack is one of the most popular WordPress plug-ins. The plug-in, available at wordpress.org/extend/plugins/all-in-one-seo-pack, allows you to enter a separate title, description, and keywords for search engines to index, which can help boost search engine traffic to your posts.

When you activate it on your blog, a new section appears when you create a new blog post, as shown in Figure 18-33.

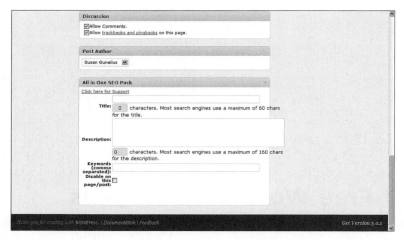

Figure 18-33 *All in One SEO Pack helps boost search engine traffic to your blog.*

WP-DB (WordPress Database)-Backup

The WP-DB-Backup plug-in, available at wordpress.org/extend/plugins/wp-db-backup, is an easy-to-configure plug-in that enables you to automate the process of backing up your WordPress database files. You can choose what gets backed up, when, and how once you install and activate this plug-in, as shown in part in Figure 18-34.

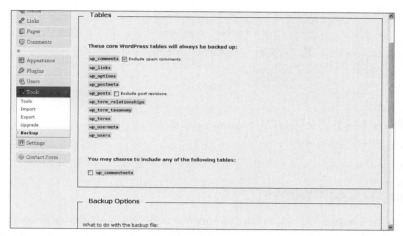

Figure 18-34 *You can configure WP-DB-Backup so you receive a weekly e-mail with your backup file attached.*

AddThis

AddThis, available at wordpress.org/extend/plugins/addthis/, enables you to add an icon in your blog posts that visitors can click so they can share your post through the social media profile or site of their choice (nearly 300 options are available), as shown in Figure 18-35.

The AddThis plug-in is very helpful in increasing traffic to your blog because it makes it easy for people to share your posts with their own audiences across the social web.

Figure 18-35 *The AddThis plug-in makes it easy for people to share your blog posts with larger audiences.*

Subscribe to Comments

Subscribe to Comments, at wordpress.org/extend/plugins/subscribe-to-comments, has been used as an example throughout this chapter. It's easy to install and lets people who visit your blog stay on top of conversations that interest them, so they can return and comment again. It's a great plug-in to help build relationships with readers and keep conversations going longer than they normally would without it. You can see Subscribe to Comments on a live blog post in Figure 18-10.

Yet Another Related Posts Plugin (YARPP)

A number of plug-ins out there add related posts to the end of your blog posts, but Yet Another Related Posts Plugin (YARPP), available at wordpress.org/extend/ plugins/yet-another-related-posts-plugin, is one of the most popular. When you install and activate this plug-in, contextually related posts appear at the end of each of your published blog posts for visitors to click and read, as shown in Figure 18-36.

YARPP is highly customizable and can help you boost the length of time people spend on your blog by making it easy to find more relevant content they're interested in. It also helps boost page views, which is important to bloggers who want to make money by selling ad space on their blogs, as discussed in Chapters 23 and 24.

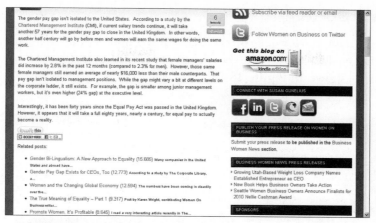

Figure 18-36   *YARPP automatically adds links to related posts at the end of each of your blog posts.*

Contact Form 7

If you want to make it easy for people to get in touch with you through your blog but you don't want to publish your e-mail address, you can use a contact form. A number of plug-ins make it easy to create contact forms, and Contact Form 7, available at wordpress.org/extend/plugins/contact-form-7, is one of the best free options. It's flexible and easy to configure, and you can create highly customizable contact forms within a few minutes of installing and activating it. You can see an example of a partial live form in Figure 18-37.

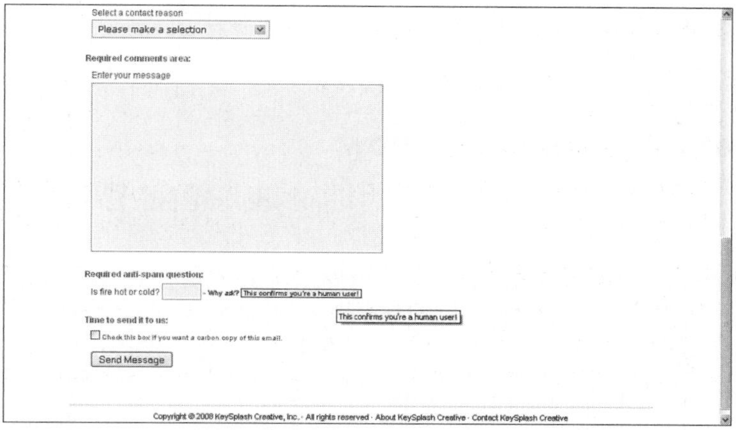

Figure 18-37   *You can create a form with a wide variety of required and optional fields with the Contact Form 7 plug-in.*

TweetMeme Button

The TweetMeme Button plug-in, available at wordpress.org/extend/plugins/
tweetmeme, enables you to add the highly popular **Retweet** button to your
blog posts, as shown in Figure 18-38.

Figure 18-38 *Make it easy for people to retweet your blog posts with the
TweetMeme button.*

You can choose where the Retweet button appears in your posts and what it looks
like. Visitors who link their Twitter accounts to free TweetMeme accounts can simply
click on the **Retweet** button to tweet your blog post to their audiences of followers.
It's a great way to drive traffic from Twitter to your blog and expose your content to a
much wider audience.

The Least You Need to Know

- WordPress plug-ins allow you to extend your site into far more than a simple
  blog.
- There are free WordPress plug-ins and WordPress plug-ins that cost money. The
  WordPress Plugin Directory offers over 10,000 free plug-ins.
- You can install, activate, deactivate, delete, or reinstall plug-ins within minutes
  and at any time. They are completely flexible!

Attracting an Audience

Your blog is set up and working just fine. Now it's time to grow your blog's audience and attract more visitors to your blog. This part shows you how to do just that.

Part 5 introduces some useful search engine optimization tricks to boost organic search traffic to your blog. You also learn how to set up your blog's feed and attract subscribers. Additionally, you learn how to use the various tools of the social web, such as Twitter, Facebook, and more, to grow your blog's audience.

At the end of Part 5, you learn how to track your blog's performance using a web analytics tool so you can make the necessary adjustments to optimize traffic to your blog.

Search Engine Optimization

In This Chapter

- Increasing traffic to your blog
- Why link building matters
- How to research keywords
- Search engine optimization don'ts

Search engine optimization (SEO) is a continually evolving practice of learning how search engines, particularly Google, index and rank web pages and content. By learning SEO techniques and applying them to your WordPress blog, you can increase the amount of traffic that comes to your blog from search engine keyword queries.

This chapter teaches you some of the most commonly recommended SEO tricks you can use to increase search traffic to your blog, including the importance of link building, writing SEO-friendly content, and researching keywords. Furthermore, this chapter explains which SEO tactics you should avoid if you want to stay on good terms with the search engines.

Boosting Blog Traffic with SEO

Google, Bing, and Yahoo! are the three most popular search engines, with Google far surpassing even its closest competitors in terms of use and the amount of traffic it sends to blogs and websites via user searches. For simplicity, this chapter frequently refers to Google, but the information in the following pages applies to other search engines as well.

Search engines like Google use proprietary algorithms (arithmetical sets of rules that aren't publicly available) to analyze every page on the web. By crawling through the contents of those pages, they rank the pages in terms of relevance for keyword searches. Sites that rank high on search engine results pages (SERPs) for keywords related to their sites and content get more traffic from search engines than similar sites that rank lower in the same keyword searches. Basically, the goal of search engine optimization is to write and publish content using SEO tactics that can push your content higher in relevant keyword searches.

How WordPress Helps SEO

There are many search engine optimization tricks you can use on your blog to boost search traffic to it, and some of those tricks are built right into the WordPress blogging application. It takes just a few minutes to set them up on your blog pages and posts.

First, be sure to configure your WordPress settings so your site is visible to search engines and pings are sent when you publish new content, as discussed in Chapters 7 and 16. This helps Google and other search engines index your content quickly and efficiently.

 INSIDER SECRET

Some WordPress themes seem more search engine friendly than others. For example, the Thesis theme from DIYthemes.com is commonly believed to be coded in a manner that aids SEO efforts.

Next, in the settings of your WordPress account, create a title for your blog that uses targeted keywords. This title appears in the bar across the top of a browser window when someone visits your blog, and it can help your search engine optimization efforts. (This is also discussed in Chapters 7 and 16.)

As you write posts on your blog, be sure to use the tools available to enhance your search engine optimization efforts. For example, as you write a post, you can add keyword tags, use heading font styles (discussed in the "SEO Tips" section later in this chapter), configure your posts and pages to accept trackbacks and pings, and use strategic links within your posts. (These tools are discussed in Chapters 9 and 10.)

When you upload images to publish in your blog posts or pages, be sure to make use of the media upload tool. You can, for example, add an image title and alternate text using keywords, as described in Chapter 10.

Finally, use plug-ins that help with search engine optimization. For example, the All in One SEO Pack, discussed in Chapter 18, is very popular among WordPress users, as is the Google XML Sitemaps plug-in (available at wordpress.org/extend/plugins/google-sitemap-generator). Both are thought to help with search engine optimization.

SEO Tips

Search engine optimization is constantly evolving as search engines update their ranking algorithms, and SEO experts work to figure out what those algorithms are and release their findings and recommendations.

Two of the most important aspects of search engine optimization you can use to your advantage are *link building* and *keyword research*. Both are discussed later in this chapter, but for now focus on specific tactics you can employ on your blog as you're writing new posts because every little bit helps!

Here are a few easy tips you can use now:

- Use keywords in your post titles.
- Use keywords in hyperlinks or around hyperlinked text.
- Use keywords in text formatted using heading styles in your WordPress post editor.
- Use keywords in alt-tags and titles of image files in the WordPress media library. (Alt-tags are discussed in Chapter 3.)
- Tag your posts with specific keywords using the Tags module in the WordPress Add a Post page.

SEO Resources

Search engine optimization requires ongoing analysis and learning to truly understand how it works, so it's a good idea to keep on top of SEO research. Fortunately, a number of websites can help you with this. Appendix C's "Search Engine Optimization Help Sites" gives you a few places to start.

If you'd like to read a step-by-step SEO guide, following are links to some useful and free guides you can access online as well as some SEO books.

- SEOmoz Beginner's Guide to SEO: www.seomoz.org/article/beginners-1-page

- *The Complete Idiot's Guide to Search Engine Optimization* by Michael Miller: www.amazon.com/Complete-Idiots-Search-Engine-Optimization/ dp/1592578357

- *The Art of SEO* by Stephen Spencer, Rand Fishkin, and Jessica Stricchiola: www.amazon.com/Art-SEO-Mastering-Optimization-Practice/ dp/0596518862

Importance of Link Building

One of the factors search engines like Google use to rank keyword search results is the number of incoming links a web page has. The theory is that pages with a lot of incoming links, particularly from popular websites, must contain good content or no one would want to link to them. So pages with a lot of incoming links are likely to be ranked higher in keyword search results than pages with fewer incoming links.

> **QUICK TIP**
>
> Find out how many incoming links your blog has according to Google by typing **link:www.yourblogname.com** into the search box on Google. On Yahoo! type **linkdomain:www.yourblogname.com** into the search bar.

Blogs are social in nature, so your readers are likely to share the posts on your blog they like with their own audiences. Therefore, it's important that you write great content and make it easy for people to share that content, thereby driving incoming links and traffic to your blog. Use plug-ins like the TweetMeme button and AddThis plug-in, as discussed in Chapter 18, to enable one-click sharing of your content on the social web.

Link-Building Tips

In addition to using the plug-ins suggested in the previous section, there are other easy tricks you can use to increase the number of incoming links to your blog. Here are a few to get you started:

- Publish amazing content on your blog other people will want to read, share, and write about on their own sites.

- Leave comments on other blogs, and include your blog's address in the comment forms' URL space.

- Accept trackbacks on your blog posts so people who link to your posts receive an incoming link to their sites in return.

- Promote your content on your Twitter, Facebook, LinkedIn, and other social networking profiles.

- Submit your content to social bookmarking sites like Digg and StumbleUpon.

- Write for multiple sites, and interlink your content.

- Write guest blog posts for other popular blogs, and include a link back to your blog in your author biography.

Anything you do to share your content with interested audiences increases the potential that people will read it. If they like it, they might write about it on their own blogs and link to it, or they might share it through their own social web connections. Each instance your content is shared and viewed increases the potential for others to write about your content and link to it. The more incoming links, the better, in terms of boosting your search engine rankings.

Link Building Versus Link Baiting

Link building and *link baiting* are two different things and serve two different purposes. While link building is a blog-growth strategy that helps boost your blog's search engine rankings and traffic in the long term, link baiting causes short-term traffic spikes. However, some of the people who arrive at your blog through your link bait might like what they read and turn into loyal readers.

DEFINITION

Link baiting is the process of writing a blog post about a hot topic for the primary purpose of driving short-term traffic and boosting incoming links.

For example, if you write a blog about business and see a hot topic about Britney Spears climbing the trending topics on Twitter, Google, or another site that tracks hot topics, you can write a post about Britney on your blog. Hopefully, you'll catch some of the traffic from people who are actively looking for online information about her.

It's best to try to write about hot topics (or link bait topics) you can associate with your blog topic in some way. In the Britney Spears example, the business blogger could tie a Britney-related post to the star's branded fragrances or personal brand strategy. This way, the post fits on the blog and also takes advantage of the potential link bait it could draw.

You can get ideas for link bait blog posts by checking the trending topics on the home page of Twitter (or in your Twitter sidebar if you're logged in to Twitter). As you can see in Figure 19-1, trending Twitter topics scroll across the Twitter home page under the search box.

Figure 19-1 *Trending topics are given on the Twitter home page.*

To learn what keyword phrases are hot at any given time, check out the Google Trends page at www.google.com/trends, as shown in Figure 19-2.

Popular online discussion topics can also be found by visiting social bookmarking sites like Yahoo! Buzz (click the **Top Buzz** link on buzz.yahoo.com) and Digg (click the **Top News** link on digg.com) to see what links are rising to the top in terms of sharing and discussion at any given moment.

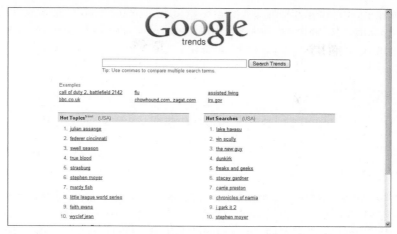

Figure 19-2   *View hot topics and search terms on Google Trends.*

Keyword Research

One of the most important aspects of search engine optimization is determining the keywords that are likely to drive the most traffic to your blog. Those keywords should be related to your blog's topic. In other words, what are the keywords people are likely to type into Google to find content like what you write about in your blog posts? Those are the keywords you need to focus on and feature in your blog content to yield the best search engine optimization results.

There's more to keyword research than simply picking the keywords you think fit your blog's content, though. For example, if you write a blog about parenting, you'd have a lot of competition from some huge and powerful sites if you focus your search engine optimization efforts on leveraging the keyword *parenting*. However, if you focus on more specific keyword phrases, you might attract less traffic, but that traffic will be more focused and more likely to be happy with the content they find on your blog. Instead of focusing on *parenting*, a blog that includes a lot of content about parenting twins could focus on that more specific keyword phrase: *parenting twins*.

INSIDER SECRET

Focusing on specific keyword phrases (three- or four-word keyword phrases are best) is called long-tail search engine optimization.

Many options are available to a parenting blogger other than *parenting twins*. The trick is finding the right keywords to maximize the focused search traffic to your blog. Keep reading to learn exactly how to do it.

What to Research

The first steps to keyword research involve determining what your blog is about, what you *want* your blog to be about, and what your desired target audience wants from your blog. Once you clearly define your objectives and your audience's needs, you can begin to research the best keyword phrases to focus on in your blog content.

You don't have to pick a single keyword phrase for your entire blog. Instead, choose a specific keyword phrase for each piece of content. Chances are, many pieces of content will use the same or a similar keyword phrase. After all, you want to drive traffic to your blog that's likely to be interested in your broader blog topic, so they stick around to read more posts, come back again, and tell their friends about it.

You need to research the popularity of keyword phrases related to your blog topic that people are currently typing into their search engines. The tools listed in the next section can help you find a variety of relevant keyword phrases.

The trick is to choose keyword phrases focused enough that bigger online publishers aren't likely to be competing for that traffic but broad enough that there's an actual audience searching for them. Look for the sweet spot, the keyword phrase that sits in the middle of the really popular and really unpopular keywords, and then start to claim that keyword as your own through targeted content.

Popular Research Tools

One of the first things you need to do is set up an analytics tool on your blog so you can track the keyword phrases people are using. (These tools are discussed in Chapter 22.) Once configured, you're ready to start writing keyword-targeted content and tracking the results of your efforts.

To determine which keywords you should focus on in your blog content, you can use two free tools offered by Google:

- Google AdWords Keyword Tool: https://adwords.google.com/select/KeywordToolExternal

- Google AdWords Traffic Estimator: https://adwords.google.com/select/TrafficEstimatorSandbox

The free Google AdWords Keyword Tool, shown in Figure 19-3, is a perfect place to start your keyword research.

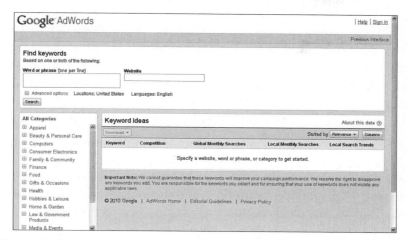

Figure 19-3   *Enter a keyword to get alternate suggestions and traffic details.*

Just type your keyword into the **Word or phrase** text box (you can enter more than one keyword phrase), and click the **Search** button to get a list of related keywords, traffic details, and cost-per-click advertising rate data, as shown in Figure 19-4.

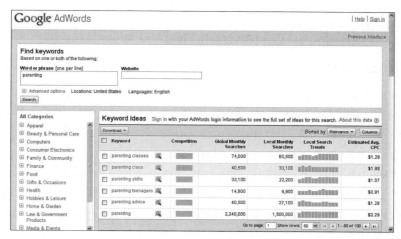

Figure 19-4   *Review the list of keyword ideas to find the right ones for your blog.*

Analyze the list of keyword ideas to find the ones best related to your blog and offer a good balance between traffic and competition. Click the **Columns** button and be sure the Keyword, Competition, Global Monthly Searches, Local Monthly Searches, Local Search Trends, and Estimated Avg. CPC columns are selected and visible. (It's likely you'll only have to add the Estimated Avg. CPC column to your display.) Click the **Global Monthly Searches** link at the top of the column to sort the results by the number of global searches conducted for that keyword each month. You can sort by clicking on the **Estimated Avg. CPC** link to view the results from a different perspective.

You want to find a keyword term that gets a decent amount of traffic but doesn't have a massive amount of competition. The Global Monthly Searches column gives you an idea about traffic, and the Estimated Avg. CPC column gives you an idea of how much advertisers are paying for that keyword. Higher average cost-per-click typically equates to more competition for traffic. Find the middle-ground sweet spot. That's the place to start your search engine optimization keyword efforts.

 INSIDER SECRET

In addition to the Google tools, check out Wordtracker (wordtracker.com) and Keyword Discovery (keyworddiscovery.com). Both of these paid keyword research tools offer free trials so you can test them out before forking over any money. Both tools offer a significant amount of information and useful features that enable you to analyze keywords in great detail. If you're serious about keyword research and search engine optimization, it might be worth it to pay for one of these tools.

The free Google AdWords Traffic Estimator, shown in Figure 19-5, allows you to enter a keyword and find out what advertisers are bidding on those keywords. Look for keywords related to your blog that fall in the middle of the pricing spread. These are the keywords that generate a decent amount of traffic but aren't excessively competitive.

Just type your keyword into the **Word or phrase** text box and click the **Estimate** button. You can type in multiple keyword phrases (one per line) to compare them. The results page, shown in Figure 19-6, delivers the traffic estimates for your chosen keywords.

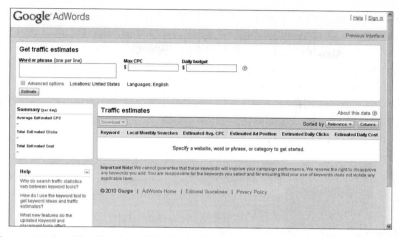

Figure 19-5 *The Google AdWords Traffic Estimator tells you the price advertisers are paying for keyword ads.*

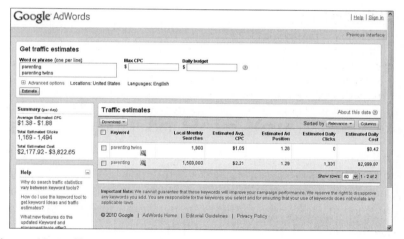

Figure 19-6 *You can view traffic estimates and advertiser bids to compare keywords.*

If you click the magnifying glass icon next to any of the keyword results shown in Figure 19-6, you can view search trends from Google Insights for Search for that keyword and related keywords, as shown in Figure 19-7.

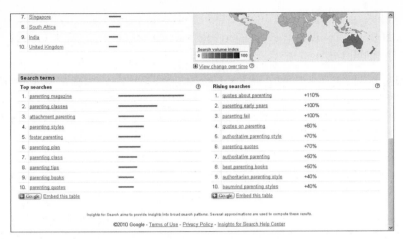

Figure 19-7 *Analyze search trends for keywords from Google Insights for Search.*

The related keyword search terms can be found by scrolling to the bottom of the Google Insights for Search page. Here you can get additional ideas for keywords you could target on your blog.

What *Not* to Do

So far in this chapter you've learned tricks and tools to help you boost your search engine optimization efforts. Now it's time to learn about all the things you *shouldn't* do unless you want your blog to get banned from search engine results.

Google and other search engines will flag your blog as spam or eliminate it from search results if you're caught using search engine optimization tactics that artificially inflate the popularity or contextual relevance of your blog. Once your blog is flagged as spam or banned from Google search results, it's nearly impossible to get back into Google's good graces.

Search engines like Google can send a lot of traffic to your blog, so if you want your blog to grow and be successful, avoid these tactics:

Keyword stuffing: Don't overuse your keywords. Including your keywords within your content is allowed, but if you overuse your keywords or publish lists filled with your keywords in your blog's sidebar or footer, Google could view that as keyword stuffing and flag your blog as spam.

Hiding keywords: Don't try to hide a list of your keywords in a very tiny font at the bottom of a page or in the same color as your blog's background. Google will find it and flag your blog as spam.

Paying for links or publishing paid links: Incoming links are an important factor in determining Google search rankings, so sites that pay for incoming links or publish links that have been paid for by another site are flagged as spam and removed from Google search results entirely.

Copyscraping: Don't republish content that's already been published on another website. Not only is that plagiarism, but Google considers it a spam tactic and will penalize your blog for it.

Publish links and ads with no real content: Google views pages filled with links and/or ads as spam. Be sure every page and post on your blog provides more original content than links and ads.

QUICK TIP

Search engine optimization professionals recommend you include no more than one link per 125 words of original text.

If you take the time to write great content, don't stress about keyword density. Allow keywords to flow into your content naturally and avoid dishonest or spam tactics, and your blog's search traffic will grow organically in time.

Heed this warning: companies that promise pie-in-the-sky results such as "We'll get your site to #1 on Google in two weeks!" are likely using spam tactics to get that fast and unnatural jump. Always remember that long-term sustainable growth is better than short-term spikes, but using honest tactics from both strategies can help you meet your blogging objectives without fearing retaliation from Google or other search engines.

The Least You Need to Know

- WordPress offers several built-in features that can help you with search engine optimization. Use them!
- Search engine optimization analysis is constantly evolving. What works today might not be recommended tomorrow.

- Link building and keyword research are two of the easiest ways bloggers can achieve search engine optimization success.

- Some search engine optimization tactics are considered spam techniques and could get your blog banned from search results entirely. Avoid those tactics at all costs!

Feeds and Subscriptions

In This Chapter

- The basics of feeds and subscriptions
- Getting started with a WordPress blog feed
- Adding a feed subscription option to your blog
- Promoting your feed and attracting subscribers

A web feed is a format for providing data from a frequently updated content source, like a blog, to users. Rather than manually visiting your blog every day to see if you've published new content, people who subscribe to your blog's feed can see your new content in their e-mail inboxes or their feed reader, depending on how they subscribe to receive content from your blog.

Feeds and subscriptions can be confusing, and this chapter teaches you the basics, in simple terms, so you can understand why people subscribe to feeds, how to set up your feed, and how to promote your feed and get more subscribers.

Understanding Feeds and Subscriptions

Feeds are typically created in RSS (Really Simple Syndication) or Atom format. Both are data formats that allow people to subscribe and receive updates when you publish new blog content, either in a feed reader like Google Reader or via e-mail. WordPress blogs most frequently use RSS feeds, which are easy to create using a tool like Google's FeedBurner, discussed later in this chapter.

In order to receive a feed and read the content within that feed, you need to subscribe to it. As you travel around the blogosphere, you're likely to notice the RSS feed icon, shown in the sidebar in Figure 20-1. This icon makes it easy for visitors to subscribe to a site's feed.

Figure 20-1 *The RSS icon makes it easy for people to subscribe to your blog.*

People subscribe to blogs primarily to save time. Rather than visiting every blog they like multiple times throughout the day, they can simply log in to their feed reader accounts and see the updates to all the blogs and websites they're subscribed to, all in one convenient place. If they subscribe by e-mail, they'll receive e-mail messages when new content is published at the time and frequency they choose when they subscribe.

QUICK TIP

Feed readers gather together all the feeds a user is subscribed to and presents them in one handy place, either on the computer or online. Most readers are available for free, but some do come with a price tag or offer premium features for a fee. Popular feed readers include Google Reader (www.google.com/reader) and FeedDemon (feeddemon.com).

Feed readers allow you to quickly and easily scroll through new updates, subscribe to new feeds, delete feeds, and more. The Google Reader account shown in Figure 20-2 shows how your feeds look in a feed reader.

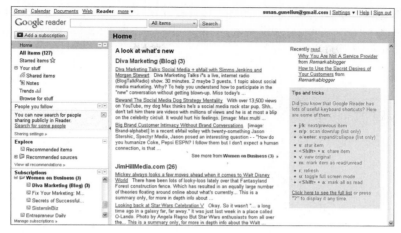

Figure 20-2 *Feeds are easy to manage in Google Reader.*

Setting Up Your WordPress Blog Feed

You can set up your WordPress blog's feed within a few minutes, and adding subscription links to your blog's sidebar takes just a few minutes more. Using a tool like Google's FeedBurner (feedburner.google.com), shown in Figure 20-3, you can create (or *burn*) your blog's feed for free.

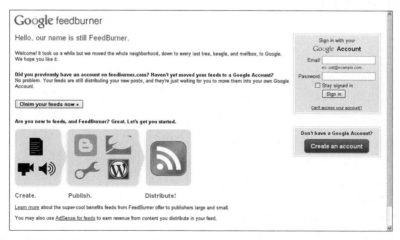

Figure 20-3 *Log in to your Google account or create a new account to burn a feed.*

If you have a Google account, sign in. If you don't have a Google account, click the **Create an account** button to open the Google Create an Account page, shown in Figure 20-4.

Required information for Google account

Your current email address:

e.g. myname@example.com. This will be used to sign-in to your account.

Choose a password:

Password strength:

Minimum of 8 characters in length.

Re-enter password:

☐ Stay signed in

Creating a Google Account will enable Web History. Web History is a feature that will provide you with a more personalized experience on Google that includes more relevant search results and recommendations. Learn More

☑ Enable Web History.

Get started with FeedBurner

Location: United States

Change

Birthday:

MM/DD/YYYY (e.g. "8/24/2010")

Word Verification: Type the characters you see in the picture below.

Letters are not case-sensitive

Figure 20-4 *Complete the form to create a Google account and get started with FeedBurner.*

Enter your information in the **Required information for Google account** and **Get started with FeedBurner** fields, read the Terms of Service, and click **I accept. Create my account.** to create your new Google account and open your new FeedBurner account page, as shown in Figure 20-5.

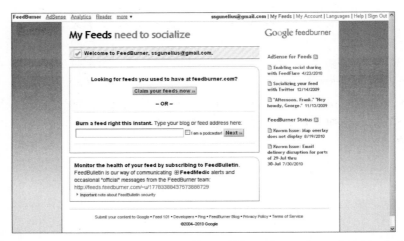

Figure 20-5 *Enter your WordPress blog's URL in the text box to burn its feed.*

To burn your WordPress blog's feed, enter your blog's URL (in www.myblogname. com format) in the **Burn a feed right this instant** field and click the **Next** button. A new Identify Feed Source page opens where you might be asked to select a feed source, as shown in Figure 20-6.

Figure 20-6   *Select your blog's main feed to burn a feed of your post content.*

Figure 20-6 shows that WordPress blogs typically have two feeds you can burn, one for your blog post content and one for comment content.

 INSIDER SECRET

You can offer post and comment subscriptions on your blog if you want, but post subscriptions are much more popular than comment subscriptions.

To burn the feed for your post content, select the radio button next to **>> Feed** and click the **Next** button to give your feed a title, as shown in Figure 20-7.

Type in the title you want to use for your feed in the field provided, and click **Next** to burn your feed. A new page opens, as shown in Figure 20-8, where you can see your blog feed URL.

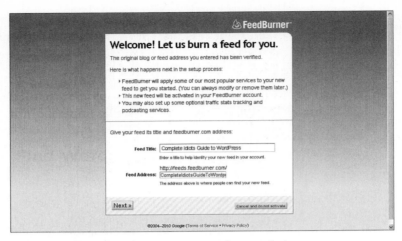

Figure 20-7 *Type the title you want to use for your feed.*

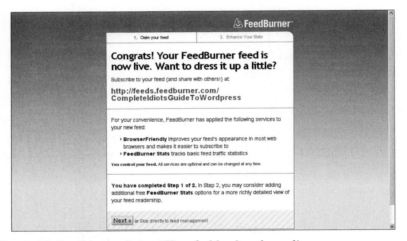

Figure 20-8 *Congratulations! Your feed has been burned!*

Click **Next** to configure additional FeedBurner stats, as shown in Figure 20-9.

If you want to set up your FeedBurner account to track some of the additional statistics related to your feed shown in Figure 20-9, check the boxes next to those options now. If not, you can always add the options later. Click **Next** to finish configuring your feed and open the page shown in Figure 20-10, where you can start the process to integrate your feed into your blog.

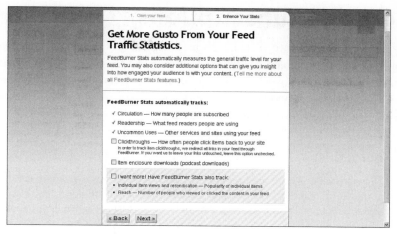

Figure 20-9 *Check the boxes for additional stats you want to track.*

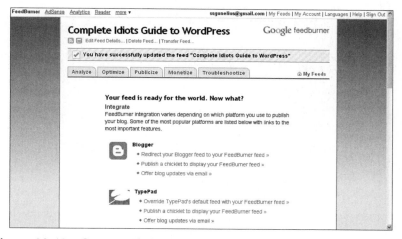

Figure 20-10 *Once your feed is configured, you can publicize it on your blog.*

You can take time now or in the future to review the various options available through the tabs across the top of the FeedBurner feed page. For example, you can review analytics, configure additional settings, add Google AdSense ads to your feed to make money, and more.

There's a lot more you can do with your feeds—too much to cover in these pages—to truly leverage them as marketing and monetization tools. Don't be afraid to try out the various features available to you through your FeedBurner account.

Inviting Feed Subscriptions

The easiest way to integrate your blog's feed into your WordPress blog is to add subscription links into your blog's sidebar. All you need to do is get the correct HTML code, copy it, and paste it into a text widget in your blog's sidebar. That's all available at your fingertips through your FeedBurner account and WordPress dashboard and takes just a few minutes to set up.

> **QUICK TIP**
>
> There are various ways to integrate your blog's feed into your WordPress blog. Some WordPress themes even offer features that simplify the process. Learn some tricks to make your subscription links look visually appealing in Appendix B.

First, click the **Publicize** tab at the top of your FeedBurner account page, shown in Figure 20-10. (If you've burned multiple feeds through this account, be sure you selected the correct feed when you first logged in to FeedBurner.) This opens the Publicize Your Feed page, shown in Figure 20-11.

Figure 20-11 *You can create links, forms, and buttons to enable visitors to subscribe to your blog with just a few easy clicks.*

To create a link inviting people to subscribe to your blog's feed in their preferred feed readers, click the **Chicklet Chooser** link in the left menu. This opens the Chicklet Chooser page, shown in Figure 20-12.

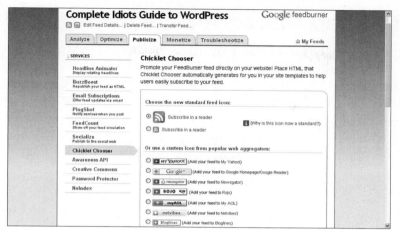

Figure 20-12 *Choose the link and RSS icon you want to display on your blog.*

In the **Choose the new standard feed icon** section of the Chicklet Chooser page, select the radio button next to the RSS icon size (large or small) you prefer.

INSIDER SECRET

Choosing one of the first two options showing the standard RSS feed icon enables visitors to choose their preferred feed readers from a list. The custom icons from popular web aggregators listed below the standard feed icon options in Figure 20-12 allow visitors to subscribe only via the feed readers whose icons are shown. The standard icons are recommended to give readers maximum flexibility in viewing your content.

Once you select your feed icon, scroll down to the bottom of the page and use your mouse to highlight and copy everything in the **Copy the HTML below for use in your own page templates** text box, as shown in Figure 20-13.

With the HTML code copied, log in to your WordPress dashboard and click the **Widgets** link in the Appearance section of your dashboard's left menu. This opens the Widgets page, shown in Figure 20-14.

Figure 20-13 *Copy the HTML code for your feed icon so you can paste it into your WordPress sidebar.*

Figure 20-14 *You first need to add a widget to your blog's sidebar before you can paste your feed icon code into it.*

Find the **Text** widget in the Available Widgets list in the middle of the page. Click and drag the **Text** widget into the **Primary Widget Area** on the right side of the page (these are the widget areas available to you on your blog), as shown in Figure 20-15.

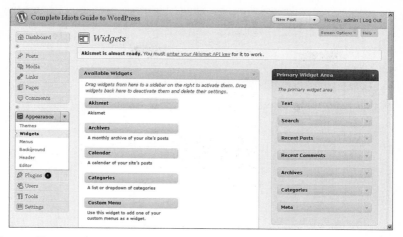

Figure 20-15 *Add a text widget to your blog's sidebar, where you can paste your feed icon's HTML code.*

 QUICK TIP

If you can only see the titles of the widget areas on the right side of your blog, you can reveal the contents of each widget by clicking the drop-down arrows in the top-right corners of each.

Click the drop-down arrow in the upper-right corner of the new text widget you just added to the widget area to expand it, as shown in Figure 20-16. You can type a title for the widget into the **Title** field and then paste the HTML code you copied from FeedBurner into the larger field.

Click the **Save** button in the text widget, and you're finished! You can visit your blog to see the new text widget with your feed subscription icon and link added to it, as shown in Figure 20-17.

 PROCEED WITH CAUTION

If your new text widget and subscription link don't appear on your live blog, refresh your browser page to be sure you're viewing the most recent version of the page. Also, be sure you clicked the **Save** button in the text widget, or your changes won't go live on your blog.

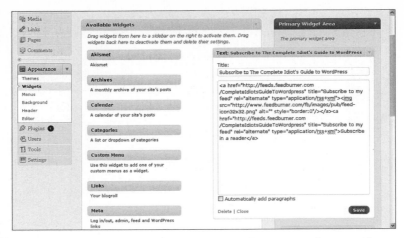

Figure 20-16 *Paste the HTML code from FeedBurner into the text widget on your blog.*

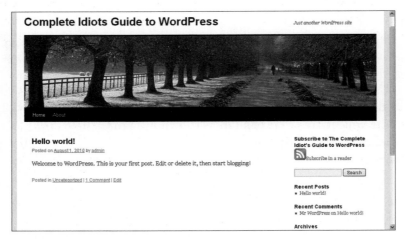

Figure 20-17 *Visitors can click* **Subscribe in a reader** *to subscribe to your blog's feed.*

Inviting E-Mail Subscriptions

Adding an e-mail subscription option to your blog's sidebar is also very easy. Navigate to the Publicize tab within your FeedBurner account, and click the **Email Subscriptions** link to open the Email Subscriptions page, shown in Figure 20-18.

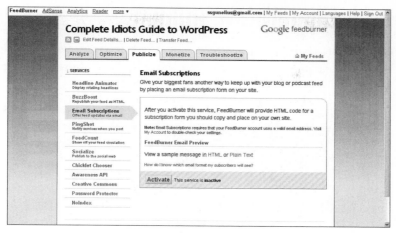

Figure 20-18 *Activate e-mail subscriptions for your blog's feed on the Email Subscriptions page.*

Click the **Activate** button to enable the e-mail subscription service for your feed. This opens a page where you can access the HTML code to paste into your blog's sidebar and also add an e-mail subscription form, as shown in Figure 20-19.

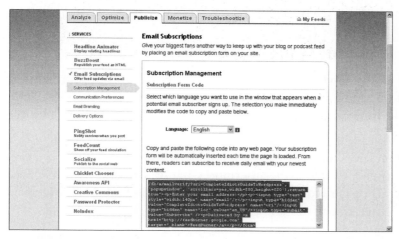

Figure 20-19 *Copy the HTML code for your feed's e-mail subscription form.*

Using your mouse, highlight everything in the text box on the Subscription Management page and copy that code. Return to your WordPress dashboard Widgets page, where you can paste that code into a text widget. Typically, e-mail subscriptions are included directly beneath feed reader subscription links, as shown in Figure 20-20.

Figure 20-20 *An e-mail subscription form works well directly beneath the feed reader subscription link.*

Keeping It Simple

Instead of including the entire e-mail subscription form in your blog's sidebar, you can just offer a link that invites visitors to subscribe by e-mail. When they click on that link, a new page opens where they can complete and submit the e-mail subscription form.

If you'd prefer to include a subscription link rather than a form, you can get the HTML code for the e-mail subscription link by scrolling down the Subscription Management page shown in Figure 20-19 until you find the **Subscription Link Code** section, shown in Figure 20-21.

Using your mouse, highlight everything in the text box in the **Subscription Link Code** section and copy that code. Next, return to the Widgets section of your WordPress dashboard, and paste the code into a text widget. In Figure 20-22, you can see that code pasted directly beneath the RSS icon subscription link code already in use.

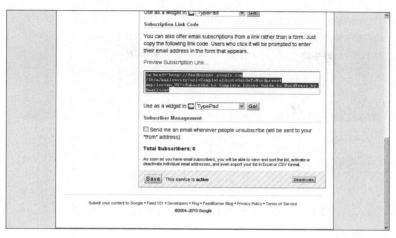

Figure 20-21 *Copy the Subscription Link Code HTML to paste into your blog's sidebar.*

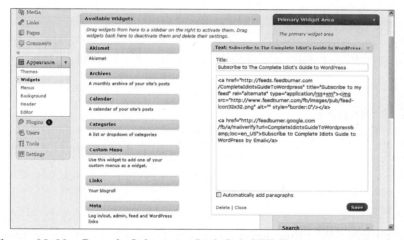

Figure 20-22 *Paste the Subscription Link Code HTML into a text widget in your blog's sidebar.*

Click the **Save** button in the Text widget, and view your changes on your live blog, as shown in Figure 20-23. Notice both the RSS icon subscription link and the new e-mail subscription link are both included in the Subscribe to the Complete Idiot's Guide to WordPress widget on the live blog.

Figure 20-23 *Feed icon and e-mail subscription links take up little space in your blog's sidebar.*

That's all there is to it! Your blog is now ready for subscribers via feed reader and e-mail.

Customizing Your Blog's E-Mail Subscriptions

One more thing we need to cover before moving on, and that's configuring the e-mail messages people receive when they subscribe to your blog via e-mail.

First, visit the Email Subscriptions section of your FeedBurner account and click the **Communication Preferences** link in the left menu. This opens the Communications Preferences page shown in Figure 20-24.

In the **Email "From" Address** field, be sure the e-mail address shown is the one you want subscribers to see your feed e-mails come from.

The **Confirmation Email Subject** field includes the text that will appear in the e-mail subject line people receive after they subscribe to your blog. This e-mail is sent primarily to confirm that the e-mail address entered in the subscription form is the correct one for sending feed update e-mails. You can change this text to say anything you want.

PROCEED WITH CAUTION

The primary purpose of the e-mail is to confirm the subscriber's e-mail address. Be sure your e-mail subject and body don't detract from that purpose.

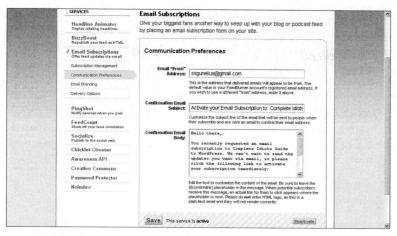

Figure 20-24 *Set up your e-mail subscription communications preferences right away.*

Finally, the **Confirmation Email Body** field is where you can enter the text you want to send within the confirmation e-mail. You can change this to say anything you want.

When you're finished editing these fields, click the **Save** button.

Next, click the **Email Branding** link in the Email Subscriptions section of your FeedBurner account left menu to open the Email Branding page, shown in Figure 20-25.

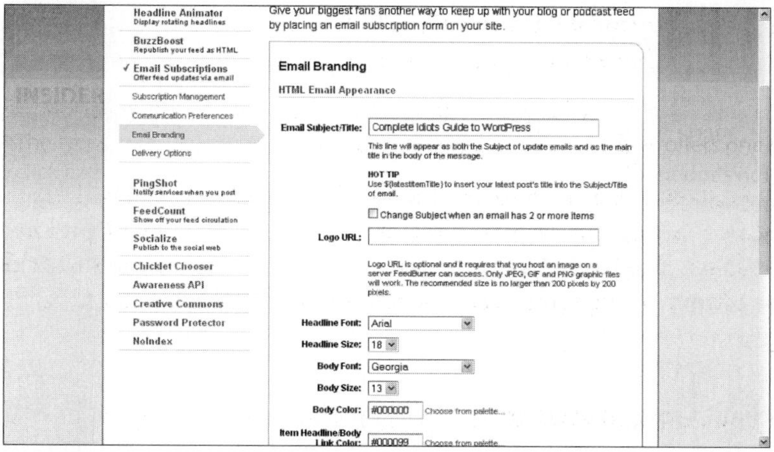

Figure 20-25 *You can edit the appearance of the e-mails subscribers receive from your feed.*

You can change the **Email Subject/Title** of the feed update e-mails subscribers receive, and you can even add a logo (which must have already been uploaded online, for example, through your WordPress account) to your feed e-mails. Just enter the URL where the logo was uploaded into the **Logo URL** field.

Also, take some time to review the fonts, font sizes, and font colors used in your subscription e-mails. You can change each of these elements to make your e-mails easier to read or match your blog's color palette for consistent branding. Just scroll down to the bottom of the page to see how your changes will look in your feed e-mails. Be sure to click the **Save** button when you're finished.

QUICK TIP

Subscribe to your blog via e-mail and take a look at the e-mails you receive to ensure they look just the way you want them to when subscribers receive them.

The last Email Subscriptions settings you need to configure can be found by selecting the **Delivery Options** link in the Email Subscriptions section of your FeedBurner account. This opens the Delivery Options page in Figure 20-26.

Figure 20-26 *Configure when your feed update e-mails are sent each day.*

The first thing you should do is choose your time zone using the drop-down menu in the **Select Timezone** section. Then use the drop-down menu in **Schedule Email Delivery** to select the time of day you want your subscription e-mails to go out. If there are updates to your blog, FeedBurner will send an e-mail with those content updates to e-mail subscribers during the time frame you select in this section.

As always, click the **Save** button to put your changes into effect, and you're done!

Tips to Boost Subscribers

Aside from the most obvious tip to boost subscribers to your blog—write great content that people want to read—there are other tricks you can use to remind and encourage people to subscribe. Following are a few easy and effective suggestions.

Make It Easy to Subscribe

Be sure to include links to subscribe to your blog via feed reader or e-mail in an easy-to-see space on your blog, such as at the top of your sidebar. You can use the subscription links and forms discussed earlier in this chapter or use creative icons and graphics, as discussed in Appendix B.

Ask People to Subscribe

Include a closing at the end of your blog posts that invites subscribers such as, "If you liked this blog post, why not subscribe to my blog via feed reader or e-mail?"

Be sure to link both "feed reader" and "e-mail" to the same URLs people land on if they click both sign-up links in your blog's sidebar.

Get Some Help from a Plug-In

A WordPress plug-in called What Would Seth Godin Do (WWSGD) can help you get more subscribers to your blog. Seth Godin is a marketing professional who advocates using browser *cookies* to identify new versus returning visitors to a website for marketing purposes. The WWSGD plug-in uses that same idea to identify new versus returning visitors to your blog.

Once installed, you can write a custom message for new visitors and a separate custom message for returning visitors, which you can position at the beginning or end of your blog posts. You can even configure how many times a new visitor will see the "new visitor" message before he or she will receive the "returning" visitor message.

DEFINITION

A **cookie** is a piece of text data stored on the computer of an Internet user's web browser. Websites store cookies on people's computers to keep track of their browsing activities on that site. For example, cookies might be used to store username and password data so you don't have to retype that information into a login page every time you visit it. You can delete cookies through the web browser at any time. Web browsers also offer an option to turn off cookies entirely, so they're never stored.

For example, you could configure a message for new visitors that says, "If you're new here, you may want to subscribe to the RSS feed. Thanks for visiting." The words "RSS feed" should link to your subscription page.

For more information, log on to wordpress.org/extend/plugins/what-would-seth-godin-do.

Offer a Freebie to New Subscribers

You can offer a special report, an e-book, or another useful resource or tool you create to all new subscribers, or you can offer a special gift that's simply a desirable giveaway. You could even tie the special gift to a contest on your blog where all new subscribers are entered into a random drawing to receive a great prize!

The choice is yours, but experiment a little to see what tactics your readers respond to when it comes to boosting subscribers. Don't be shocked to see the number of subscribers to your blog fluctuate significantly. The key to success is to remember that long-term sustainable growth is most effective, so try not to sweat the numbers. Your subscribers will grow in time.

The Least You Need to Know

- You can set up your blog's feed and publicize it on your blog within minutes.
- FeedBurner is the most popular tool for burning feeds and analyzing feed statistics.
- Visitors to your blog can subscribe to your blog's feed via feed reader or e-mail.
- Don't sweat the numbers. Feed subscriptions are likely to rise and fall sporadically. Growth over time should be your primary goal.

Networking and Community Building

In This Chapter

- Using social networking to boost blog traffic
- Sharing content via social bookmarking
- Tweeting for blogging success
- Linking to your social media profiles on your blog

One of the best ways to ensure your blog's long-term growth and success is to work to build relationships not only with your blog readers, but with a wider audience across the social web as well. A variety of methods are available to help you communicate with people around the world, thanks to the free tools of social media.

This chapter teaches you what social networking, social bookmarking, and microblogging are all about, and how you can use tools like Facebook, LinkedIn, and Twitter to increase your blog's readership—and achieve your overall blogging goals!

Social Networking

The term *networking* typically refers to in-person communications and relationship-building efforts, but thanks to the tools of the social web, networking can happen online and from the privacy of your own home. Facebook and LinkedIn are two of the most popular social networking websites where you can create a free profile, connect with other people, join conversations and niche groups, and even share your blog content through automated feeds.

INSIDER SECRET

In addition to Facebook (www.facebook.com) and LinkedIn (www.linkedin. com), some other popular social networking sites are MySpace (www.myspace. com), Bebo (www.bebo.com), Foursquare (www.foursquare.com; a location-based mobile social network), and Ning (www.ning.com; a fee-based site where you can create your own social network).

When you create a personal profile on Facebook and LinkedIn, you can search for people you know and send them friend or connection requests. You can publish short updates on your personal profile, which your connections can comment on, and you can comment on your connections' updates as well. You can also upload photos, videos, and more. Social networking tools are very easy to use, but they give you an incredible reach across the world to a huge potential audience. For example, more than 500 million people around the world use Facebook.

Social networking sites also enable you to create and join smaller, targeted groups where you can connect with people and start or join conversations related to specific topics. You can even create a group for your blog! Alternately, you can create a fan page on Facebook for your blog where anyone can click the **Like** button to add the page to their own list of Likes.

Promoting Your Blog with Social Networking

There are so many opportunities available to you via social networking to meet people and spread the word about your blog! But simply creating a profile on popular social networking tools like Facebook and LinkedIn isn't enough, especially if you want to use social networking to increase awareness of your blog and traffic to it. Following are a number of tips you can use to take full advantage of the promotion potential social networking offers:

Create a relevant profile: If your primary purpose in joining Facebook or another social network is to promote your blog, you need to be sure the profile you create on that site is relevant to your blog's topic. Lead with your strengths, and clearly demonstrate through your profile why you're qualified to write about and discuss your blog's topic.

Find people to connect with: Take some time to conduct searches of users on the social network you join. Some social networks allow you to search by keywords to find people discussing topics related to your blog or area of expertise. As you find people who are likely to be interested in your blog and your content, send them connection requests so you can begin conversing with them through your social network profiles, private messages, and more.

Be active, and publish relevant and useful content: One of the most important aspects of social networking success is being an active participant. That means you should start conversations and join conversations by providing more content that adds value to the online discussion. Simply creating a profile and never updating it won't help you build awareness of your blog and drive traffic to it at all.

Just be sure far more of the content you publish is *not* self-promotional compared to how much *is*. Follow the classic 80–20 rule of marketing. When applied to social media marketing (including social network participation), no more than 20 percent of your overall activities and content should be self-promotional. Feel free to publish links to your blog content, but be aware of the 80–20 rule.

Create and join groups: Search for existing groups related to your blog's topic, and join active, relevant groups. Participate in the conversations happening in those groups. If you can't find an existing group related to your blog's niche, create your own! You can even create a group named after your blog.

Leverage site-specific features: Each social networking site offers the ability to create a profile and make connections, but some offer extra features that can be very helpful in building an audience for your blog. For example, you can create a Facebook page for your blog. You can answer questions on LinkedIn or give and request recommendations. Some sites even allow you to link your other social media profiles to your social networking profile so people can connect with you across the social web.

QUICK TIP

Learn about Facebook features in the online Facebook Help Center at www. facebook.com/help/?page=414. Also, check out LinkedIn features in the online LinkedIn Learning Center at learn.linkedin.com.

Take advantage of automated processes: Many social networking sites allow you to automatically feed your blog content or other social media profiles' content streams into your social networking updates. Some even allow you to feed the updates you publish on your social networking profiles to your blog or other social media profiles. Feeding content from one site to another is a great way to appear more active and create new opportunities for people to interact with you or share your valuable content with their own audiences. I cover some of these processes later in this chapter.

Feeding Your Blog to Your Facebook Profile

The easiest way to feed your blog content to your Facebook profile updates is to import your blog's RSS feed to your Facebook wall. That's where your updates are published within your Facebook profile.

To do so, log in to your Facebook account. Type "Notes" into the search box at the top of your screen, and click the **Edit import settings** link on the left side of the page, as shown in Figure 21-1.

Figure 21-1   *Click the **Edit import settings** link to configure your blog's feed to publish on your Facebook profile wall.*

Next, type your blog's URL into the text **Web URL** box and check the box to agree to the terms and conditions, as shown in Figure 21-2.

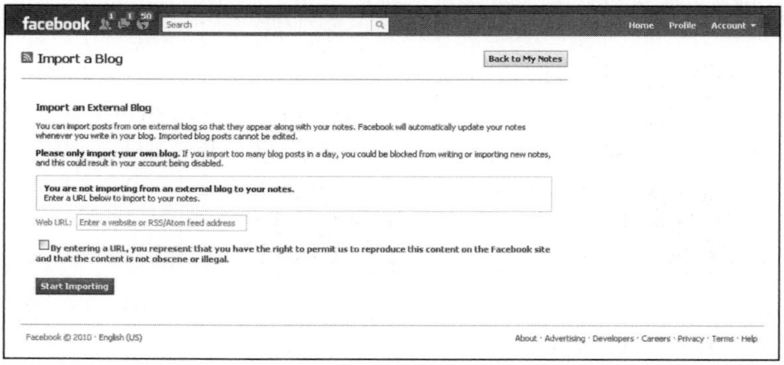

Figure 21-2   *Type in your blog's URL.*

Finally, click the **Start Importing** button. Your previous blog posts will appear as notes in your profile and as updates on your wall, and new posts will automatically display as you publish them.

> **INSIDER SECRET**
>
> Another option to automatically publish blog updates to your Facebook profile and page is to use the RSS Graffiti Facebook app (www.facebook.com/RSS. Graffiti). This makes it easy to manage multiple blog feeds on multiple profiles and pages. The Networked Blogs app (www.facebook.com/networkedblogs) is another alternative.

You can import your blog feed into Facebook pages and Groups, too. For example, log in to Facebook and visit your blog's page (assuming you already created one). Click the **Edit Page** link beneath the page profile picture, and find the Notes application in the list. Click **Edit** and then click **Import a blog** from the Notes Settings box on the right side of your screen. Follow the remaining instructions to enter your blog's URL and finish configuring your settings. That's all there is to it!

Feeding Your Blog to Your LinkedIn Profile

If you're using WordPress.com as your blogging application, you can easily import your blog feed to your LinkedIn profile using the handy WordPress app for LinkedIn. Just log in to your LinkedIn account and click the **More** link in the top navigation bar to reveal the drop-down menu. Then click the **Applications Directory** link to open the Applications Directory, shown in Figure 21-3.

Figure 21-3 *Open the LinkedIn Applications Directory, and find the WordPress app.*

Click the **WordPress** app to open the WordPress app page, shown in Figure 21-4. Click the **Add application** button to add it to your LinkedIn account. Once installed, you can click the radio button to publish all your blog posts on your LinkedIn profile or just posts you tag with a "LinkedIn" tag when you write them. Click the **Save** button, and you're done! Your blog posts will now be published as updates to your LinkedIn profile.

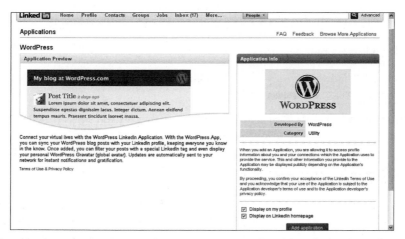

Figure 21-4 *With a single click, you can add the WordPress app to your LinkedIn account.*

If you use WordPress.org as your blogging application, you can import your blog's feed using the Blog Link application for LinkedIn. Just visit the LinkedIn Applications Directory, shown in Figure 21-3, and click the **Blog Link** application to open the Blog Link app page, shown in Figure 21-5.

Once added to your LinkedIn account, the Blog Link app indexes the sites you list in the "Websites" section of your LinkedIn profile and searches for RSS feeds for those sites. When an RSS feed is found (such as the feed for your blog), it's automatically included in the Blog Link section of your LinkedIn profile. So new blog posts you publish will automatically display on your LinkedIn profile as well.

Figure 21-5　*Add the Blog Link application to your LinkedIn profile.*

Social Bookmarking

Social bookmarking is the process of saving web pages you like using an online book-marking tool like Digg (www.digg.com) or StumbleUpon (www.stumbleupon.com). Instead of saving pages you like in your web browser Bookmarks or Favorites menu, where you can only access them from the computer where you saved them, you can bookmark pages using a social bookmarking tool and access them from any computer with an Internet connection.

You can make your bookmarked pages private or public (for all users to view), but where social bookmarking truly gets social is through the sharing of other people's content with wider audiences and even commenting on bookmarked content. This is where conversations happen. Pages bookmarked on popular social bookmarking sites have the potential to be seen by very large audiences, which could bring large bursts of traffic to your blog.

Increasing Blog Traffic with Social Bookmarking

The first step to drawing traffic from social bookmarking sites using an online book-marking tool like Digg (www.digg.com) or StumbleUpon to your blog is to publish amazing content people want to read and share. If your content isn't good, no one will want to bookmark it or share it with their own audiences.

Here are several more tips to help you get more traffic to your blog from social bookmarking:

Share more content from other people than your own: Don't use social bookmarking strictly as a self-promotional tool. A big part of leveraging social bookmarking to grow your blog is building relationships with other users who, in time, will help you spread your content even further.

Therefore, it's essential that you spend more time bookmarking and sharing content from sites other than your own. If the content you share is interesting, often related to your blog's topic, and not just self-promotional, other users will get to know you and come to expect valuable bookmarks from you. That's the first step to growing your blog through social bookmarking: consistently sharing great content that adds value to the online conversation.

Share content from a variety of sources: Just as you don't want to only share information from your own blog, you also shouldn't only share content from any other single website. Instead, vary your bookmarks, sources, and shared content so it doesn't appear that you're trying to boost traffic to a single site (even if that's not your intention).

Write great titles and descriptions: If you want people to perceive your bookmarks as click worthy, you need to write interesting, useful titles and descriptions when you submit them. It's not necessary to use the same title from the original piece of content you're sharing. Instead, create titles and descriptions that pique people's interests and encourage them to click through and read the content you've shared.

Use relevant tags: It's easy to skip adding keyword tags to your link submissions to save a few seconds, but tags are extremely useful in helping get your content found and shared by other users. Tags are used to categorize content and make it available to users who are searching for content related to specific topics. Take a few seconds to add keyword tags that accurately match your content and are likely to be used by people searching for content like the links you share.

Make friends and comment on other users' submissions: Don't just submit new links to social bookmarking sites. Take the time to resubmit (also called voting up) other users' submissions, too. Send connection requests to other users who consistently share content you enjoy, and leave comments on other users' submissions to start conversations. By taking time to build a band of supporters on social bookmarking sites, you'll have an engaged audience who looks for your bookmarks and actively shares those bookmarks with others.

Don't try to get around the bookmarking system: Social bookmarking sites have a few written and unwritten guidelines you should follow if you want your accounts to stay in good standing. Take the time to read the rules on individual social bookmarking sites, and avoid activities that might be flagged as spam. For example, don't create multiple user accounts so you can resubmit your content more than one time on the same social bookmarking site.

Ask people to share your content: Be sure you ask people to share your best content and make it easy for them to do so. Include links visitors to your blog can simply click on to share one of your posts with their preferred social bookmarking sites in seconds. Chapter 18 includes information about a popular WordPress plug-in that allows WordPress.org users to add social sharing links to every post on their blogs.

Final Thoughts on Social Bookmarking Sites

Many social bookmarking sites allow users to share content from across the World Wide Web. Some niche social bookmarking sites enable users to share content related to specific topics or areas of interest. Take the time to test multiple social bookmarking sites to determine which ones seem to drive the most traffic to your blog from your submissions, which generate the most conversations, and so on.

 INSIDER SECRET

> Some of the most popular social bookmarking sites include StumbleUpon (www.stumbleupon.com), Digg (www.digg.com), Reddit (www.reddit.com), Yahoo! Buzz (buzz.yahoo.com), and Delicious (www.delicious.com).

The key is to remember that social bookmarking can drive a large and sudden burst of traffic to your blog, but it's far more likely that a big increase in traffic won't happen. Social bookmarking should be viewed as a long-term blog marketing strategy.

Twitter and Microblogging

Microblogging is the process of publishing short updates (usually of 140 characters or less) on a personal profile using a microblogging tool. Accounts can typically be public or private, and you can publish updates to your profile or send private messages to other users.

The microblogging craze has grown to become a global activity, with Twitter leading the way as the most popular microblogging tool.

INSIDER SECRET

Popular microblogging tools include Twitter (www.twitter.com), Jaiku (www.jaiku.com), Plurk (www.plurk.com), and Tumblr (www.tumblr.com; a little blogging application and a little microblogging tool).

All A'Twitter

Twitter is a free microblogging tool anyone can join. It takes just a few seconds to create a Twitter profile and begin publishing updates (called *tweets*) of 140 characters or less. When you create a Twitter account, you can make your account public (so anyone with Internet access can view your updates) or private (so only people you approve can see your tweets).

Microblogging through Twitter is more open than publishing updates on social networking sites like Facebook or LinkedIn because other users don't have to accept you before you can follow their update stream on Twitter. As long as a person's Twitter profile is public, you can just click the **Follow** button on that person's profile, as shown in Figure 21-6, and his or her tweets will start to appear in the stream of updates from people you follow on your Twitter profile home page (when you're logged in to your Twitter account).

Figure 21-6 *Just click the **Follow** button to follow another Twitter user's tweet stream.*

Promoting Your Blog with Twitter

Twitter is an amazing tool for connecting with other people, starting conversations, joining conversations, sharing content, and building relationships. The more great content you share in your own Twitter update stream, the greater the chances your followers will share that content with their own audiences.

That means more people will find your content, and some of those people might even start to follow your Twitter stream. In time, your online persona will grow and traffic to your blog will increase both indirectly *and* directly from your Twitter activities.

Following are a number of tricks you can use to directly promote your blog on Twitter. Just remember, only 20 percent or less of your Twitter activities should be self-promotional, and the other 80 percent should *not* be self-promotional.

* Make your Twitter profile public.

* Share links to your best content.

* Share great content other Twitter users have published.

* Follow people who tweet about your blog's topic.

* Communicate with other Twitter users who are actively engaged with your blog's topic through direct messages, @*replies*, *retweets*, and *hashtags*.

* Respond to direct messages and acknowledge people who follow you, publish @replies and mentions directed at you, and retweet your updates.

* Track the traffic to the links you share with a URL shortener such as bit.ly (www.bitly.com).

* Make use of the many Twitter apps available to help you track conversations (such as Monitter), organize your Twitter activities (TweetDeck), and more.

* Automatically feed your blog updates to your Twitter stream, as discussed later in this chapter.

DEFINITION

Typing @ followed by a Twitter user's username (for example, @susangunelius) at the beginning of the tweet indicates the tweet is a direct reply to that user and is referred to as an **@reply** (pronounced *at-reply*). You can **retweet** updates published by other Twitter users within your own Twitter update stream by typing **RT** at the beginning of the retweeted update or clicking the **retweet** button. **Hashtags** include the # symbol followed by a keyword such as #world-cup and help users find tweets related to topics of interest.

You can automatically feed your blog posts to your Twitter update stream using a variety of methods. One of the easiest ways is by using the free Twitterfeed app (www.twitterfeed.com). Just visit the Twitterfeed home page and create a new account by clicking the **sign up** link in the top-right corner of the home page, as shown in Figure 21-7.

Figure 21-7   *Click the **sign up** link to create a free Twitterfeed account.*

Simply enter your e-mail address and a password in the sign-up form to create your account. When your account is created and you're logged in to Twitterfeed, click the **Create New Feed** button to open the New Feed configuration page, shown in Figure 21-8.

Name your feed, copy and paste the URL for your blog's feed (discussed in Chapter 20), and click the **Advanced Settings** link to expand the page. Enter any additional information related to update frequency, formatting, and more. Next, click the **Continue to Step 2** button at the bottom of the page. This takes you to another page where you can select Twitter and your specific Twitter account as the destination for your Twitterfeed and complete the configuration process. Your new blog posts should begin publishing on your Twitter update stream shortly. Note, however, that sometimes there is a delay before a new Twitterfeed starts to work.

A variety of other tools and even some WordPress plug-ins can help you automatically update your Twitterfeed when you publish a new blog post. If you're not happy with Twitterfeed, don't be afraid to test other options.

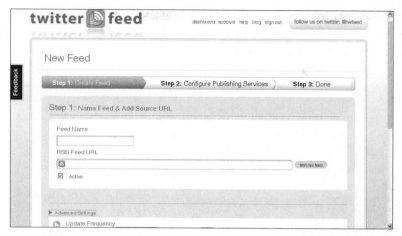

Figure 21-8 *Complete the form to configure your blog's feed to publish to your Twitter stream.*

Promoting Your Social Media Profiles on Your Blog

To fully integrate your online marketing strategy, you should not only promote your blog content on your social networking and social bookmarking profiles, but also promote those profiles on your blog. In other words, surround consumers with your branded online destinations so they can easily reach any and all of your content and conversations.

A number of widgets are available through some of the most popular social media tools. These are easy to insert into your WordPress blog's sidebar to promote the content you publish there and invite people to connect with you on those profiles.

INSIDER SECRET

To look through and add some of the most popular badges and widgets to your blog, check out Twitter Goodies (twitter.com/goodies; offers Twitter buttons and widgets), Facebook Badges (www.facebook.com/badges), and Facebook Social Plugins (developers.facebook.com/plugins).

You can also promote your social media profiles in your blog's sidebar by publishing social media icons that link to your profile on various sites. Take a look at Figure 21-9 for an example of how social media icons can look in a blog's sidebar.

Figure 21-9 *Insert social media icons into your blog's sidebar to boost connections to those sites.*

Find free social media icons you can use on your blog (meaning the copyright licenses allow you to use them for free) by searching for "free social media icons" using your preferred search engine. The "Social Media Icons" section in Appendix C gives you some other sites that offer a wide variety of links to excellent social media icon resources.

To insert social media icons into your blog's sidebar, you need to save the icon image files you want to use to your hard drive. Then upload those files to your WordPress Media Library, just as you would with any other image you upload to WordPress, as described in Chapter 10.

QUICK TIP

Some WordPress themes include features that make it easy to add your social media profile URLs for promotion on your blog.

When you upload the icon files, you need to copy the URL where the image file is saved because later you'll need to paste it into a text widget in your blog's sidebar.

Copy the URL for each icon file you upload, and save it to your Notepad or elsewhere so it's easy to copy from later. The URL is located in the upload window, as shown in Figure 21-10.

Figure 21-10   *Copy the URL for the image file you upload.*

Next, click the **Widgets** link in the Appearance section of your WordPress dashboard left menu to open the Widgets page, shown in Figure 21-11.

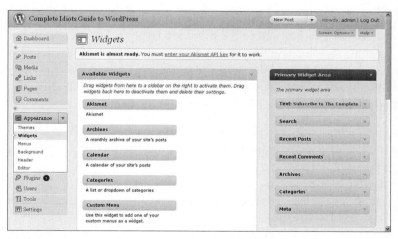

Figure 21-11   *Open the Widgets page in your WordPress dashboard.*

Click and drag a new text widget to the sidebar box where you want your social media icons to appear. In this example, they'll be added to the top of the first sidebar, as shown in Figure 21-12.

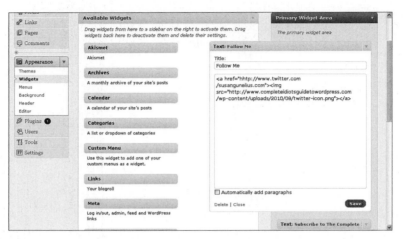

Figure 21-12 *Add a new text widget to your blog's sidebar.*

Click on the right arrow in the new text widget title bar to expand it. Enter a title for the new text widget to invite people to connect with you. "Connect with Me" or "Follow Me" might work.

Next, enter the HTML code to display the social media icon you uploaded to your WordPress Media Library and make that icon hyperlink to the correct social media profile page. To do this, you'll need the URL for the uploaded image you copied from the image upload window earlier. You also need the URL for your specific social media profile. For example, the uploaded Twitter icon in this example will link to my Twitter profile at www.twitter.com/susangunelius.

Type the following code into the new text widget where the first URL should be replaced with your social media profile URL and the second URL should be replaced with your image URL:

```
<a href="http://www.twitter.com/susangunelius"><img src="http://www.
    completeidiotsguidetowordpress.com/twitter-icon.png"></a>
```

Click the **Save** button in the new text widget to save your changes and then visit your live blog to see your new social media icon added, as shown in Figure 21-13.

Figure 21-13 *View your new social media icon in your live blog.*

Click the icon to confirm that it correctly leads to your specific profile.

You can add additional icons using the same HTML code but replacing the image URL with the URL for a different social media icon (remember, you have to upload the image from your hard drive first to be able to copy the URL) and replacing the social media profile URL with the one that matches the different icon. It's that easy!

QUICK TIP

To learn more about social media tools and using social media for marketing purposes, pick up a copy of my book *30-Minute Social Media Marketing.*

More Options

There is more to the social web than blogging, Twitter, and Facebook. In fact, you can promote your blog by writing guest blog posts on other popular blogs, giving away prizes in contests you host on your blog, syndicating your content, and more. You can even create, upload, and share videos, audio content, images, presentations, and more.

A number of resources can help you build your online presence, increase your online connections, and enhance relationships with other social web users. Together, these activities can help grow your blog's audience both directly and indirectly.

- Guest blogging: www.myblogguest.com and weblogs.about.com

- Blog contests: www.online-sweepstakes.com and www.contestblogger.com

- Syndication: www.newstex.com and www.demandstudios.com/freelance-work/bloggers.html

- Online video: www.youtube.com and www.tubemogul.com

- Audio and podcasts: www.blogtalkradio.com and www.blubrry.com

- Images: www.flickr.com and www.picasa.com

- Presentations: www.slideshare.com

This list is not all-inclusive. Many tools can help you share content and build relationships across the social web, so don't be afraid to test tools and find the ones you like *and* successfully boost awareness of and traffic to your blog.

Remember, think strategic and long term rather than tactical and short term, and you'll be more likely to reach your blogging goals.

The Least You Need to Know

- Social networking is just like face-to-face networking, but you do it from your computer.

- Social bookmarking makes it easy to find content you like and share content across a wide audience.

- Microblogging with Twitter is an easy and popular way to grow your online audience, relationships, and blog.

- You can promote your blog and build your blog audience both on and off your blog using the tools of the social web.

Web Analytics

In This Chapter

- Introducing web analytics
- Knowing what to track on your blog
- Testing, tweaking, and trying again
- Popular web analytics tools

If you want your blog's audience to grow, you need to do more than publish great content, network, and build relationships. You also need to keep track of what is and what isn't working on your blog. In other words, by analyzing traffic trends and the behavior of the users when they visit your blog, you can create more of the content they want, continually meet their expectations, and build your audience.

The type of data you track, how frequently you do so, and what you do with that information is entirely up to you and depends on your blogging goals. This chapter teaches you what kind of data is available for you to track and introduces you to some of the most popular web analytics tools so you can get started tracking immediately.

What to Track and Measure

If you create an account with a web analytics tool, you're likely to be overwhelmed at first by the amount of data available to you. Don't worry! You don't need to look at all the numbers immediately. In fact, depending on your blogging goals, there's likely to be a lot of data you'll never look at, and that's absolutely fine. The key is knowing that just because all this data is available, doesn't mean you have to use it.

Sit down and think about your blogging objectives. Are you just blogging for fun and have no goals for building an audience? Are you hoping to build a highly successful and popular site? Do you want to make money from your blog? Your answers to these questions, along with your ultimate blogging objectives, will determine what data you should begin tracking.

For example, if you want to build a successful blog and make money from it, you need to work on growing your blog's audience of new and repeat visitors. With that in mind, you'll want to track three things:

- The keywords people are typing into their preferred search engines that lead them to your blog

- What sites other than search engines are sending traffic to your blog

- Which of your blog posts are getting the most views

Starting with just these three areas will keep you from getting overwhelmed with mountains of data. You can add additional tracking efforts as you get more comfortable tracking and analyzing the data.

What Am I Looking At?

Most web analytics tools offer similar types of data for you to track. In fact, when you create a new account with a web analytics tool, you'll be bombarded with links, tabs, and data overflowing with terminology you may not be familiar with.

Here are some of the most common terms you should be aware of as you start analyzing your blog's performance statistics:

hit   Web analytics tools count a hit to your blog every time a file downloads from your site, including image files, flash files, data files, and more. Hits cause an inflated view of your blog's popularity and are no longer used as a reliable measure of a site's traffic patterns.

visit   A visit is counted each time your blog is accessed. If a person accesses your blog more than once, two visits are counted.

visitor   Anyone who visits your blog at any time is considered a visitor. Visitors can be counted multiple times if they visit your blog more than once.

unique visitor   Unique visitors are counted only once, regardless of how many times they visit your blog.

return visitor   Visitors who access your blog more than once are called return visitors.

page view   Each time a visitor views an individual page on your blog (including blog posts), a page view is counted.

 INSIDER SECRET

The page views metric is most commonly viewed to determine the true popularity of a website or blog in comparison to others. Advertisers also use it to compare apples to apples when purchasing online ad space because page views tell them exactly how many times their ads will be displayed to visitors.

referrers   The search engines, websites, blogs, or other online destinations that lead a visitor to your blog via a link to your blog content.

keywords, keyword phrases   The word or words visitors typed into their preferred search engines that produced the search results that brought them to your blog.

top pages viewed   The pages within your blog that have been viewed the most.

bounce rate   The percentage of visitors to your blog who leave immediately after arriving at it.

What's Working … and What Needs to Change?

It's important to understand that traffic spikes might appear in your web analytics data. There are many reasons why your blog might suddenly get a burst of traffic, and it's important to determine what the catalyst was. Doing so helps you determine if the traffic spike can be replicated (assuming it came from a positive source and reason).

For example, if one of your blog posts is linked to from a highly popular website or blog, you might see a huge spike in traffic for a day or more. You'd be able to identify this by reviewing the top pages viewed and referrers statistics in your web analytics data.

Alternately, if you see a jump in a keyword that doesn't usually drive significant traffic to your blog and an increase in traffic to a specific post, you may have written a post about a hot topic that became a form of link bait, driving traffic from a variety of sources to your blog. (See Chapter 19 for more on link baiting.)

QUICK TIP

A traffic spike is usually significant and very noticeable. Take a few minutes to determine what changed during the time traffic increased to your blog so you can adjust your content and promotional strategies in the future.

Just as you want to keep track of surprising changes to your blog's performance, you should also look for trends that will help you create a better long-term blogging strategy. For example, if you see specific keywords start to pick up more traffic, older posts staying strong and continuing to perform well into the future, or continual traffic from a specific referrer, shift your attention to those areas and leverage them. Something is clearly working to cause these trends, and those are activities you want to continue doing.

Similarly, if you see negative trends, those are activities you need to change. For example, if links at the top of your sidebar lead to pages or posts that get very little traffic over time, move those links and put other content into that prominent spot in your sidebar. Or delete those links entirely if they're getting very little activity.

When you make changes to your blog, be sure to track the results. Part of developing a successful blog is testing new layouts, links, designs, content, and so on. Fortunately, many web analytics tools can help you determine if those changes are helping or hurting your blog.

Tools to Track Your Blog's Performance

As mentioned earlier, many free and low-cost tools enable you to track a wide variety of statistics related to your blog's performance. As always, analyze your goals and your budget and confirm that a web analytics tool will work with the version of WordPress you're using before you pay for an account. Appendix C's "Web Analytics Tools" section lists some of the most popular options.

PROCEED WITH CAUTION

Some web analytics tools, like Site Meter, use JavaScript coding to work. WordPress.com does not allow JavaScript, so these tools might not work on your blog. Be sure you check the most recent WordPress rules and offerings as well as the current documentation for web analytics tools before you pay for a web analytics account.

If you try multiple web analytics tools, don't be surprised to see different statistical data for your blog from tool to tool. No web analytics tool is perfect. I've used many of the tools in this chapter (both free and paid versions), and I've been happiest with Google Analytics for tracking the performance of my personal blogs and websites. Of course, it's always best to test tools on your own blog and choose the tool that works best for you.

Adding Google Analytics to Your WordPress Blog

Google Analytics is the most comprehensive free web analytics tool. Not only does the Google-owned analytics tool offer tons of data, but it's also easy to insert the necessary tracking code into your WordPress blog. Furthermore, you can access Google Analytics along with all other Google tools, such as FeedBurner (discussed in Chapter 20), Google AdSense (discussed in Chapter 24), and more, all with the same user account.

The process of adding the necessary code to your WordPress.org blog so a web analytics tool can begin tracking your blog's traffic and performance is fairly similar from one tool to the next. Typically, you have to create an account, provide some configuration information (such as your blog's URL), and copy and paste some provided code into your blog. As an example, the following directions teach you how to create and copy Google Analytics tracking code into your self-hosted WordPress blog.

 QUICK TIP

Some WordPress themes offer special features that make it very easy to insert your Google Analytics tracking code into your blog. If the option exists in your theme, go ahead and use it! Usually, themes that offer this feature provide a special text box within your WordPress dashboard configuration settings where you can simply paste the requested information related to your Google Analytics account.

First, you need to sign in to your Google Analytics account, which takes you to your Account Overview page. Here your new account is shown in the list of accounts at the center of the page. Click on your account link to open it, scroll to the bottom of the page, and click the **Add Website Profile** link to open the Create New Website Profile page, which is shown in Figure 22-1. Note that the Add Website Profile link is also available to the right of your account listing.

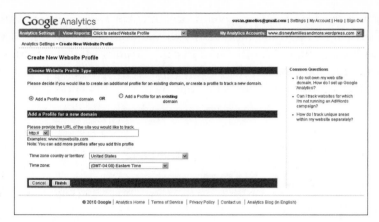

Figure 22-1   *Enter the information for your blog into the Create New Website Profile form.*

When you're done entering the required information, click the **Finish** button to proceed to the Tracking Code page, shown in Figure 22-2.

Figure 22-2   *Copy the tracking code so you can paste it into your WordPress theme.*

Scroll down to the tracking code listed under #2 on the right side of the Tracking Code page. Highlight and copy all the text within the box. This is the code you need to paste into your WordPress.org theme.

Next, log in to your WordPress account and click the **Editor** link in the Appearance section of your dashboard's left menu to open the Edit Themes page. This is the area of your dashboard where you can make changes to your blog's CSS files. Click the **Header** link in the Templates list on the right side of your screen to open the header. php file for editing, as shown in Figure 22-3.

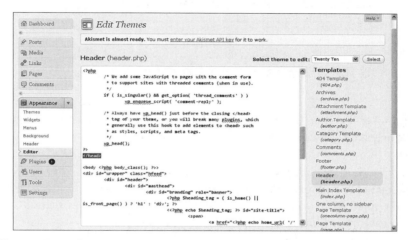

Figure 22-3 *Paste your tracking code before the* `</head>` *tag in your theme's header file.*

Google recommends that you paste the tracking code immediately before the `</head>` tag in the header.php file. Just place your cursor immediately before the `</head>` tag and paste the code you copied from your Google Analytics account in that position. Click the **Save** button to save your changes.

That's all you have to do! Google will begin tracking your blog's statistics, and you should be able to view data in your Google Analytics account within a day or two.

Many bloggers prefer to insert their tracking code in their WordPress theme's footer file. You can do the same by clicking on the **Footer** link in the Templates list on the right side of the Edit Templates page in your WordPress account. This opens the footer.php file for editing, as shown in Figure 22-4.

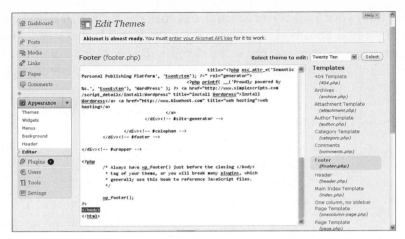

Figure 22-4 *Paste your tracking code before the* </body> *tag in your theme's footer file.*

Just place your cursor immediately before the </body> tag and paste the tracking code you copied from your Google Analytics account in that position. Click the **Save** button to save your changes.

QUICK TIP

The tracking code you paste into your WordPress theme's header or footer files is invisible on your live blog unless you view the source page on your browser. If you scroll through the source HTML, you'll find your tracking code exactly where you pasted it in your WordPress dashboard.

If you're not comfortable editing your blog's CSS files, some other alternatives are available to insert your Google Analytics code. For example, if your sidebar appears on every page of your blog, you could insert the code at the bottom of an existing text widget, as shown in Figure 22-5. The code will be invisible on your live blog.

Some plug-ins make it very easy to link your Google Analytics account to your blog. Both the Google Analytics for WordPress plug-in (wordpress.org/extend/plugins/google-analytics-for-wordpress) and the Google Analyticator plug-in (wordpress.org/extend/plugins/google-analyticator) receive good reviews.

Wherever you decide to paste your Google Analytics tracking code, be sure you don't paste it in more than one place on your blog or your statistics will be skewed.

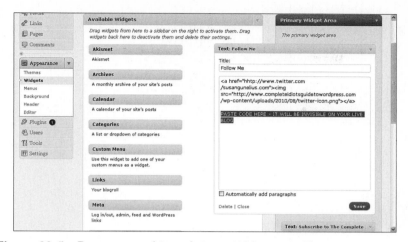

Figure 22-5   *Paste your tracking code into a sidebar text widget.*

Finally, don't sweat the numbers. Spend more time creating great content, engaging your audience with conversation, and building relationships, and you'll find your blog continuing to grow consistently over time.

The Least You Need to Know

- Web analytics tools offer a lot of data most bloggers don't use immediately or ever use.

- No web analytics tool is perfect, and no two tools will give you the exact same data.

- Many free tools are available for you to use. If you choose a fee-based tool, always be sure the tool works with your version of WordPress before you invest any money.

- Adding web analytics tracking code to your WordPress blog usually takes just a few minutes and is as easy as copying and pasting some code into your web analytics account.

Blogging for Big Bucks

Many bloggers want to learn how to make money from their blogs, and Part 6 introduces you to some of the easiest ways to monetize your blog. First, you learn some of the most popular monetization methods as well as the pros and cons of varied money-making opportunities. You also learn about the things you shouldn't do when you monetize your blog.

In addition, Part 6 shows you how and where to place ads on your WordPress site and points you in the direction of blog advertising programs and networks you can join right now.

Finally, you learn how to sell ad space on your blog without the use of a blog advertising program, network, or middleman.

Making Money with Your Blog

In This Chapter

- Making money from your blog
- Choosing a blog monetization method
- Warnings to heed
- Where to display ads on your blog

Many people publish blogs with the hope that one day they'll be able to make a passive income from their efforts by publishing ads, product reviews, and similar content on their blogs in exchange for payment. If you'd like to make money from your blog one day, this chapter is for you.

In this chapter, you learn about the most popular blog monetization methods and how the various opportunities differ in terms of effort and payment. You also learn about the negative aspects of blog monetization you should be aware of before you get started. Blogging can lead to earning money, but there are precautions you should take to ensure your blog *benefits* from monetization rather than being hurt by those efforts.

Popular Monetization Methods

There are a number of different ways to make money from your blog. Some are easier to implement than others, and some are more noticeable than others. The trick is testing different monetization methods to find the ones that generate revenue without damaging your blog's reputation or the user's experience.

Following are some of the most common forms of blog monetization.

Advertising: Image ads, text link ads, video ads, and flash-animated ads are just a few options.

PROCEED WITH CAUTION

If you use WordPress.com as your blogging application and host, know that the WordPress terms of use state that you cannot place ads of any kind on your blog. Be sure to read the most recent terms of use to ensure you're not breaking them with blog monetization efforts.

Reviews and paid posts: You can write reviews about products, services, websites, and more on your blog in exchange for a product sample or money.

Selling merchandise: Websites like Cafepress.com, Prinfection.com, and Zazzle.com make it easy for you to create your own online storefront and link it to your blog so you can sell merchandise from that company (or your own designs).

Accepting donations: Accept monetary donations on your blog by placing a donation button or message in your blog's sidebar.

INSIDER SECRET

PayPal offers donation buttons you can link to your PayPal account, so visitors can donate via PayPal with the click of a button. Simply follow the directions at www.paypal.com/us/cgi-bin/webscr?cmd=p/xcl/rec/donate-intro-outside, and paste the provided code into a text widget in your blog's sidebar to add a donation button to your blog.

These are by no means the only ways to make money from your blog, but they're the most commonly used methods beginner bloggers can experiment with.

Analyzing Monetization Methods

Before you dive into the world of blog monetization, there are some things you need to understand so you can effectively analyze opportunities and pick the monetization methods most likely to help you meet your blogging goals.

As mentioned earlier, a lot of blog advertising and monetization opportunities can be found online, and not all programs are created equal. Venture into the world of blog monetization bearing in mind the following criteria:

Payment models: How you get paid matters. For example, you could be paid a flat rate for publishing an ad for a specific amount of time, or you might only be paid if a visitor to your blog clicks on an ad and then makes a purchase.

Payout thresholds: Some advertisers set payout thresholds that define a specific dollar amount you must earn through their ads displayed on your site before you're paid for those ads. If a payout threshold is set, be sure it's one you can reach within a period of time acceptable to you.

Relevance to your blog: If ads are irrelevant to the blog topic, they're unlikely to be of interest to your visitors and may not help you earn money at all.

INSIDER SECRET

It's unlikely you'll make much money from any form of blog monetization until your blog traffic increases to approximately 10,000 or more page views per month ... but you never know!

Audience: Use the information you have about your visitors to gain a better understanding of who your audience is and what they want and need from you and the ads on your blog.

Reputation: Do some research and be sure the reputation of the company or advertising program or network you're considering working with is in good standing.

Customer service and help: Choose an advertising program that offers readily available customer service support.

Reports: Be sure the ad programs you use provide reports so you can track the performance of published ads and your earnings to ensure you couldn't make better use of that space with a different ad.

Competition: Some online advertisers set rules telling you that you can't display similar ads, competitor ads, or other specific types of ads while their ads are running on your blog. This can be very limiting for your earnings potential.

Warning! Warning!

Making money from your blog might sound like a great idea, but there are things you should not do if you want to ensure your blog retains its audience, continues to attract new visitors, and stays in the good graces of search engines such as Google. Furthermore, you need to be aware of online advertising laws that affect bloggers—and follow them!

Here are some things you should avoid when it comes to blog monetization:

Getting too intrusive: Your blog monetization efforts shouldn't interrupt the user experience on your blog.

Detracting from the user experience: Ads and monetization tactics should enhance the user experience on your blog and add value to it, not damage it.

Being mistaken for spam: Search engines like Google identify websites that publish more ads than original content as spam. Even if only one page of your blog contains more ads than original content, visitors, Google, or other search engines could flag your entire blog as spam. If that happens, your blog might be removed from search engine results entirely, and the traffic that comes to your blogs from search engines will plummet.

Breaking the law: Even bloggers must follow the law, and the onus is on the publisher, or the blogger, to know what laws apply to them. Pleading ignorance won't work in a court of law, so be certain you understand the legalities related to any monetization program or tactic you use on your blog.

PROCEED WITH CAUTION

If you publish paid reviews or endorsements, you need to follow the Federal Trade Commission guidelines in the Code of Federal Regulations (CFR), Title 16, Part 255, which can be found in the Electronic CFR at ecfr.gpoaccess.gov.

Placing Ads in Your WordPress.org Blog

Some WordPress themes make it extremely easy to insert ads into multiple areas of your blog by offering configuration settings where you can simply paste the requested information from your advertising program. Others are not as easy and require that you edit your blog theme's CSS files to do so.

Fortunately, there are some simple ways to add advertisements to various areas of your blogs.

Inserting Ads in Your Blog's Sidebar

Inserting ad code into a text widget in your blog's sidebar, like those shown in Figure 23-1, is a very easy way to publish ads on your blog.

Figure 23-1   *Insert ads into text widgets in your blog's sidebar.*

Simply click the **Widgets** link in the Appearance section of your WordPress dashboard's left menu to open the Widgets page, where you can click and drag a text widget to your blog's sidebar. Simply paste the ad code from the advertiser into the text widget, and the ads should begin displaying.

Inserting Ads Between Blog Posts

Some bloggers like to put ads in between blog posts. This isn't hard to do if you're comfortable pasting code into your theme's CSS files. One of the easiest ways to do it is simply inserting an ad immediately after a blog post.

> **QUICK TIP**
>
> I've said it before, and I'll say it again: always copy and paste the original code in your theme file before you edit it. If you make a mistake, it's easy to go back to the original code.

Log in to your WordPress dashboard, and click the **Editor** link in the Appearance section of your dashboard left menu to open the Edit Themes page. Click the **index. php** file under the list of Templates on the right side of your screen to open the index. php file, as shown in Figure 23-2.

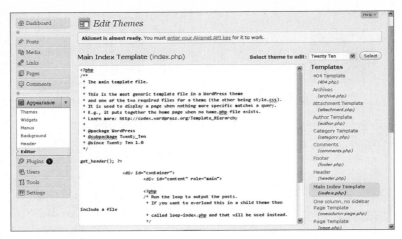

Figure 23-2 *Insert code into the index.php file to display ads between posts.*

Locate the code in the file that says `<php if (have _posts ()) : ?>`, and place your cursor immediately before that code, as shown in Figure 23-3. Type the following code where your cursor is placed: `<?php $count = 1; ?>`

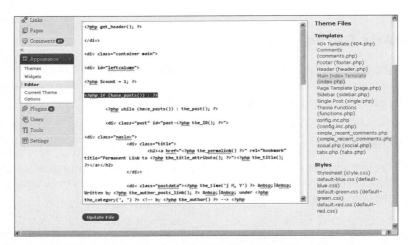

Figure 23-3 *Insert code into the index.php file to identify which post you want your ad to display after.*

> **QUICK TIP**
>
> To place the ad under a specific post on your blog, you can change the number
> in the code you insert from "1"—meaning the ad will appear beneath the first
> post on your blog—to another number.

Once that code is added, you can paste the code for the ad you want to display into
the index.php file. Locate the code that says `<!-- end .entry -->` in your index.php
file, as shown in Figure 23-4.

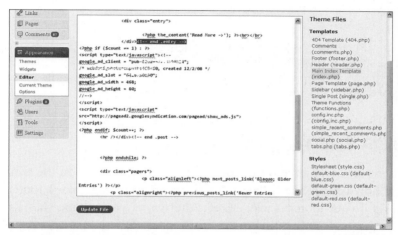

Figure 23-4   *Insert your ad code into your theme's index.php file.*

Place your cursor immediately after that code, and paste the ad code in that position.
Click the **Update File** button to save your changes. Ads will start to display below
your first blog post similar to the example shown in Figure 23-5.

Some WordPress theme CSS files are structured differently from the example shown
in this chapter. If the code you need isn't in your theme's index.php file, it may be in
a separate loop.php file. If your theme is not as clear as the one used in this example,
contact the theme developer for help or try to use one of the plug-ins listed later in
this chapter to position ads on your blog.

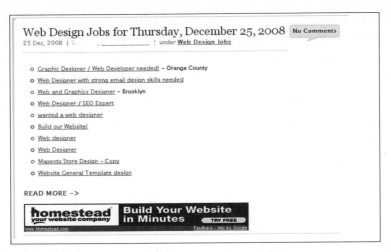

Figure 23-5 *You can insert ads after a post in your blog.*

Insert Ads in Your Blog's Header or Footer

The process of inserting ads into your blog's header depends on the theme you're using and how your header is laid out. Inserting ads in your blog's footer is easier, particularly if your footer is widgetized. Alternately, you can use the WP Footer Ad plug-in (wordpress.org/extend/plugins/wp-footer-ad) to insert ads into your blog's footer.

INSIDER SECRET

The WordPress support forum at wordpress.org/support is a great place to search for specific steps to insert ads on your blog or to post your own question and get help from other users.

Inserting Ads in Blog Posts

You can insert ads into your blog posts by editing your post.php file in your WordPress CSS editor so ads always appear in the same location in all your blog posts. The spot where you insert your ad code varies depending on where you want ads to appear. For example, you can insert ads at the beginning of your posts, right aligned, left aligned, at the end of your posts, and so on. It's up to you. Just remember that you don't want ads to detract from the content in your posts and interrupt or damage the user experience on your blog.

Fortunately, a number of WordPress plug-ins can help you manage ads and place ads in a variety of locations on your blog. Here are a few plug-ins you can test to see if they offer the help you need for the ad program you participate in:

- Advertising Management: wordpress.org/extend/plugins/advertisement-management

- Wp-Insert: wordpress.org/extend/plugins/wp-insert

- All in One Adsense and YPN: wordpress.org/extend/plugins/all-in-one-adsense-and-ypn

Remember, the WordPress Codex is an excellent resource to get answers to questions about editing theme files. Additionally, you can find resources to learn CSS in Chapter 17, which will make it even easier for you to insert ads anywhere you want on your WordPress blog.

The Least You Need to Know

- WordPress.com users cannot place paid ads on their blogs per the WordPress.com terms of service.
- You can monetize your blog through ads, reviews, selling merchandise, donations, and more.
- Ads should enhance the user experience on your blog, not damage it.
- Inserting ad code typically involves using widgets or plug-ins or editing your blog's theme CSS files.

Advertising, Affiliate Programs, and More

In This Chapter

- Understanding ad payment models and ad formats
- Choosing an ad program or network
- Cutting out the middleman: selling ad space
- Joining affiliate or sponsored post programs

As you begin to search for ways to make money from your blog, you'll discover a wide variety of programs and opportunities. In order to effectively evaluate them, you need to understand the types of ad formats and payment models you're likely to come across.

This chapter teaches you about the most common monetization programs and payment models available for your blog. You also learn how to effectively sell ad space on your blog to cut out the middleman and keep 100 percent of your earnings.

Types of Ad Payment Models

When it comes to online advertising, advertisers pay publishers in a variety of ways. Payment typically depends on clicks, impressions, or actions (more on these in a little bit). Alternately, an advertiser might agree to pay you a flat fee to publish an ad for a predetermined length of time.

It's important to understand that the amount of money you can make from blog advertising depends on two primary variables: traffic and placement. The more traffic your blog gets, the more advertisers are willing to pay for ad space on your blog, and the more money you can make from clicks, impressions, and actions. Furthermore, advertisers usually pay more for ads placed in positions where the most people will see them.

Here are some of the most popular ad payment models:

Pay-per-click: Some advertisers only pay you for each click their ad gets on your blog, which is referred to as pay-per-click (PPC) advertising.

> **PROCEED WITH CAUTION**
>
> Don't click on pay-per-click ads on your blog yourself or ask others to click on them for you. This practice is a violation of pay-per-click advertisers' policies, as discussed in Chapter 23.

Pay-per-impression: With pay-per-impression (PPM) ads, you earn money every time the ad displays on your blog. For example, if a pay-per-impression ad appears in your blog's sidebar, an impression is counted every time someone views a page on your blog that includes your sidebar.

Pay-per-action: Pay-per-action (PPA) advertisers pay every time a specific action is completed related to their ads. For example, if a visitor to your blog clicks on a pay-per-action ad, which takes them to an inquiry form on the advertiser's website, the visitor needs to complete and submit the inquiry form before you're paid.

Popular Ad Formats for Blogs

Ads come in various shapes and sizes and can appear just about anywhere within your blog. The choice is yours, but don't forget to follow the suggestions and warnings in Chapter 23 to ensure you publish ads that add value to the user experience on your blog rather than damaging it. The last thing you want to do is drive traffic away from your blog because of the ads you publish.

Display ads: Display ads include any kind of graphic or image ads. They can be static images or flash-animated graphics. Display ads often appear in the header, in the footer, in the sidebar, between posts, or within posts. Also, display ads can be pay-per-click, pay-per-impression, or pay-per-action ads, depending on the advertiser or advertising program.

Text ads: Text ads look like regular hyperlinks. They could appear within your blog posts, in your blog's sidebar, in your blog's footer, or anywhere else you can insert a text link. Many bloggers like text links because they take up very little room on their blogs.

PROCEED WITH CAUTION

Not only do text link ads fail to disclose to visitors that they are, in fact, clicking on an ad—which could annoy them when they realize it—but text link ads also are disliked by search engines, which view paid links as spam and could negatively affect your blog's search traffic.

Video ads: Video ads are one of the newer forms of blog monetization. Typically, they're pay-per-click ads that might require visitors to simply click on the ad for you to be paid. It's important that you read the earnings method requirements for specific video advertising opportunities because advertisers are testing new payment models and methods all the time.

Which Ad Program Is Right for You?

There are many advertising programs bloggers can join in an effort to make money from their blogs. While some programs require that your blog receives a minimum amount of traffic each month in order to participate, other programs are open to anyone who publishes a blog or website.

In other words, there are money-making opportunities for every blogger. You just have to be willing to do your research, find the programs that match your audience's wants and needs, and experiment with ad content, placement, and payment models to learn what delivers the best earnings for you.

Popular Ad Programs and Networks

A variety of advertising programs and networks are open to bloggers to help you get started in your efforts to become a revenue-generating blogger. Appendix C's "Sites to Help Monetize Your Blog" section gives you a list of some of the more popular ad programs and networks.

PROCEED WITH CAUTION

Keep in mind that program guidelines and participation requirements can change at any time, so be sure to check each website to learn the current restrictions.

Some blog advertising programs offer pay-per-click, pay-per-impression, or pay-per-action opportunities, while others only offer one type of payment model. Similarly, some programs offer display ads or text link ads, while others offer a wide variety of options for both display and text ads as well as video. Be sure to read through all the options and experiment with the monetization opportunities that fit best with your blog's content, design, and audience in order to best position yourself to reach your long-term blogging goals.

Inserting Google AdSense Ads into Your Blog's Sidebar

Most advertising programs for bloggers work in a similar manner. You sign up for an account, copy some code provided to you through your new account, and paste it into your blog where you want ads to appear.

The following example shows you how to create and insert code for a Google AdSense ad unit into your blog's sidebar, so you can see how easy it is. Different ad programs are likely to have specific nuances that affect how you create and insert their ad code into your blog, but this example should take some of the confusion out of the process.

INSIDER SECRET

Ad programs such as Google AdSense might place ads contextually, meaning the ads are served based on the content found on the page where they're displayed.

First, log in to your Google AdSense account at www.google.com/adsense and click the **AdSense Setup** tab in the top navigation bar. This opens the AdSense Setup page, shown in Figure 24-1.

Figure 24-1 *You can create a new ad unit from the Google AdSense Setup Page.*

Click the link that matches the type of ad unit you want to create for your blog to open the corresponding configuration page. In this example, a new AdSense for Content ad (the most popular ad unit used by bloggers) is created, as shown in Figure 24-2.

Select the type of AdSense for Content ad you want to create from the options provided, and click the **Continue** button to set up the design of your ad unit, as shown in Figure 24-3.

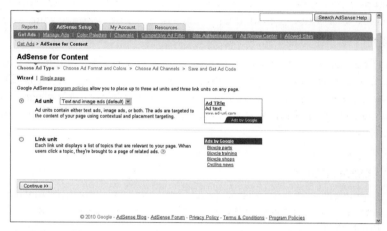

Figure 24-2   *Choose the type of ad unit you want to place on your blog.*

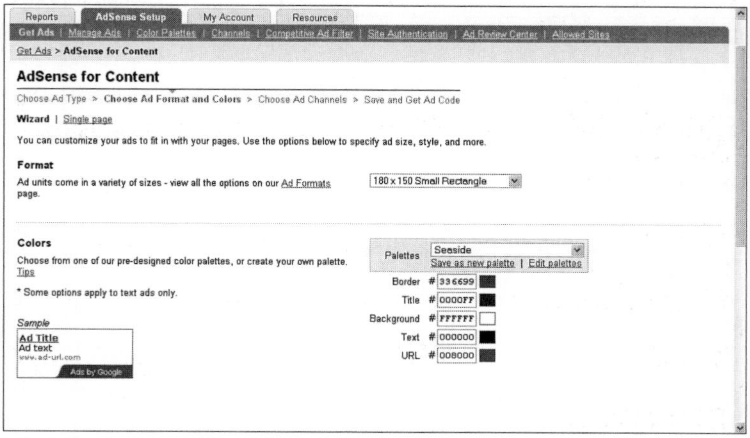

Figure 24-3   *Choose the design settings for your new ad unit.*

Click the **Continue** button when your configurations are complete, and choose a channel (or create a new channel) if you want to be able to track this ad unit as part of a larger program, as shown in Figure 24-4.

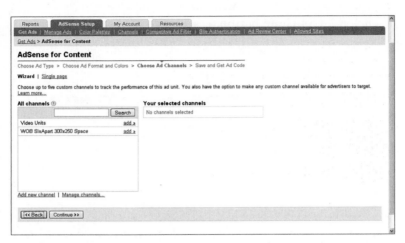

Figure 24-4   *Choose the channel you want to associate your ad unit with for tracking purposes.*

If you don't want to specify a channel, just click the **Continue** button to give your ad unit a name, as shown in Figure 24-5.

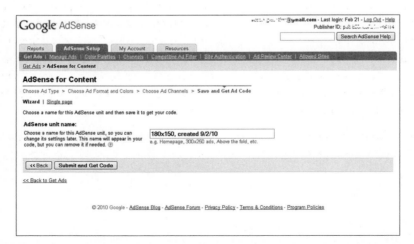

Figure 24-5   *Give your AdSense ad unit a name so you can identify it in your account later.*

Click the **Submit and Get Code** button to access your AdSense unit code, as shown in Figure 24-6.

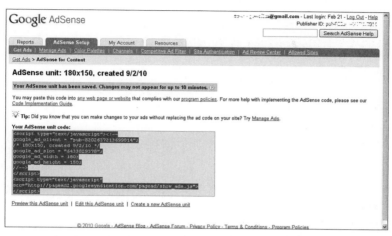

Figure 24-6   *Copy the code for your new AdSense ad unit so you can insert it into your WordPress blog.*

Highlight all the content in the Your AdSense Unit Code text box, and copy it. This is the code you need to insert into your WordPress blog in order for ads to begin appearing to visitors.

Next, log in to your WordPress dashboard, and select the **Widgets** link in the Appearance section of your dashboard's left menu to open the Widgets page. Click and drag a new text widget into the position in your blog's list of sidebar widgets where you want your new ad unit to appear. (You can also simply paste the ad code into an existing text widget if you prefer.) Paste the ad code you copied from your Google AdSense account into the new text widget, as shown in Figure 24-7. You can also give your new text widget a name if you'd like.

Click the **Save** button at the bottom of the new text widget and then view your live blog to see your ad unit in its new place on your blog, as shown in Figure 24-8.

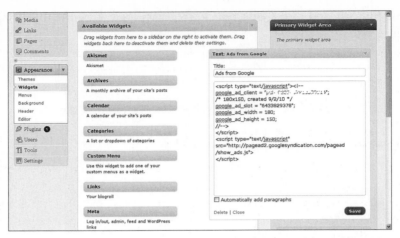

Figure 24-7 *Paste your ad unit code into a text widget.*

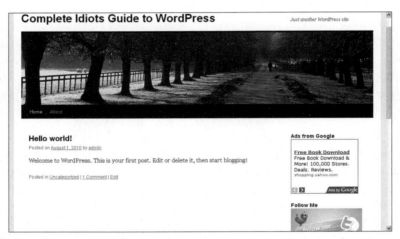

Figure 24-8 *Your new ad unit appears in your blog's sidebar.*

Keep in mind, you might need to refresh your browser to see the new ad unit on your live blog.

PROCEED WITH CAUTION

Some advertising programs might have a delay in serving ads to your new ad unit, particularly if your site has to be indexed for contextual advertising, so don't be surprised if it takes a day or so before ads begin appearing in your live blog.

Selling Ad Space Directly

It can be difficult for beginner bloggers to attract advertisers without the help of an advertising program or middleman, but it can be done. As traffic to your blog grows, you'll be able to attract more advertisers and increase your advertising rates. As long as you set realistic expectations for your earnings potential from selling ad space directly to advertisers, you'll be successful.

Pros and Cons of Selling Directly

The biggest benefits to selling advertising space directly to advertisers is being in control and keeping all the money you make. When you participate in advertising networks and programs, you only make a percentage of the program's overall earnings, or you have to give up a percentage of your earnings to the advertising program. Both scenarios mean you lose money, but that's not a problem when you sell ad space directly to advertisers.

On the other hand, bloggers whose blogs don't attract at least tens of thousands of visitors each month can have a very difficult time attracting advertisers to their blogs. Advertising networks and programs give you access to advertisers smaller bloggers can't always get on their own.

Furthermore, when you participate in a blog advertising network or program, you significantly reduce the amount of work you have to do. Often you just have to sign up, copy some ad code, paste it into your blog, and you're done. When you sell ad space directly, you have to promote your ad space for sale, communicate with advertisers, approve ads, handle payment processing, respond to problems, and do the technical work to publish and remove ads based on the specific run time of each ad published on your blog. If you don't have a lot of free time, selling ad space directly could be challenging for you.

Many beginner bloggers choose to pursue the best of both worlds. They offer ad space for sale directly on their blogs, knowing it's unlikely they'll get a lot of inquiries, and they also participate in one or more advertising networks or programs. Even some of the most popular and well-trafficked blogs diversify their earnings by participating in multiple revenue-generating activities. That's just good business.

Setting Rates

There's no single recipe for success when it comes to setting advertising rates on your blog, particularly if your blog is new or not well trafficked yet. It is important to set the rates for your ad space competitively, so take some time to visit other blogs about your topic and that attract similar audiences. Search those sites to see if they offer advertising rates. This can help you set competitive rates for your own ad space.

> **QUICK TIP**
>
> Search for blogs similar to yours on a site like BuySellAds.com (discussed in detail later in this chapter) to see what advertising rates those blogs are charging. Use that information as a benchmark when setting rates for your own blog.

It's a good idea to set your rates low at first in order to attract the most advertisers. For example, if your blog traffic is under 1,000 page views per day, you could set a rate of $10 per 30 days for a 125×125 pixel button ad in your blog's sidebar (above the fold) or $20 for a 250×300 pixel square ad in your sidebar. Set rates for premium locations (above the fold or in the header) higher than other locations on your blog.

Using a Middleman

As mentioned earlier in this chapter, it can be difficult for new bloggers to attract advertisers. Fortunately, there are some companies that link online publishers with advertisers so even low-trafficked blogs can connect with advertisers. An advertising program like the one offered by BuySellAds.com (www.buysellads.com), for example, is an excellent option for small blogs.

You can sign up for a free publisher account on BuySellAds.com, create a listing for your blog, enter the ad sizes and placements you're willing to accept on your blog along with pricing for each, and you're done! Be sure to include a great description and tag your blog listing with keywords related to your topic and audience that advertisers are likely to search for. Also, take the time to see what other blogs similar to yours in terms of traffic and audience are charging for ad space so you can set competitive fees.

A site like BuySellAds.com takes care of all the technical aspects of advertising on your blog. You paste code into your blog once, and BuySellAds.com does the rest. However, BuySellAds.com does keep a percentage of your earnings from each ad sold on your blog. If you have trouble attracting advertisers to your blog, using a middleman like BuySellAds.com might turn your blog from a site that earns no money to one that earns a bit each month. Of course, you can stop using BuySellAds.com at any time.

Automating Ad Space Sales

Selling ad space directly to advertisers can take up a lot of your time. Fortunately, some WordPress plug-ins make it easier to manage the monetization of your blog through ads. If you visit the WordPress Plugin Directory and type in keywords such as "ad" or "advertising," you'll find many free plug-ins that can help you sell and manage ad space on your blog.

The free WP125 plug-in (wordpress.org/extend/plugins/wp125) makes it very easy to sell and manage 125×125-pixel button ads on your blog. You can configure the placement and quantity of ads on your blog as well as track clicks for pay-per-click ads. Furthermore, you can automate the process of taking down expired ads as well as set up e-mail notifications when expired ads are removed from your live blog. Even unsold space is automatically promoted on your blog with a special "Your Ad Here" image.

For more control and customization, the OIOpublisher plug-in (www.oiopublisher. com), which is offered for a reasonable fee, provides complete automation of your direct advertising sales and publishing. Using OIOpublisher, you can sell and manage display ads of all sizes, text link ads, and even paid posts. You can even automate payments through PayPal with OIOpublisher. Also, you can track ad performance and set up ads so they're only displayed to specific audiences. It's easy to create custom ad zones with different prices and options. If you're serious about selling ad space directly, this is a great plug-in to help you.

Affiliate Programs

Affiliate advertising is a popular blog monetization method. Many companies pay bloggers to become their affiliates. Affiliate advertising programs also link online publishers, such as bloggers, with a wide variety of companies looking for affiliates.

In simplest terms, bloggers can become affiliates of one or more companies and place ads for those companies on their blogs. When a visitor clicks on one of those ads and completes a predetermined action (for example, makes a purchase), the blogger is paid a percentage of the sale or a predetermined fee. Companies of all sizes use affiliates to advertise their products across the web.

While some affiliate programs have participation requirements related to your blog's traffic, others are open to all online publishers. Furthermore, some affiliate programs are open for anyone to join, but the specific companies that participate in those programs that are looking for affiliates might have their own requirements you have to meet in order to work with them. It's important that you read the current guidelines and restrictions for not only any program you join, but also for each specific affiliate advertiser you consider working with.

Finding an Affiliate Program and Network

Appendix C's "Sites to Help Monetize Your Blog" section offers a list of some of the most popular affiliate programs and networks for bloggers.

Inserting Amazon Affiliate Links in Blog Posts

Many affiliate advertising programs simply require that you create an account, copy some ad code, and paste it into your blog to begin serving their ads to your audience. However, some unique opportunities are available to you as well. For example, as an Amazon Associate, you can include your affiliate ID in text links within your blog posts so you can make it easy for people to find and purchase products *while* they're reading a post on your blog that refers to a specific product.

INSIDER SECRET

If you're already logged in to Amazon when you start your blog post, you can easily get ad code for any Amazon product with a simple mouse click and without leaving your blog using the Amazon Associates Site Stripe (affiliate-program.amazon.com/gp/associates/promo/sitestripe.html). It even adds a handy toolbar to your web browser!

To begin, log in to your Amazon Associates account and click the **Links & Banners** tab in the navigation bar to open the Product Links page, shown in Figure 24-9.

Figure 24-9   *Search for the product you want to link to in the Amazon Associates Product Links page.*

Use the **Search** drop-down menu and keyword text box to enter search criteria to find the product you're looking for. Click the **Go!** button to see your search results, as shown in Figure 24-10.

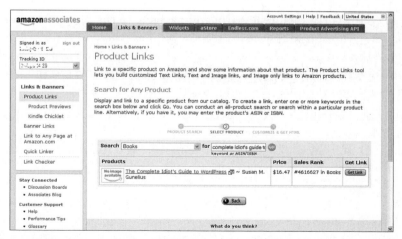

Figure 24-10   *Click the **Get Link** button to get the link code for the product you want to advertise on your blog.*

When you find the product you want to link to from your blog post, click the **Get Link** button next to it. The Customize and Get HTML page opens, as shown in Figure 24-11.

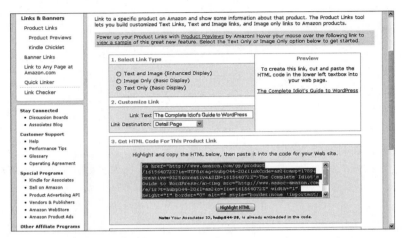

Figure 24-11 *Copy the ad code provided.*

Click the radio buttons and drop-down menu to customize your ad link. You can see how your ad will look in the Preview section of the page. When the ad looks the way you want it to on your blog, highlight all the text in the **Get HTML Code For This Product Link** text box. This is the code you need to insert into your blog post.

Log in to your WordPress dashboard, and navigate to the blog post where you want to display the Amazon ad. For text link ads, be sure you're in the HTML editor by clicking on the **HTML** tab in the top right of the post editor. Position your mouse where the text link should begin, and paste the code you copied from your Amazon Associates account into that position, as shown in Figure 24-12.

Once your post is published, the Amazon product link will look like all other links on your blog, as shown in Figure 24-13, but the actual link includes your Amazon Associates ID in it, so you'll get credit if someone who follows that link from your blog post to Amazon makes a purchase.

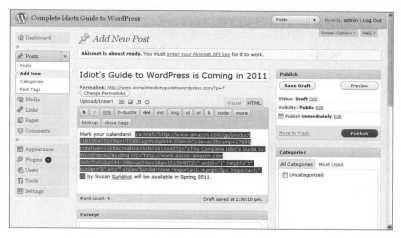

Figure 24-12 *Insert Amazon text link ad code into your HTML blog post editor.*

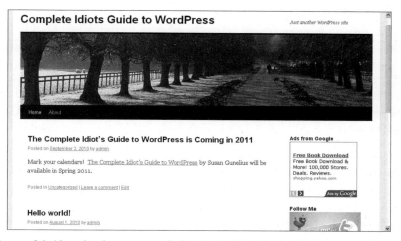

Figure 24-13 *An Amazon text link ad looks like all other links on your blog.*

Paid Reviews and Sponsored Posts

As discussed in Chapter 23, if you publish blog posts in return for monetary or other forms of compensation, you need to disclose that relationship to stay compliant with the law and the ethics of the social web. If you're willing to do that, writing posts for payment can be a great way to make money from your blog. The trick is to be sure you publish paid posts that actually add value to your blog and your audience.

Paid reviews are simply reviews of any kind of products, services, companies, or other items or entities published in return for compensation. Sponsored posts don't necessarily have to be reviews. Instead, they're considered any blog post published in exchange for compensation. In other words, if you're getting paid by a company or individual to write a post, you're participating in paid posting, paid reviews, and/or sponsored post advertising, and you need to disclose those activities on your blog.

> **PROCEED WITH CAUTION**
>
> Be sure any paid posting program you join requires that participants provide full disclosure within paid posts to ensure you're working with a reputable company.

A number of websites connect online publishers, such as bloggers, with companies and people who are looking for sites willing to publish content about their products and services. Appendix C's "Sites to Help Monetize Your Blog" section gives you sites where bloggers can find paid posting opportunities.

Some paid posting programs pay you as soon as your published post is approved, while others require you to reach a payout threshold to receive payment. Always take the time to not only read the guidelines set by the paid posting program but also of each specific opportunity you consider to ensure it's right for your blog.

Also, be careful not to publish too many paid posts on your blog or your audience might begin to think you have nothing to offer but paid reviews and posts that read like ads. Remember, without valuable content, no one will want to read your blog, and without readers, you won't be able to attract any advertisers or make any money at all.

The Least You Need to Know

- Advertisers could pay you each time a visitor clicks on an ad on your blog, each time an ad is displayed on your blog, or each time a visitor completes a specific action after clicking on an ad on your blog.
- You keep all your earnings if you sell ad space directly, but joining an ad program can help you sell *more* ad space.
- Affiliate advertising and publishing paid posts are popular blog monetization methods, but remember to disclose compensated links and posts as such.

Glossary

@reply Pronounced *at-reply*. A Twitter update that begins with @username, which identifies a tweet as being directed at a specific Twitter user. @username used *within* a tweet is considered a mention.

above the fold The area on a web page that can be seen by visitors in their browser windows without having to scroll down.

add-on domains New domains added to the primary domain in a web hosting account that enable a user to manage multiple websites from a single hosting account.

affiliate advertising A blog monetization method wherein bloggers sign up through advertising programs agreeing to display ads for advertisers. Those advertisers pay the bloggers each time a visitor to their blogs follows an affiliate ad link and makes a purchase or performs a specified action. Popular affiliate advertising programs include Amazon Associates and Commission Junction.

alt-tag The alternate tag is a piece of HTML code typically used to display relevant text when an image cannot be displayed in a web browser.

Amazon Associates A popular affiliate advertising program for bloggers.

archive The location on a blog where posts that are not current are stored for easy access by visitors.

attribution A citing of the source of a story, quote, or image used within a blog post.

audio blog *See* podcast.

bandwidth The amount of data, typically measured in bits per second, or bps, that can be transmitted through a network, modem, or online connection.

blog Originally called weblogs for the fusion of the words *web* and *log*, blogs began as online diaries with entries listed in reverse chronological order. Today, blogs are written and published by individuals, groups, businesses, and more. Blogs are considered a social media because they provide a two-way conversation between the author and visitors through the comment feature. Blogs are viewed as one of the first methods of bringing user-generated content to the mainstream.

blog contest   A blogging promotional event wherein a giveaway is raffled off in order to drive traffic to the hosting blog.

blog host   A company that provides space on its servers to store and maintain blogs. Also called host, web host, or third-party host.

blog posts   Individual entries written by a blogger and published on a blog.

blog statistics   The data used to track the performance of a blog. Also called web analytics.

blogger   A person who writes content for a blog.

blogging   The act of writing and publishing blog posts or entries.

blogging application   The program bloggers use to create and maintain blogs such as WordPress, Blogger, TypePad, MovableType, and LiveJournal. Also called blogging platform or blogging software.

blogosphere   The online blogging community made up of bloggers from around the world creating user-generated content as part of the social web.

blogroll   A list of links created by a blogger and published on his or her blog. Links in a blogroll are typically related to the blog topic or other sites the blogger enjoys or recommends.

bounce rate   The percentage of people who leave a blog immediately after finding it.

browser   A program used to surf the Internet. Popular browsers include Internet Explorer, Firefox, Opera, Google Chrome, Safari, and more. Also called web browser.

category   A division used to separate similar blog posts so it's easier for readers to find them.

comment   An opinion or reaction by a blog reader to a specific post. Comments can be submitted at the end of blog posts, if the blogger has chosen to allow them. Comments are what make a blog interactive.

comment moderation   The process of holding comments for review prior to publishing them on a blog. Comment moderation is typically used to ensure spam and offensive comments are not published on a blog.

comment policy   A set of rules and restrictions published on a blog to set visitor expectations related to the types of comments allowed on the blog and what types of comments are likely to be deleted.

contextual advertising   Ads served based on the content found on the web page where the ads appear. Popular contextual advertising programs include Google AdSense and Kontera.

copyright   Legal ownership of intellectual property giving the owner exclusive right to reproduce and share that property.

Creative Commons license   A form of copyright license created to give copyright holders more flexibility in allowing reproduction and sharing of their property.

CSS (cascading style sheets)   The structured documents WordPress designers use to create blog layouts.

custom field   Specific fields in the WordPress database that include customization data for a post, a page, or an entire theme.

dashboard   The primary online management page of a WordPress account where users can access the tools and functionality to modify settings, create content, and more.

domain   The part of a URL that represents a specific website. Domain names are typically preceded by *www.* and end with an extension such as *.com* or *.net*.

domain registrar   A company that registers domain names for users and has the authority to do so by the Internet Corporation for Assigned Names and Numbers (ICANN).

fair use   An exception to copyright laws that allows limited use of certain copyrighted materials for editorializing, commentary, education, and similar activities.

feed   The syndicated content of a blog. *See also* RSS *and* feed reader.

feed reader   A tool used to collect RSS feeds for viewing. Feed readers receive feeds from blogs and deliver them to subscribers in aggregated format for quick and easy viewing in one place.

flash   Streaming animation that appears on web pages.

footer   The area spanning the bottom of a blog page, which typically includes copyright information and may include other elements such as a contact link or ads. Some WordPress themes include widgets within the footer.

forum   An online message board where participants post messages within predefined categories. Other participants respond, creating an online conversation between a potentially large group of people led by one or more moderators.

FTP (file transfer protocol)   The process used to transfer files from one computer to another across the World Wide Web.

Google   A California-based company that produces software, programs, tools, and utilities to help people leverage the Internet to accomplish tasks. The Google search engine is the most popular search engine in the world.

Google AdSense   A contextual advertising program offering text, display, and video ads, popular with bloggers and online publishers.

guest blogging   The process of writing free posts to appear on another person's blog or accepting free posts from another blogger to publish on your blog, with the purpose of networking and driving blog traffic.

hashtag   An informal categorization system for Twitter that helps users identify tweets related to topics of interest. Hashtags include the # symbol followed by a keyword such as #worldcup.

header   The area spanning the top of a blog page where the blog title, graphics, and possibly navigational links or ads appear.

hit   A statistic counted each time a file is downloaded from your blog. Each page in a blog or website typically contains multiple files.

home page   The first page a visitor sees when he or she enters a root domain name.

HTML (hypertext markup language)   A programming language made up of tags used to create websites and blogs.

HTML editor   The area within a WordPress dashboard where users can enter the content for a blog post or page using HTML code.

impression-based advertising   An ad model wherein bloggers publish ads for advertisers and get paid based on the number of times those ads are displayed to visitors. Popular impression-based advertising programs include ValueClick and TribalFusion.

keyword   A word or phrase used to help index a web page, allowing it to be found by search engines.

link   A connection between two websites. When selected, a link takes the user to another webpage. Also called hyperlink.

link bait   A post written for the primary purpose of attracting traffic and links. Link bait posts are typically related to hot and current topics.

microblogging   The process of publishing short updates (typically 140 characters or less) through sites such as Twitter and Plurk.

multiuser blog   A blog authored by more than one person and accessible to multiple users through the blogging software.

navigation bar   A set of links arranged across all or a portion of a web page to make it easier for visitors to find content.

niche A specific and highly targeted segment of an audience or market. A niche blog is written about a focused topic and appeals to a very specific group of people.

Nofollow An HTML tag that makes links invisible to web browsers.

open source Computer applications and technologies for which the original developer code is freely available.

page Content on a WordPress blog that's completely separate from the chronological blog post archive.

page rank A ranking some search engines and advertisers use to determine a blog's popularity typically based on traffic and incoming links.

page view A statistic that tracks each time a web page is viewed by anyone at anytime.

paid post A blog post written and published in exchange for some form of compensation.

parked domain An Internet domain address that's been registered but is either not in use and leads to a static page with no information, or leads to a page filled with ads.

pay-per-action (PPA) An online advertising payment model that pays the publisher each time a visitor clicks an ad and a corresponding, predefined action is performed (e.g., a sale is made or a lead form is submitted).

pay-per-click (PCC) An online advertising payment model that pays the publisher each time a visitor clicks an ad.

pay-per-impression (PPM) An online advertising payment model that pays the publisher each time an ad is displayed.

permalink A link to a specific page in a blog that remains unchanged over time. Formed by a fusion of the words *permanent* and *link*.

php Hypertext preprocessor (php) is a scripting language web developers use to produce web pages.

ping A signal sent from one website to another to ensure the other site exists. Pings are used to notify sites that receive notice from ping servers of updates to a blog or website.

plug-in A tool created by web developers that enhance the functionality of WordPress.org.

podcast An audio file that's recorded digitally for online playback. Bloggers use podcasts to create audio blog posts. Also called audio blogging.

post   An entry on a blog, typically published in reverse chronological order and accessible until deleted through the blog's archives.

post editor   The section of the WordPress dashboard where a user can enter the content for a blog post in a manner similar to using a traditional word processing application or using HTML code. *See also* HTML editor *and* visual editor.

professional blogger   A person who writes blogs as a career.

profile   A blogger's About Me page, which usually describes who the blogger is and why he or she is qualified to write the blog.

referrer   Any website, blog, or search engine that leads visitors to your blog through a link.

retweet   A Twitter term used to identify updates copied from another user's Twitter stream and republished. Retweets are preceded by *RT.*

RSS (Really Simple Syndication)   The format used to create web feeds, which allows users to subscribe to syndicated websites and blogs and view new content from those websites and blogs in aggregated format within a feed reader. *See also* feed *and* feed reader.

search engine   A website used to find online content related to specific keywords or keyword phrases. Search engines use proprietary algorithms to spider the Internet, index content, and return relevant results, which are typically presented in a ranked order. Google, Bing, and Yahoo! are popular search engines.

search engine optimization (SEO)   The process of writing online content, designing web pages, and promoting both to boost rankings within search engine keyword searches and generate an increase in traffic to a specific site.

server   A computer program that provides services to other computer programs; can also be the computer or equipment a server program runs on. A web server is the computer program that serves requested web pages or files.

sidebar   A column on a blog to the right, left, or flanking the largest, main column on a blog. Sidebars typically include a blogroll, archives, ads, and more.

social bookmarking   A method of saving, storing, and sharing web pages for future reference. Popular social bookmarking sites include Digg, StumbleUpon, Reddit, and Delicious.

social networking   The process of communicating with, connecting with, and building relationships with people online using specific tools and websites. Popular social networking sites include Facebook and LinkedIn.

social web   The second generation of the World Wide Web, which focuses on interaction, user-generated content, communities, and building relationships. Also called web 2.0.

spam   Comments submitted on your blog for no reason other than to drive traffic to another website. Spam can also come in other forms such as e-mail spam.

sponsored review   A blog post written in exchange for some form of compensation that may or may not require an actual review of a product, company, item, or entity. Popular sponsored review networks include PayPerPost, ReviewMe, and SponsoredReviews.com. Also called sponsored post or paid post.

sticky post   A post that always appears as the first (or top) post on a blog or online forum.

subscribe   When a person signs up to receive a blog's feed in his or her feed reader or via e-mail.

tag   Keywords used to identify and informally categorize a blog post. Tags are also used for search engine optimization because search engines read and include them in their indexing and ranking processes.

text link ads   Ads that appear as simple text links on blogs and websites.

theme   A predesigned blog layout created to make it easy for people with little to no computer knowledge to start and maintain an aesthetically pleasing blog. Also called template.

third-party host   *See* blog host.

trackback   A reference link or shoulder tap used to notify a blog when another website or blog has linked to it. Trackbacks appear as links within the comments section of blog posts, if they are enabled within the WordPress dashboard settings.

tweet   A Twitter update.

Twitter   A microblogging application.

Twitter app   A tool developed by a third party to enhance the functionality of Twitter.

unique visitor   A visitor to a website or blog who is counted one time regardless of how many times he or she visits. *See also* visitor.

URL (uniform resource locator)   The unique address of a specific page on the Internet consisting of an access protocol (e.g., http), a domain name (e.g., www.sitename.com), and an extension identifying the specific page within a website or blog (e.g., /specificpage.htm).

URL shortener   A tool used to shorten lengthy URLs for republishing in microblogging updates such as Twitter.

visit   Each time a page on your blog is accessed by anyone and at any time, a visit is counted.

visitor   A person who views a page (or multiple pages) on a website or blog.

visual editor   The section of the WordPress dashboard where bloggers can create posts or pages using a common word processing interface. *See also* WYSIWYG.

vlogging   A fusion of the words *video* and *blog*. The process of creating and publishing videos rather than written blog posts. Also called video blogging.

web 2.0   *See* social web.

web analytics   *See* blog statistics.

web browser   *See* browser.

weblog   *See* blog.

widget   A tool used in WordPress to add additional features and functionality to a blog, particularly in the blog's sidebar.

WordPress   A blogging application from Automattic, Inc. Two versions are available: Wordpress.com, which is hosted by WordPress, and Wordpress.org, which bloggers must host through a third-party hosting provider.

WYSIWYG (what you see is what you get)   The visual editor provided by most blogging applications that allows users to create blog posts in a manner similar to traditional word processing software, where the format seen on-screen during the editing process looks similar to how the final, published post will appear.

XML (extensible markup language)   A generic set of rules for encoding documents, such as online content, to provide that information in a wide variety of formats and applications.

Frequently Asked Questions

The more you use WordPress, the more features and options you'll discover to make your blog look and perform exactly how you want it to. While many of the advanced questions and answers provided in this appendix refer to the self-hosted WordPress.org application, I've noted when the information applies to WordPress-hosted blogs using the free WordPress.com application without paid upgrades.

This appendix answers questions that might arise as you begin to use WordPress on a daily basis, with information on feeds, subscriptions, plug-ins, Twitter applications, text formatting, and more. Of course, you're likely to have additional questions that couldn't fit into the scope of this book, so helpful resources are provided in Appendix C if you can't find the information you need elsewhere in this book.

What Kind of Theme Layout Should I Use on My Blog? (WordPress.org and WordPress.com)

Many types of WordPress theme layouts are available. If you use the free WordPress.com, you're restricted to using the themes in the WordPress themes directory, although a good variety can be found there. Alternately, if you self-host your blog using WordPress.org, there are thousands and thousands of themes (both free and with a fee attached) that you can choose from. The most common theme layouts are explained in the remainder of this section.

Note that theme examples shown in the following screenshots include both free and premium themes offered by reputable theme designers and are well coded.

One-column: One-column WordPress themes include just one column of content, with no sidebars. Some WordPress themes offer a number of page and post layouts you can choose from. An example of a premium WordPress theme that includes multiple page configurations, including a one-column layout, is the Education Child theme from Studiopress (www.studiopress.com/themes/education), shown in Figure B-1.

Figure B-1   *One-column WordPress theme layouts focus on post content above all else.*

Two-column: Two-column WordPress themes include one column for the main post or page content and a second column that appears to the right or left of the main column as a sidebar. Note that the main column typically takes up at least 75 percent of the screen width. An example of a two-column WordPress theme is the free Bueno theme from WooThemes (www.woothemes.com/2009/11/bueno), shown in Figure B-2.

Figure B-2   *Two-column WordPress themes can display a sidebar to the right or left of the main content column.*

Three-column: Three-column WordPress themes include one column for the main post or page content and two smaller columns used as sidebars. The two sidebar columns can appear to the left or right of the main column, or one sidebar can appear on each side of the main column. The main column should be the widest. An example of a three-column WordPress theme with both sidebars positioned to the right of the main content column is the premium Simple Site theme from Templatic (templatic.com/portfolio-themes/simple-site), shown in Figure B-3.

Figure B-3 *Three-column WordPress themes can display sidebars on one side or both sides of the main content column.*

Magazine: Magazine WordPress themes include a wide variety of boxes of content on the home page to simulate a page in a newspaper or magazine, while interior pages and post pages typically use a traditional one-, two-, or three-column layout. An example of a magazine-style WordPress theme is the premium bSocial theme from iThemes (ithemes.com/purchase/bsocial-premium-wordpress-social-magazine-theme), shown in Figure B-4.

Figure B-4 *Magazine WordPress themes allow you to highlight a wide variety of content on your home page.*

Photo: Photo WordPress themes (sometimes called portfolio themes) include many boxes where images can be displayed across the home page and interior pages. Most photo WordPress themes also include layouts for one-, two-, or three-column pages and post pages, and many can be used for video content as well as photo content. An example of a photo and video WordPress theme is the premium Object theme from WooThemes (www.woothemes.com/2009/09/object), shown in Figure B-5.

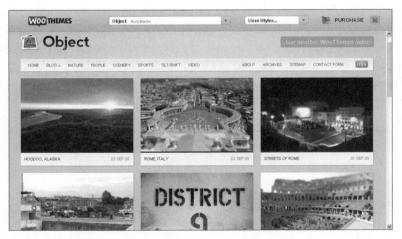

Figure B-5 *Photo WordPress themes allow users to display a variety of images neatly.*

Website or business: Website or business WordPress themes look like traditional websites on the home page. Interior pages and post pages can have a variety of layouts, including one-, two-, or three-column. An example of a website or business WordPress theme is the premium Agency theme from Studiopress (www.studiopress.com/themes/agency), shown in Figure B-6.

Figure B-6 *Business WordPress themes look like traditional websites.*

E-commerce: E-commerce WordPress themes are designed to enable users to highlight many products in different ways. For example, home pages can look like traditional retail websites, and interior pages can include a variety of product images and details or a single product image and detail. A shopping cart is usually built into an e-commerce WordPress theme. An example of an e-commerce WordPress theme is the premium eStore theme from ElegantThemes (www.elegantthemes.com/gallery/estore), shown in Figure B-7.

Figure B-7   *E-commerce themes include built-in shopping carts.*

Choosing Your Theme Layout

Before you choose your WordPress theme layout, you need to define your blogging goals and your audience's expectations for your blog. If you're creating a business website with a blogging component, a business theme is your best option. If you publish a lot of content every day or you have multiple bloggers contributing content in specific categories each day, a magazine theme will allow you to highlight more of that content on your home page.

However, if you're simply publishing a traditional blog, a two- or three-column layout should work for you. Avoid the one-column layout that limits the amount of information you can publish outside your blog posts.

Whether you choose a two- or three-column WordPress theme depends on how much information you think you want to include in your blog's sidebar. If you have a lot of content in your sidebar, you don't want people to have to keep scrolling to find it, and you don't want the length of the sidebar to be excessively long in comparison to the length of your post column. If a single sidebar gets very long, it's time to delete some content from that sidebar or switch to a three-column WordPress theme.

Why Does Content I Copy and Paste from Microsoft Word Look Strange When Published in One of My Blog Posts?

As mentioned in Chapter 10, when you copy and paste text directly from Microsoft Word into your blog post visual editor, the published post looks like a formatting mess on your live blog. That's because when you copy and paste directly from Word, a bunch of HTML code is added to the post content. Even though the post content looks fine in your visual editor, that extra HTML code is still there. You won't be able to see that HTML code unless you switch to the HTML post editor in your WordPress dashboard.

If you don't know the basics of HTML tagging, you won't be able to recognize all the extra code in your HTML editor responsible for making your post look terrible on your live blog. Even if you do know HTML, cleaning up the mess in your HTML editor is time-consuming. There's a lot of extra code you need to delete and fix.

It's best to avoid copying and pasting text directly from Word to your WordPress post editor entirely. Instead, take an extra step in the copy and paste process to ensure that extra code doesn't make it to your post editor at all. Here's how to do it:

1. Copy the content from Microsoft Word.

2. Open Notepad (for PC users) or Text Editor (for Mac users), and paste the content into a new document.

3. Copy the content from Notepad or Text Editor.

4. Paste the content into your WordPress post editor.

The content will paste into your WordPress post editor free of all that extra HTML coding if you take the extra step to paste it into Notepad or Text Editor first. It's possible you'll need to reapply some formatting if you had bullets, numbers, headings, or type formatting in your Word document, but those tasks take less time than trying to clean up messy HTML code.

Why Did My Post Column Move So It's Not Next to My Sidebar Anymore?

If your post column has moved so you have to scroll down to the bottom of your sidebar to see it (or vice versa), an element in your post column (or sidebar) is too wide. For example, if an image file is wider than the width of your post column or sidebar, as defined in your theme's style.css file, it will push the content in the columns next to it out of the way so it can fit. The column(s) that gets pushed out of the way has to go somewhere. Usually, it ends up appearing at the bottom of the column with the too-wide image. You have to scroll down to see the missing column(s).

If you use Mozilla Firefox as your web browser, you can easily check the width of your blog's columns in pixels using the MeasureIt ruler add-on (addons.mozilla.org/en-US/firefox/addon/539). A Google search for "pixel ruler" provides a number of other resources if you don't use Firefox. Otherwise, you can view your blog's Stylesheet in your

WordPress dashboard Editor to find the layout information where your blog's column widths are defined.

Once you learn the widths of your blog theme's columns, be sure any images, videos, or other content you place in those columns is narrower than the width of the columns where those elements will appear.

Why Is the Text Formatting for My Blog Posts Messed Up? My First Post Is Fine but After That, All My Posts on My Home Page Are in Boldface (or Another Text Attribute), but I Didn't Make Them That Way.

This happens frequently, and the culprit is almost always an HTML tag that's not been closed. Locate the point in your posts where the formatting begins. There's probably an HTML tag designating that formatting to begin in that position but the closing HTML tag was not included.

Open the post where the problem begins and insert the closing HTML tag in the proper position. Save your changes and refresh your blog's live home page. (You might have to clear your cache, too.) The text in your posts should be corrected now.

My WordPress.org Blog Is Acting Strange and Looks Wrong. What's Going On?

Sometimes third-party code can cause a blog to load strangely. For example, flash ads might cause your blog to load only partially or very slowly. If third-party code is causing a problem on your blog, you can notify the provider to try to find a solution, or you can delete it entirely.

If third-party code isn't the problem, there might be a problem with your hosting account. These are often temporary. Most hosting providers offer updates on known problems somewhere on their websites. Check with your hosting provider to learn if a problem is the cause.

Another possible culprit could be a plug-in. Deactivate all your plug-ins, clear your web browser's cache, and refresh your browser to view your live blog again. If your blog appears to be okay, reactivate each plug-in one at a time and check your blog after each is reactivated to ensure it still looks and works the way it should. Chances are, the problem will start again after the troublesome plug-in is reactivated.

Less likely but possible causes of the problem include issues with your theme files, which might require a reinstallation of your theme. It's also possible that a hacker has gotten access to your blog. Before you panic, take a deep breath, test plug-ins, contact your host, and reach out to a WordPress designer or developer who might be able to troubleshoot the problem quickly and save you a lot of time, money, and headaches. Often a problem that appears huge to you is actually very easy for a seasoned WordPress designer or developer to fix.

Which Widgets Should I Use in My Blog's Sidebar? *(WordPress.org and WordPress.com)*

When you log in to your WordPress dashboard and click the **Widgets** link under the Appearance section of your dashboard's left menu, you'll see a big selection of widgets you can add to your blog's sidebar (or footer, depending on the WordPress theme you're using). Some widgets are fairly standard from one WordPress theme to the next, but you might see some widgets you're not familiar with on your list. For example, WordPress.com users have access to a variety of WordPress community-related widgets unavailable to WordPress.org users. Which ones should you use, and why?

In this section, I go over what some of the most popular standard widgets do, as well as some of the other widgets you're likely to find in your WordPress theme. You can't know if you want to use them on your blog unless you know what they do!

When you visit the Widgets page in your WordPress dashboard, you can see that each available widget includes a short description that explains what it can be used for. Often, you can do more with these widgets than meets the eye. Following are tips for each of the widgets offered in the default Twenty Ten WordPress theme for self-hosted WordPress.org bloggers.

Akismet

The Akismet widget adds a small flash button to your blog that displays a current count of how many spam comments Akismet has detected on your blog. There's really no reason why you'd need to add this widget to your blog unless you like it. It adds no real value to the user experience on your blog and doesn't offer you any information you can't access through your WordPress dashboard.

My recommendation: skip it.

Archives

There are two schools of thought on the Archives widget, which enables you to display links for visitors to your blog to access your older posts by date. As shown in Figure B-8, you can configure the Archives widget to display your archived posts in the standard format, as a list of links by month, or you can check the box next to **Display as a drop down** so visitors can only access monthly links through a drop-down menu. You can also check the box next to **Show post counts** if you want the number of posts published each month to appear next to that month's link.

Test both options on your live blog to see how they look, and choose the style you prefer. However, be sure your blog can benefit from displaying archives before you do so. Use the decision points discussed in the remainder of this section to decide whether or not it's a good idea to show your archives in your sidebar and in what manner to display them.

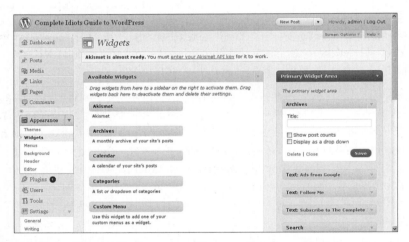

Figure B-8   *You can display your archives as a list of monthly links or in a drop-down menu.*

If your blog is brand new and has no archives or only a small number of posts in your archives, don't waste the space in your sidebar for the archives widget. If your visitors can click through all your blog posts within 5 to 10 pages of posts, it's not necessary to offer links to your blog archives. Also, some bloggers don't like to advertise that their blogs are brand new, thinking it might turn off visitors.

On the flip side, if your blog has been around for a long time or has a huge number of archived posts, displaying your archive links in your blog's sidebar could be useful. It establishes your blog as one that has staying power because visitors can see links to archives for many years. Second, it enables visitors to quickly find content published at a specific time. For example, visitors to a blog about toys might be interested in finding specific posts about toy recalls. If they know when the recall happened, they can search the archives for that month to find the post they need.

If your archive links are few in number, using the list option won't take up a lot of room and should be fine for your blog's sidebar. For blogs with a large number of archive links, the drop-down option offers a better use of sidebar space. Imagine a 5-year-old blog that displays a list of monthly archive links in its sidebar. That's 60 links! Surely that blogger could make better use of that space by publishing an archive drop-down menu.

Some bloggers prefer not to display archive links in their sidebars at all. Maybe their archives are not deep enough, or maybe they're too deep. Instead, they offer a search tool that enables visitors to search for older post content using keywords. In fact, a search tool is a must-have on all blogs. You can learn about the WordPress Search widget later in this section.

My recommendation: use the drop-down menu option and place the widget near the bottom of your sidebar so more useful information appears in priority positions.

Calendar

The Calendar widget might be a nice addition to your blog if you like calendars, but otherwise it doesn't add much value. When you add the Calendar widget to your blog's sidebar, a calendar appears in its place on your live blog. You can click on each date when a blog post was published to open a page with those posts on it.

My recommendation: skip it.

Categories

The Categories widget allows you to include a list of links to all the posts saved in specific categories in your blog's archives. Remember, as you write new blog posts, you can—and should—categorize them to help readers find related information. The Categories widget enables visitors to do just that!

Of course, you can play around with the settings to see how the widget display changes on your live blog before you decide how to set up your final configuration. When you configure the Categories widget, you'll have three options to choose from, as shown in Figure B-9.

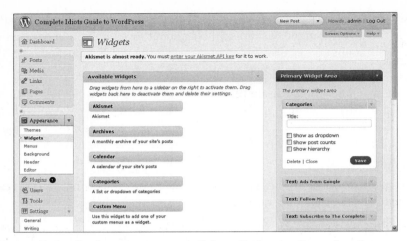

Figure B-9 *Configure your category links to display as a list or drop-down menu.*

If you have a long list of categories that would take up a lot of space in your blog's sidebar, check the box next to **Show as dropdown** to display links to your categories in a drop-down menu. If you want to show a count of the number of posts in a specific category, check the box next to **Show post counts**. If you set up your categories to include parent-child relationships (meaning some of your categories are subcategories of other categories), and you want that relationship to be evident to visitors using your categories links, check the box next to **Show hierarchy**. Click the **Save** button, and your category links will appear in your sidebar in the format you chose.

My recommendation: use the link list unless you have a long list of categories. If that's the case, use the drop-down option. If your categories include parent-child relationships, be sure you use the hierarchy option, too. You can place your category widget below the fold and save the above-the-fold space for ads or other priority information.

Custom Menus

Custom menus were introduced in Chapter 8 as an easy way to create fully customized navigation bar links on your WordPress blog. With the Custom Menus widget, you can add any of the custom menus you create from the Menus link in the Appearance section of your WordPress dashboard's left menu to your blog's sidebar.

My recommendation: it's unlikely you'll need this widget if your custom menus already appear in your blog's navigation bars. However, if your custom menus are not visible on your blog, your visitors might be happy to find the inclusion of those links in your blog's sidebar.

Links

You can use the Links widget to display any list of links you created using the tools in the Links section of your WordPress dashboard's left menu, including your blogroll, as discussed in Chapter 16.

My recommendation: if you created a list of links your visitors will find useful, adding it to your blog's sidebar is quick and easy.

Meta

The Meta widget provides a link to access your blog's WordPress dashboard login page, a link to log out of your WordPress account, a link to view your blog's RSS feed and comments feed, and a link to WordPress.org.

My recommendation: bookmark each of the links offered in the Meta widget in your local browser instead, and save the space in your blog's sidebar for information that adds value to the user experience rather than saves you some time.

Pages

The Pages widget adds a list of links to each of the pages published on your blog. If your pages aren't accessible through your blog's navigation bar or custom menus, but you want it to be easy for visitors to find them, the Pages widget could be useful.

As shown in Figure B-10, you can change the order your page links are sorted in your sidebar, and you can exclude specific pages from the list if you want to.

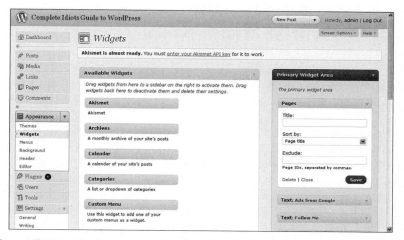

Figure B-10   *You can change the order of page links and exclude pages from the list in your sidebar.*

My recommendation: offer page links in your blog's top navigation bar and save the space in your sidebar for ads or other information that can't be accessed quickly and easily elsewhere on your blog.

Recent Comments

The Recent Comments widget allows you to display a list of links to the most recent comments visitors have left on your blog posts. You can configure the widget to display any number of recent comments you want; three to five is most common. The live widget will display the name provided in the comment submission form with a link to the URL provided. The title of the post where the comment was published appears as well, along with a link to that post.

Many bloggers like to display recent comments in their blogs' sidebars to show visitors that conversation is happening on their blogs. The theory is that visitors who find active blogs are more likely to perceive them as being good (or no one would join the conversation) and might even join the conversations, too. However, sometimes bloggers prefer not to highlight comments because they might not update frequently enough or they might not draw attention to the posts the blogger wants to make the focal point of the blog.

Some WordPress plug-ins can enhance the appearance of recent comments in your blog's sidebar. For example, the free Recent Comments with Gravatar WordPress plug-in (wordpress.org/extend/plugins/recent-comments-with-gravatar) adds gravatar images next to comments in the sidebar widget.

My recommendation: if comments on your blog are submitted frequently enough that the content of your blog's Comment widget changes at least several times a week, include it on your blog below the fold. If comments are very infrequent or may lead to spam, don't bother using the space on your sidebar to display comment links.

Recent Posts

The Recent Posts widget displays a list of links to the most recently published posts on your blog. You can choose how many post links to display in the widget, which will determine how long the list is. Of course, if your blog post titles are long, the list will take up more space in your sidebar.

My recommendation: most bloggers display 5 to 10 posts on their blog's home page. Some WordPress themes allow bloggers to display links and snippets to even more blog posts right on the home page. Skip this plug-in because it takes up space on your blog's sidebar with a list of posts a visitor can easily access from your blog's home page.

RSS

The RSS widget allows you to display links to recent posts on any other blog that has an RSS feed. As shown in Figure B-11, you can easily configure the RSS widget as long as you have the RSS feed URL for the feed you want to display.

You can get the RSS feed URL for any site that has an RSS feed by clicking the RSS icon in the web browser search field. This opens the XML feed page. Copy the URL for that page, and paste it in the **Enter the RSS feed URL here** text box. Enter a title for the feed in the **Give the feed a title (optional)** text box, and use the drop-down menu to select how many post links you want to include in your sidebar.

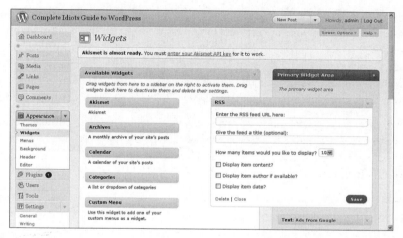

Figure B-11 *Just enter the RSS feed URL you want to display, and choose your display options.*

Depending on how much space you want the RSS widget to take up in your blog's sidebar, you might want to check the box next to one or more of the other options available to you as you configure the widget. If you select the **Display item content?** box, a snippet of content appears with each link item in the list in your blog's sidebar. If you select the **Display item author if available?** box, the author of the item will appear with the link. If you select the **Display item date?** box, the publication date will appear with the item link. Feel free to play around with these configurations and view the changes on your live blog to see what works best in your sidebar.

When you click the **Save** button, the widget goes live on your blog. Figure B-12 shows what three different RSS widgets look like in a blog's widgetized footer with just links displayed in each widget without item content, item author, or item date.

RSS widgets are helpful in promoting your other websites or blogs because they display links to your content. You can build traffic to another site or blog, or simply offer links to content you think your blog readers will find useful.

My recommendation: if you want to build traffic to another blog or website, use the RSS widget in your blog's sidebar or footer.

Figure B-12 *The RSS widget is a great way to send traffic to other sites and offer more valuable information to your readers.*

Search

The Search widget adds a keyword search box to your blog. Users can only search within your blog's contents using this search tool. It takes up very little space and can be very helpful to visitors.

My recommendation: use it if your blog's theme does not come with a built-in search box or tool.

Tag Cloud

The Tag Cloud widget enables you to display a bunch of links in your blog's sidebar that help visitors find relevant posts you've tagged with specific keywords. Tags used most often appear in larger and bolder font in the tag cloud than tags used infrequently.

Some bloggers like tag clouds because they're very precise with their tagging efforts. In fact, some bloggers display tag clouds rather than a Categories widget. Whether you choose to display a tag cloud or not depends on how you tag and categorize posts when you write them. Only you can decide if tag or category links would be more helpful to your blog visitors when they're looking for content related to specific keywords or topics.

My recommendation: use a Tag Cloud or Categories widget, depending on whether your tagging or categorization efforts are more useful to visitors. Using both in your sidebar is redundant and steals space from other information and monetization efforts.

Text

The Text widget is the catch-all widget that can help you extend your blog's sidebar in many ways. As discussed throughout this book, you can use Text widgets to display ads, images, videos, links, and much more.

My recommendation: use it, and use it often.

What Is a Favicon, and How Can I Get One for My Blog? (WordPress.org)

A favicon is a small image that appears before your blog's URL in visitors' web browser search bars and next to your blog's bookmark listing in their browser bookmarks or favorites drop-down lists. Favicons help people who have a lot of saved bookmarks or favorites easily find your blog in a long list. They also make your blog look a bit more professional.

To add a favicon to your blog, you first need to create your favicon file, which is a 16×16-pixel image. Once you have your favicon file, you need to convert it into .ico format and name it favicon.ico. Fortunately, a number of websites automate the conversion process for you. I've used the Dynamic Drive FavIcon Generator (tools.dynamicdrive.com/favicon), as shown in Figure B-13.

Figure B-13   *Upload your favicon image to create your blog's favicon.ico file.*

Click the **Browse...** button to locate your favicon file on your hard drive. You can upload files in .png, .jpg, .gif, or .bmp format, but the uploaded file must be less than 150 kilobytes. Select your file, and click the **Create Icon** button.

Once your new favicon.ico file has been created, log in to your web hosting account, navigate to your blog's root directory, and upload the file to that directory. For example, your favicon file should be accessible at yoursitename.com/favicon.ico after it's uploaded.

Next, you need to add some code into the header.php file of your WordPress theme that tells web browsers where to find your favicon. To do this, log in to your WordPress dashboard and click the **Editor** link in the Appearance section of your dashboard's left menu to open your theme editor. Find the **header.php** file in the list of files on the right side of your screen, and click it to open it in your editor, shown in Figure B-14.

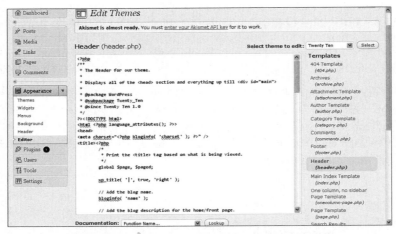

Figure B-14   *You'll insert the necessary HTML code in your header.php file.*

Enter the following code between the <head> and </head> tags in your header.php file:

```
<link rel="shortcut icon" type="image/x-icon" href="/favicon.ico">
```

Click the **Save** button, and you're done. You can refresh your live blog's browser page to see your favicon, but it might take a couple days for your favicon to show up in front of your blog's URL in your browser address bar.

What Free WordPress Plug-Ins Are Recommended for Blogs Starting to Receive Some Traffic and Comments? *(WordPress.org)*

Congratulations! Your blog is beginning to attract visitors and conversations, and you're on your way to becoming a successful blogger. It's safe to say you're passed the "beginner blogger" stage and you're ready to start testing some additional WordPress plug-ins that can make your life easier and help your blog grow even more. This section introduces you to a variety of plug-ins to get you started, depending on your objectives and needs. Be sure to read Chapter 18 for more plug-in suggestions.

Plug-Ins to Make Blog Management Easier and Enhance the User Experience

Fortunately, you can speed up many maintenance tasks or make those tasks less noticeable to your blog visitors with a variety of free WordPress plug-ins. Blogging can take a lot of time. Why not streamline activities when you can with some handy plug-ins?

Theme Test Drive (wordpress.org/extend/plugins/theme-test-drive): Give a theme a test drive on your blog without visitors seeing it with the Theme Test Drive plug-in.

WP Maintenance Mode (wordpress.org/extend/plugins/wp-maintenance-mode): Don't worry about visitors seeing your blog mid-redesign. Instead, show a customized splash page letting them know your blog is temporarily under construction with the WP Maintenance Mode plug-in. You can see two example splash pages in Figure B-15.

Figure B-15 *You can customize the splash pages available with the WP Maintenance Mode plug-in with your own information.*

WP-DB-Backup (wordpress.org/extend/plugins/wp-db-backup): Use the WP-DB-Backup plug-in to automatically back up your core WordPress files.

Math Comment Spam Protection (wordpress.org/extend/plugins/math-comment-spam-protection): Reduce the number of spam comments submitted to your blog posts with the Math Comment Spam Protection plug-in.

W3 Total Cache (wordpress.org/extend/plugins/w3-total-cache): To speed up the load time of your pages so visitors won't get impatient and click away, use the W3 Total Cache plug-in.

Bad Behavior (wordpress.org/extend/plugins/bad-behavior): The Bad Behavior plug-in helps block spam link comments and the robots that submit them.

WordPress Plug-Ins to Boost Traffic

A number of free plug-ins can help you get more search engine traffic to your blog, as well as traffic from across the social web. By enhancing SEO on your blog and allowing visitors to share your posts and e-mail them to friends, traffic will grow organically.

All in One SEO Pack (wordpress.org/extend/plugins/all-in-one-seo-pack): The All in One SEO Pack plug-in adds a special section to your blog post editor where you can add a better search optimized title, description, and keyword tags. It's one of the most popular free WordPress plug-ins.

Google XML Sitemaps (wordpress.org/extend/plugins/google-sitemap-generator): You can add a linked sitemap to your blog, which is a great way to boost search engine rankings and help search engines like Google crawl and index your blog content. The Google XML Sitemaps plug-in is another of the most popular free WordPress plug-ins.

AddThis (wordpress.org/extend/plugins/addthis): Make it easy for visitors to share your blog posts with their social media audiences with the AddThis plug-in.

TweetMeme Button (wordpress.org/extend/plugins/tweetmeme-button): The retweet button from TweetMeme is one of the best tools for enabling blog visitors to share your posts with their Twitter audiences.

AddToAny: Share/Bookmark/Email Button (wordpress.org/extend/plugins/add-to-any): The AddToAny: Share/Bookmark/Email button enables visitors to easily share links to your blog posts with their social media audiences, *and* it enables them to e-mail those links using a variety of e-mail applications.

SubHeading (wordpress.org/extend/plugins/subheading): You can add a subtitle to any blog post, which can make your blog post more intriguing and could help with search engine optimization, too.

WordPress Plug-Ins to Increase Interactivity

These plug-ins provide different opportunities for visitors to get involved in the activities happening on your blog. Increased interactivity enhances relationships and reader loyalty.

CommentLuv (wordpress.org/extend/plugins/commentluv): Many bloggers like this plug-in because it automatically displays a link to a blogger's most recent blog post (based on the URL they include in the post comment form) with his or her published comment on your blog. You can see the CommentLuv plug-in on a live blog in Figure B-16.

Subscribe to Comments (wordpress.org/extend/plugins/subscribe-to-comments): To keep visitors apprised of new comments added to blog posts they already submitted a comment to, use the Subscribe to Comments plug-in. This helps them stay active in ongoing conversations on your blog.

Figure B-16 *The CommentLuv plug-in provides incoming links to comment authors' blogs.*

WP Greet Box (wordpress.org/extend/plugins/wp-greet-box): Display a special message to visitors depending on how they arrived on your blog. For example, a visitor who finds your blog from a Digg submission receives a different message from a visitor who arrives to your blog from a Google search. Figure B-17 shows screenshots of the WP Greet Box plug-in in action.

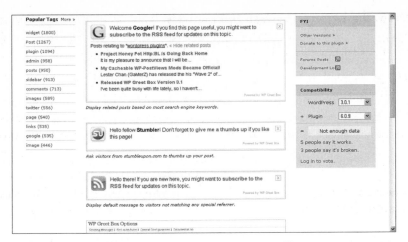

Figure B-17 *The WP Greet Box plug-in displays a different message to visitors coming to your blog from different sites.*

The Events Calendar (wordpress.org/extend/plugins/the-events-calendar): If you attend events or want to promote events related to your blog, then you can display an interactive calendar on your blog using The Events Calendar plug-in.

TDO Mini Forms (wordpress.org/extend/plugins/tdo-mini-forms): This free WordPress plug-in enables visitors to your blog to submit more than traditional contact form information. With the TDO Mini Forms plug-in, visitors can also submit draft posts and pages, which you can edit, approve, and publish on your blog.

Snazzy Archives (wordpress.org/extend/plugins/snazzy-archives): Make your archives interactive with the Snazzy Archives plug-in that allows you to create a calendar sitemap complete with images, videos, special effects, and more.

WordPress Plug-Ins to Help Make Money from Your Blog

Try any of these plug-ins to make it easier to place and fill ad space on your blog. More ad space = more money!

WP125 (wordpress.org/extend/plugins/wp125): This plug-in makes it easy to display and manage 125×125-pixel button ads in your blog's sidebar.

Another WordPress Classifieds Plugin (wordpress.org/extend/plugins/another-wordpress-classifieds-plugin): Place classified ads on your blog in a snap with the Another WordPress Classifieds Plugin.

Advertising Manager (wordpress.org/extend/plugins/advertising-manager): This plug-in makes the process of placing and rotating Google AdSense ads quick and easy.

Easy Ads (wordpress.org/extend/plugins/easy-ads): You can manage the placement of ads from multiple ad programs from your WordPress dashboard (including Google AdSense, Bidvertiser, Chitika, and Clicksor) using the Easy Ads plug-in.

Wp-Insert (wordpress.org/extend/plugins/wp-insert): Manage multiple ad networks, place ads in multiple locations on your blog, style ads, and much more.

All in One Adsense and YPN (wordpress.org/extend/plugins/all-in-one-adsense-and-ypn): Automatically insert Google AdSense and Yahoo! Publisher Network ads into multiple positions on your blog at any time. You can also configure color, position, and display options with the All in One Adsense and YPN plug-in.

WP e-Commerce (wordpress.org/extend/plugins/wp-e-commerce): Add a shopping cart to your WordPress blog with the WP e-Commerce Shopping Cart plug-in.

Should I Set Up My Blog for a Full or Partial Feed? *(WordPress.org and WordPress.com)*

As mentioned in Chapter 7, the debate over whether online publishers should offer full or partial feeds has been ongoing for many years, with people on both sides of the discussion. Only you can decide whether you want to offer subscribers a full or partial feed to your blog based on your blogging goals. There are pros and cons to both feed options. Take some time to evaluate your long-term blogging goals against the pros and cons of both feed options so you can make the best decision for your blog.

When you provide a full feed to subscribers of your blog, the entire content of your blog posts is visible in their feed readers or e-mail messages, depending on the method they choose to receive subscription updates. That means they can read all your new content without visiting your blog at all. Many bloggers view this as a guaranteed way to reduce the amount of traffic and page views a blog gets each day, and that's a valid argument in the defense of partial blog feeds. If blog traffic and page views are your top blogging goals, a partial feed might be a better choice for your blog.

On the other hand, partial feeds deliver only a truncated version of your new blog posts to subscribers, followed by a **Read More** link, subscribers must click to visit your blog and read the remainder of the posts that interest them. Certainly, partial feeds can retain some of your blog's traffic (assuming your new posts are interesting enough that subscribers actually click on the **Read More** links in their feeds to visit your blog and read the rest).

However, partial feeds can also frustrate subscribers, particularly those viewing your feed on mobile devices. It takes more time and effort to click on the **Read More** link to finish reading your posts. It can be difficult to retain a loyal audience if readers are not motivated enough to click through to finish all your content. If they don't actually visit your blog, they can't leave a comment and build your blog through comment conversations.

Also, if subscribers don't actually visit your blog to read your entire post, they're less likely to share your posts through social networking, Twitter, social bookmarking, and so on, which reduces the reach of your content. Partial feeds might hurt your long-term blogging growth goals because they can reduce conversations and sharing of your content both on and off your blog.

Years ago, the number of subscribers a blog had was a badge of honor to be displayed proudly in the blog's sidebar. Today, that's not necessarily as true. That's because the *reach* of your blog, meaning how far your content spreads across the social web, can be a much bigger factor in the growth and success of a blog than the number of subscribers.

If long-term growth is most important to you, offering full feeds is probably a better choice for your blog. However, if ensuring you get as many page views as possible in the short-term is most important to you (for example, if you're trying to increase interest and potential earnings from advertisers in the near future), partial feeds could be more beneficial to you today.

The most important factor when choosing between full and partial feeds for your blog is goal setting and evaluation, but you must constantly reevaluate those goals and track your feed's performance. You won't know if you should change from a partial to a full feed or vice versa unless you analyze performance and communicate with your audience. This helps you better understand what they want and need from your blog so you can configure your blog, including feeds, to meet their expectations.

Do I Need to Submit My Blog to Search Engines to Get Included in Search Results? *(WordPress.org and WordPress.com)*

No. It can speed up the process of getting included in search results, but most search engines find new content quickly enough that manual submission isn't necessary. Instead, spend that time creating great content on your blog and linking together your blog, Twitter profile, Facebook page, and so on.

How Can I Change the RSS Feed Icon and Subscription Links in My Sidebar So They Look Nicer?

As you travel across the blogosphere, you'll undoubtedly find many blogs with RSS feed subscription icons and links that look a lot better than the standard ones offered through your FeedBurner account. That's because bloggers like to draw attention to their feed subscription links to boost subscribers, and the icons offered through FeedBurner are boring in comparison to some of the options freely available to you through a simple Google search for "social media icons."

Also, many bloggers like to list links to their RSS feed subscription page alongside links for their Facebook, LinkedIn, Twitter, and other social media accounts. Using a set of icons meant to be displayed together looks much better than using a random selection of icons placed haphazardly in your blog's sidebar.

Fortunately, it's not hard to change your feed subscription icon and links in your blog's sidebar in the vast majority of WordPress themes. If a subscription box is already included in your blog, delete it and replace it with your own. For most themes, you can simply add a new text widget to your blog's sidebar and paste in code for the image you want to use as your subscription link. It really is that easy.

Find a great selection of free subscription icons and other social media icons at www. wpmods.com/ultimate-social-media-icon-list; scroll to the bottom of the post to see RSS icons only. For example, the list includes a link to the creative RSS/Feed Icon set created by Dirceu Veiga for Smashing Magazine and a great Mini Cooper RSS icon from www.s-w.deviantart.com, shown in Figure B-18.

Figure B-18   *Some RSS/feed icons take on the shapes of everyday objects.*

Simply download the RSS icon you want to use on your blog, and save it to your computer hard drive. Next, upload that icon to your WordPress account by selecting the **Add New** link in the Media section of your WordPress dashboard's left menu. Upload the file as you would any other image file, and copy the URL of the uploaded file.

Next, add a text widget to your blog's sidebar, and enter the following code where the first URL represents the page where people can subscribe to your blog via feed reader or e-mail and the second URL represents the image file you just uploaded.

```
<a href="http://feeds.feedburner.com/YourSiteHere"><img src="http://
    www.YourSiteName.com/IconImageName.png"></a>
```

The page you want to link your RSS icon to is shown in Figure B-19. Note that this page is the FeedBurner URL for your blog's feed and is typically formatted as http://feeds. feedburner.com/SiteNameUsedinYourFeedBurnerAccount. You can get this URL from your FeedBurner account if you need to confirm it.

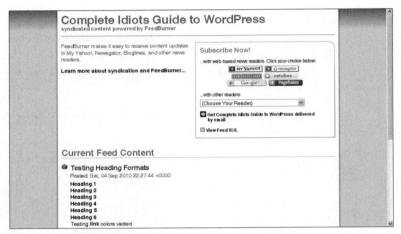

Figure B-19 *Link your RSS icon to your blog's FeedBurner subscription page.*

To add icon links to your other social media profiles, simply follow the same steps and add the necessary code immediately following the RSS feed code provided earlier. Just replace the image URL with the URL for the appropriate social media icon after uploading it to your WordPress account, and replace the link URL with the URL for the appropriate social media profile page.

For example, the complete code inserted into a text widget to display the social media icon links shown in Figure B-20 follows:

```
<a href="http://www.facebook.com/profile.php?id=634924440"><img
    src="http://www.womenonbusiness.com/facebook7.png"></a><a
    href="http://www.linkedin.com/in/susangunelius"><img src="http://
    www.womenonbusiness.com/linkedin.png"></a><a href="http://www.
    twitter.com/susangunelius"><img src="http://www.womenonbusiness.
    com/twitter10.png"></a><a href="http://www.keysplashcreative.
    com"><img src="http://www.womenonbusiness.com/keysplash1.png"></
    a><a href="mailto:susan@womenonbusiness.com"><img src="http://www.
    womenonbusiness.com/email.png"></a>
```

Figure B-20 *Feed and social media icons look great displayed together in a blog's sidebar.*

Notice that each image appears immediately next to the image before it in this example. You can do the same with a text widget on your blog. Just be sure the image icons you use are small enough to fit across your blog's sidebar by comparing their width to the width of your blog's sidebar.

Many web users are accustomed to finding subscription and other social media icon links grouped together in an easy-to-find place on blogs and websites. It's a good idea to provide yours to increase your online relationships, which then helps build your blog's audience in the long term.

Which Twitter Apps Should I Use to Make My Blog More Successful?

Many Twitter applications are available for free. Depending on your blogging goals, some Twitter apps will be more helpful to you than others. Don't be afraid to test a variety of Twitter apps. You can't break your Twitter account by doing so!

Also, don't be surprised if applications require access to your Twitter account information in order for them to work. Just as WordPress plug-ins have to be connected to your WordPress account to work, Twitter apps must be able to connect with your Twitter account to work. If you're concerned about the security related to a specific Twitter app, take a few minutes to conduct a Google search on that Twitter app to see what other Twitter users have to say about it before you make your decision to experiment with it.

Keep in mind, the purpose of using Twitter and many Twitter apps is to build your online audience and create more opportunities for your blog content to be shared across the web. Some Twitter apps can help you find people and conversations happening at any given moment in time. You can join those conversations and offer links to your useful blog content, or simply begin building relationships with people who are likely to be interested in your blog content in the future.

TweetDeck (www.tweetdeck.com): TweetDeck is an excellent Twitter app for time management and organization. With TweetDeck, you can separate your Twitter audience into groups so it's easier to stay on top of conversations. TweetDeck must be downloaded to your computer desktop to work, but you can manage all Twitter activities without leaving your TweetDeck screen, including posting tweets, retweeting, and sending direct messages. You can see TweetDeck in action in Figure B-21.

TweetDeck only works with Windows-based PCs. If you use a Mac, twhirl (www.twhirl. org) is a good alternative.

Monitter (www.monitter.com): Monitter is one of the best apps to keep track of real-time local conversations on Twitter related to keywords you select.

Twellow (www.twellow.com): You can use Twellow to create a listing for your blog, similar to how you might create a listing in the Yellow Pages.

Localtweeps (www.localtweeps.com): Localtweeps enables you to search for Twitter users by keywords, zip code, or city. You can also publish local events you might be holding on Localtweeps.

Figure B-21   *TweetDeck can help you stay organized.*

Twitterfeed (twitterfeed.com): Twitterfeed is a must-have Twitter app you can use to automatically feed your blog post content to your Twitter and Facebook profiles.

WeFollow (wefollow.com): You can use WeFollow to find Twitter users based on keywords and categories they use to flag their own WeFollow listings. You can also create your own WeFollow listing. Be sure to use keywords the target audience for your blog would be likely to search for.

SocialOomph (www.socialoomph.com): SocialOomph offers a wide variety of useful tools. For example, you can use SocialOomph to schedule tweets to publish in your Twitter stream at a specific time in the future. This is a great feature if you want to be sure tweets publish throughout the day even though you can't always be logged in to your Twitter account and actively participating.

TweetMeme (tweetmeme.com): This is another must-have Twitter application. With TweetMeme, you can add the **Retweet** button to your blog, and you can retweet content you like to your own Twitter followers with a click of your mouse. You need to create a TweetMeme account and link your Twitter profile with TweetMeme in order to be able to retweet content you like using the **Retweet** button found on other websites and blogs.

Should I Pay for WordPress.com Upgrades, or Switch to WordPress.org? *(WordPress.org and WordPress.com)*

WordPress.com is a great tool for blogging novices who want to test the blogging waters to determine if they like being an online publisher or not. Once you decide you want to take blogging seriously, you need to evaluate your long-term blogging goals. Switching from WordPress.com to WordPress.org is easy, but there are inherent negatives to making the switch you need to be aware of.

For example, if your blog's URL changes (which it will if you switch from WordPress.com to WordPress.org), you'll lose all your blog's search engine rankings, incoming links, bookmarks from visitors, and so on. Your blog feed URL will also change. If you think you might want to blog for any reason other than to have some fun, you need to consider using WordPress.org sooner rather than later.

In terms of paying for WordPress.com upgrades, I don't recommend it. You can get all the functionality WordPress.com upgrades provide and much more by self-hosting your blog and using the blogging application from WordPress.org. It's also cheaper in the long run to use the self-hosted WordPress.org application than it is to pay for WordPress.com application upgrades.

The problem for most beginner bloggers is that they've never dealt with blog hosting and don't even understand many of the terms they have to encounter as they create a self-hosted WordPress blog. Fortunately, everything you need to know is included in Part 4 of this book. If you follow those chapters as you set up your WordPress.org blog, the process of dealing with web hosting, using FTP, and creating your blog is easy! Once WordPress is installed, you'll find that blogging with the WordPress.org application is the same as blogging with the WordPress.com application. You just have more options available to you to enhance your blog!

So I guess my answer to this question is simple. If you're new to blogging, start a new test blog on any subject you enjoy using the free application at WordPress.com. You can set up your test blog to be private if you want and even delete it later. Play around with the various features and functions available to you, so you get comfortable using the WordPress application.

When you feel somewhat confident with WordPress, you can decide if blogging is right for you or not. If you decide to join the blogosphere with a real blog (rather than your test blog), and you have blogging goals that include growing your online audience or making money, start your real blog with WordPress.org. Once you get over the process of creating your actual first self-hosted blog, you'll realize how easy it actually is!

Why Should I Let Other People Write Guest Blog Posts on My Blog? Why Should I Try to Write Guest Posts on Blogs I Don't Own? *(WordPress.org and WordPress.com)*

In simplest terms, a guest blog post is an unpaid post written by one blogger to be published on another blogger's site. Guest blogging is an excellent way to boost traffic to your blog because it puts your amazing content, your name, and a link to your blog in front of a new audience. Guest blog posts usually include a link back to the writer's blog and a brief writer's biography.

If you look for blogs with larger audiences than your own who are interested in the same type of content you publish on your blog, offering your knowledge and perspective to that audience with a guest post puts you in front of an audience who is likely to be interested in what you have to say. Many of them will want to hear more from you or engage in conversations with you, which means they'll follow the link in your guest post to read more of your blog. They might even start to follow you on Twitter or connect with you on Facebook.

A guest post can directly and indirectly increase traffic to your blog and help you build relationships with a wider audience than you can reach on your own. When your guest posts are published on sites more popular than your own, you'll also get valuable incoming links to your blog, which can help boost your Google search rankings and drive more traffic to your blog from keyword searches in the future.

Furthermore, guest blogging puts you on the radar screens of the owners of blogs related to your blog topic. Some of those bloggers might be influential in the online community and are likely to be important connections for you to make.

Looking at guest blogging from the other side, accepting guest posts on your own blog can help you, too. Some guest bloggers might bring their own audiences to your blog when they promote their guest blog post. Publishing guest blog posts also gives you a day off from writing content and can bring a fresh new voice and perspective to your blog that could elicit comments and sharing from your audience. Just be sure to create a page on your blog that explains any requirements related to submitting guest posts for possible publication on your blog. Remember, it's your blog, and you reserve the right to publish or not publish guest posts as you see fit.

Bottom line: you have nothing to lose and everything to gain from guest blogging. Be sure to check Chapter 21 for links to sites that can help you find guest bloggers or offer your services as a guest blogger.

How Can I Hold a Blog Contest? *(WordPress.org and WordPress.com)*

Blog contests can drive a significant amount of short-term traffic to your blog, particularly if you're offering a great prize and promote your contest on some of the sites mentioned in Chapter 21. The key to running a successful blog contest is making sure you set it up for success from the beginning.

The first steps are to secure a prize, define the entry rules, establish how the prize will be shipped to the winner, and write the blog contest announcement post. For example, you need to know if you'll be responsible for shipping the prize to the winner or if the company providing the prize (if there is a sponsor) will ship the prize. Keep in mind, shipping a contest prize might be tax deductible; check with your tax professional for confirmation.

Once your contest is structured, you can announce it on your blog with a call for entries. Be sure to explain the contest and rules in detail in the announcement post. For example, include the following elements:

Prize description: Be honest and thorough.

Eligibility: If there are age or shipping restrictions, include them in your post.

Entry method: Explain what people have to do to get an entry into the contest.

How winners are chosen: Explain if winners are chosen in a random drawing of all comments left on the contest post (recommended for ease), randomly amongst entrants who complete a specific task (such as following you on Twitter or tweeting the contest link to their followers; recommended for the best promotional results), or using a subjective method (for example, the best response to a specific question).

How alternate winners are chosen: Let people know how winners will be contacted and what they must do to claim their prizes. Also, explain how alternate winners are chosen if the original winners don't respond within a specified time frame.

Entry deadline: Give a specific time and date, and be sure to include the time zone.

Once your contest post is published, you can promote your giveaway on the sites listed in Chapter 21. Be sure to promote your contest with an intriguing title that tells readers what the prize is so you get the most traffic and entries!

Should I Create a Facebook Profile, Page, or Group for My Blog? Do I Have to Use LinkedIn, Twitter, and Other Social Tools, Too? *(WordPress.org and WordPress.com)*

If you want to achieve maximum growth for your blog, the more activities you can participate in across the social web, the better. However, it's unrealistic to think a blogger can effectively manage a blog, Facebook profile, Facebook page, Facebook group, LinkedIn profile, LinkedIn group, Twitter profile, and more. There simply aren't enough hours in the day for a typical blogger to stay active on all the social sites available and still create amazing blog content.

The answer to these questions depends on your blogging goals and personal preferences. Test the various tools available, and learn which ones you actually enjoy using. For example, if you love Twitter, that's great! Use it! However, if you don't enjoy using Twitter but you like Facebook, that's fine, too.

Quality trumps quantity when it comes to building long-term sustainable growth to your blog. Focus your efforts on the tools you enjoy, and your conversations and interactions will come naturally rather than forcefully when you use a tool you don't like.

If you do enjoy Facebook, you'll be faced with three types of destinations: a profile, a page, and a group. You have to have a Facebook profile because that's your personal space on Facebook. Without a profile, you can't create a page or group. So create your profile and start interacting!

Next, create a page for your blog. Pages are open to anyone and have a wider reach than groups. Anyone can "like" your Facebook page.

Groups are great for smaller niche users who want to discuss specific topics in more detail. As your blog grows, you might want to start Facebook groups where your audience can interact in greater detail about specific areas of interest. Some of your blog readers might even start Facebook groups related to your blog or your blog's topic, which you should join.

Start small and be sure the quality of your content and conversations doesn't deteriorate because you're spreading yourself too thin. You can always add more accounts and social destinations to your repertoire at a later date.

Comment Moderation Takes Too Much Time. Is It Really Necessary? *(WordPress.org and WordPress.com)*

The simple answer to this question is no. Comment moderation is not necessary. Remember, it's your blog, and you can configure it to perform anyway you want. However, for the best user experience on your blog, it's important to moderate comments.

Comment moderation is important to your blog's readers because it ...

- Removes spam comments that add nothing to the conversation.

- Removes comments that are ads or published for no reason other than to build incoming links to another site.

- Removes offensive comments.

- Removes comments that are hateful or attack a person or entity.

The conversations that happen on your blog through the commenting feature are what make your blog interactive and help you build relationships with your readers. Comments also help your readers build relationships with each other. When a community develops around a blog, that blog has hit a significant success milestone. That community of loyal readers is likely to share content on your blog with their own audiences, talk about you and your blog with other people, and keep the conversation going when you're too busy to join it. It's essential that you moderate comments to ensure your loyal readers don't have to sift through spam and negativity to find the valuable conversations they expect on your blog.

Comment moderation can be time-consuming as your blog attracts more legitimate and spam comments. You can teach yourself how to identify spam comments, so you can spot them and delete them more quickly by following these tips:

- *Gibberish comments:* These comments are filled with text and words that make no sense.

- *Excessively complimentary comments:* Over-the-top complimentary comments that add nothing to the conversation.

- *Off-topic comments:* Comments that have nothing to do with the blog post topic.

- *Suspicious URL comments:* Comments that include a suspicious URL in the comment submission form for the sole purpose of driving traffic to that site or to a spam site.

- *Link-filled comments:* Comments that include more than one or two links related to the blog post topic.

Also see Chapter 7 for a variety of suggestions related to configuring your comment moderation settings to reduce spam and make the moderation process more streamlined.

Is It Okay to Require Visitors to Register in Order to Leave Comments on My Blog Posts? *(WordPress.org and WordPress.com)*

Let me put it this way: the more restrictions and requirements you put in place in an effort to reduce spam or useless comments from being submitted to your blog, the more overall comments and conversation will decrease. If your goal is to grow your blog and the traffic to it, leave commenting open to anyone, as recommended in the configuration suggestions found in Chapter 7.

Requiring registration, log in, or personally identifying information absolutely helps keep comments on point and helpful. However, even honest visitors don't always like to identify themselves or take the time to register or log in to submit a comment on a blog post. People expect a free flow of information across the social web without barriers to entry or sharing. Most expect that from blog commenting as well. Therefore, open the doors and let them in, but be sure to moderate closely!

Of course, if you're writing your blog simply for fun with no objectives related to growth or monetization, then by all means, go ahead and restrict commenting to registered users or visitors who identify themselves with an Open ID username and password or other personal information.

Should I Allow Pings and Trackbacks on My Blog Posts? *(WordPress.org and WordPress.com)*

I'm going to answer that question with a question: do you want to grow your blog's audience and increase traffic? If your answer to that question is yes, the answer to whether you should allow pings and trackbacks on your blog post should also be yes.

Trackbacks are basically comments published on your blog posts from other blogs. When another blogger links to one of your blog posts on her blog, that blogging application pings your blog to confirm it exists and to provide an electronic notification that the link has been published. If your blog accepts pings, it will receive the ping from the other blogger's blog. If your blog accepts trackbacks, a comment will automatically be published on your blog post that includes a link back to the other blogger's blog.

Let me try to explain using fictitious blogs and bloggers. Imagine that John writes a blog about Hawaii travel called "Aloha from John," and he published a post about a luau he attended and enjoyed. Now, imagine that Ann writes a blog about family travel, called "Family Travel Tips" and found John's post about the specific luau he attended with his review of it. She decides to write a post on "Family Travel Tips" about luaus in Hawaii that are perfect for families and, after reading his review, wants to include the luau John referenced. Ann writes her post and decides to link back to John's post where her audience can get more details from John's personal review. When Ann publishes her post, her blog pings John's "Aloha from John" blog. John's blog is configured to accept pings and trackbacks, so Ann's trackback comment, complete with a link back to her post on "Family Travel Tips," is published in the post comments section on John's blog.

Both John and Ann benefit from the trackback. John's blog might get incoming traffic from Ann's link, and he learns who Ann is and that she's interested enough in his content to share it in a link to her audience. Ann benefits from the published trackback on John's blog, which could send some traffic to her blog. The trackback also puts her on John's radar screen, which could lead to more opportunities for sharing content, links, and so on with John and his audience in the future.

Now, back to the question of whether you should accept pings and trackbacks on your blog. The answer is always yes if you want to grow your blog's audience and traffic. Just be sure to keep your eyes open for spam trackbacks that come from sites that simply republish content from other blogs and websites along with lots of ads in an effort to get incoming links and traffic to those plagiarized spam sites.

Can I Really Make Money from a WordPress Blog? (WordPress.com and WordPress.org)

If you use the WordPress.com blogging application, the answer to this question is no. The WordPress.com terms of service clearly state users may not monetize their blogs in any way.

If you use the self-hosted WordPress.org blogging application, the answer to this question is yes. Of course, the amount of money you can make ranges from a few dollars per month to thousands of dollars per month, depending on several factors:

- The amount of traffic your blog gets.
- The content of your blog.
- The demographics of your audience.
- The amount of time you dedicate to monetizing your blog.

In simplest terms, the more traffic your blog gets, the more advertisers are willing to pay for ad space on your blog and the more people are likely to click on ads on your blog. That means more money for you. Also, blogs that offer highly focused, niche content to an audience advertisers really want to reach can make more money than blogs about broad, highly competitive topics or blogs with less-coveted consumer audiences.

Making money from your blog is possible, and many bloggers have worked hard for years to reach a point where they make full-time incomes from their blogs. However, it takes time, patience, and dedication to reach that point. You need to continually tweak your efforts, test new opportunities, track performance, and adjust your strategy to find the recipe for success for your blog.

Keep in mind, that recipe might not be the same one that works for another blogger. There's no single road map for blog monetization success. It's up to you to carve out your own path. If you stick with it, you'll get there. Remember, the foundation of all your efforts comes from your amazing content and audience relationships.

Do I Need to Know HTML and CSS to Use the Self-Hosted WordPress Application? *(WordPress.org)*

You do not need to know HTML or CSS to use the self-hosted WordPress application from WordPress.org. However, every little bit of HTML and CSS you learn can make your life a bit easier and enable you to customize your blog a bit more.

For example, if you don't like the size of your blog's sidebar or can't figure out why text formatted with a header tag can't appear on the same line in a blog post with any other content, a tiny bit of CSS knowledge can help you make the necessary adjustments to fix both problems.

Frankly, much of the coding within the CSS files of your WordPress blog's theme is fairly intuitive. While the code in the php files is a bit harder to interpret, even the most technologically impaired individuals can read CSS code and make simple changes.

The Parts of a WordPress Theme

It's important to point out that some tricks to CSS can make what appears to be a simple change more complicated. For example, CSS is called cascading style sheets because code *cascades* down from one to the next. Parent codes influence child codes, and sometimes making a change in one place won't produce the effects you want in your live blog. You also need to know where to look for code, because your theme includes multiple template files.

Here are the most common files you'll find in your WordPress dashboard Editor screen:

Stylesheet: Style.css is the file that provides all the layout and global attribute settings for your blog, including fonts, layout, spacing, and so on.

Main index: Index.php is the file that pulls your blog together. It pulls your posts (referred to as "the loop" part of your theme's code) and inserts them into the appropriate place on your blog. It includes a direction to display the header, the posts in reverse chronological order with post author, and so on (depending on the specific theme code), the sidebar, and the footer.

Loop: Loop.php is used in some WordPress themes to save the loop code used in the Index.php template file.

Header: Header.php is the file that tells browsers your blog's title (to display in the title bar), the RSS feed URL, the blog URL, the tagline, the header image, and where the CSS Stylesheet is.

Footer: Footer.php is the file responsible for displaying the content that runs across the width of the bottom of your blog.

Sidebar: Sidebar.php is the file that sets up your blog's sidebar. If your blog uses more than one sidebar, your theme will have multiple sidebar files.

Single Post: Single.php is the file that displays one post on a single post page with comments (if enabled) and the comment form.

Comments: Comments.php is the template file that displays comments published on posts.

Page: Page.php is the template file used to display single pages in WordPress blogs (separate from single post pages). If your WordPress theme offers more than one page layout, your theme will have more than one page template file.

Search: Search.php is the template file used to display search results conducted using the search widget.

404 Template: 404.php is the template file that displays a special 404 Page Cannot be Found error message if a link within your blog leads to a URL that cannot be found (for example, the link URL is wrong or the page was deleted).

Archives: Archives.php is included in some WordPress themes to display archived posts when called up by date.

Category: Category.php is used in some WordPress themes to display archived posts when called up by category.

Tags: Tag.php is used in some WordPress themes to display archived posts when called up by tag.

Author: Author.php is used in some WordPress themes to display archived posts when called up by author.

Attachment: Attachment.php is used in some WordPress themes to display uploaded image files by individual URL.

Functions: Functions.php is used in some WordPress themes to define functions used in several template files of the theme or enable extra features such as post thumbnails, custom header, custom background, and navigation menus. Furthermore, the functions. php file can create an options menu, so you can set up colors, styles, and other attributes of the theme.

Teaching HTML and CSS is beyond the scope of this book, but resources are offered in Chapter 17. You can also find resources to locate WordPress designers and developers to help you in that chapter. And most WordPress theme questions are answered online and can be found through a Google search. Just remember to always copy the original code to another text file or HTML editor before you make any changes so you can revert to the original format if you make a mistake.

Should I Upgrade to the Newest Version of WordPress? *(WordPress.com and WordPress.org)*

If you use the WordPress-hosted application from WordPress.com, your blog is automatically upgraded for you. However, if you use WordPress.org, you'll see a message at the top of your WordPress Dashboard, as shown in Figure B-22, and also in the Updates section of your dashboard, notifying you that a new version of WordPress has been released and you can upgrade when you're ready.

Figure B-22 *A message appears on your WordPress Dashboard when an upgrade is available.*

New versions of WordPress include great new features, but they also often include security updates, so upgrading is a good idea. However, upgrading immediately might not be a good idea, for a couple reasons.

First, problems with the new version of WordPress often aren't noticed and fixed until a large number of users actually work with the application. It's a good idea to wait a few weeks before you upgrade to ensure any bugs are fixed.

Second, your plug-ins might not work correctly with the new version of WordPress. If you rely on plug-ins that have not been tested with the new version, you might want to wait until those plug-ins are updated or look for substitutes that do work with the new version of WordPress. When you're ready to upgrade, be sure to back up your blog first using a plug-in like WP-DB-Backup, discussed earlier in this appendix.

The websites and books listed in this appendix will help you find additional information so you get the most from your WordPress application and your blogging experience.

WordPress Help Sites

en.support.wordpress.com

codex.wordpress.org/Main_Page

www.wpmods.com

lorelle.wordpress.com

www.performancing.com

CSS and HTML Help Sites

www.w3schools.com

www.davesite.com

www.cssbasics.com

www.westciv.com (fee-based)

Blog Host and Domain Registrar Sites

www.bluehost.com

www.godaddy.com

www.hostgator.com

www.dreamhost.com

www.justhost.com

WordPress Theme Sites

wordpress.org/extend/themes

www.eblogtemplates.com (free)

www.wpthemesfree.com (free)

www.freewordpressthemes.com (free)

www.studiopress.com (premium)

www.ithemes.com (premium)

www.elegantthemes.com (premium)

www.woothemes.com (premium)

www.templatic.com (premium)

www.diythemes.com (premium)

WordPress Forum Tools

www.phpbb.com

simple-press.com

bbpress.org

www.vbulletin.com

WordPress Plug-Ins and Reviews

wordpress.org/extend/plugins

weblogs.about.com/od/
wordpressplugins/Wordpress_Plugins.
htm

www.wpmods.com/category/wordpress-
plugins

www.bloggingpro.com/archives/
category/wordpress-plugins

FTP Tools

www.coreftp.com

www.filezilla-project.org

www.smartftp.com

Social Media Icons

www.freeiconsdownload.com/
free_web_icons.asp

www.wpmods.com/ultimate-social-
media-icon-list

webdesignledger.com/freebies/the-best-
social-media-icons-all-in-one-place

weblogs.about.com/od/bloggingtools/
tp/FreeSocialMediaIcons.htm

Social Networking Sites

www.facebook.com

www.linkedin.com

www.myspace.com

www.bebo.com

www.ning.com

www.foursquare.com

Social Networking Help Sites

www.allfacebook.com

www.facebook.com/help/?ref=pf

learn.linkedin.com

faq.myspace.com/app/home

support.foursquare.com/home

Social Bookmarking Sites

www.stumbleupon.com

www.digg.com

www.reddit.com

www.delicious.com

buzz.yahoo.com

www.newsvine.com

Microblogging Sites

www.jaiku.com

www.plurk.com

www.tumblr.com

www.twitter.com

Twitter Apps, Tools, and Reviews

twitdom.com

twittown.com/social-networks/twitter/
twitter-applications

weblogs.about.com/od/twitterapps/
Twitter_Apps.htm

www.twitip.com/category/twitter-tools

Twitter Help Sites

weblogs.about.com

pistachioconsulting.com

www.twitip.com

support.twitter.com

URL Shorteners

bit.ly

ow.ly/url/shorten-url

www.snurl.com

tinyurl.com

Free Image Sites

www.sxc.hu

www.morguefile.com

www.dreamstime.com

www.picapp.com

www.freefoto.com

Image-Sharing Sites

www.flickr.com

www.photobucket.com

www.picasa.com

Image-Editing Tools

www.picnik.com

www.shrinkpictures.com

www.getpaint.net

www.gimp.org

Video-Sharing Sites

www.blip.tv

www.dailymotion.com

www.tubemogul.com

www.vimeo.com

www.youtube.com

Podcast and Online Talk Show Sites

www.blogtalkradio.com

www.blubrry.com

www.podbean.com

WordPress Freelancer Sites

jobs.wordpress.net

www.elance.com

www.freelanceswitch.com

www.guru.com

www.ifreelance.com

www.craigslist.org

General Blogging Help Sites

weblogs.about.com

www.problogger.net

www.dailyblogtips.com

Search Engine Optimization Help Sites

www.seomoz.org

www.searchenginejournal.com

www.searchengineland.com

weblogs.about.com/od/
searchengineoptimization/Search_
Engine_Optimization_Tips.htm

Web Analytics Tools

www.google.com/analytics

www.statcounter.com

sitemeter.com

www.omniture.com

awstats.sourceforge.net

www.webtrends.com

www.w3counter.com

Feed Reader Tools

www.google.com/reader

feeddemon.com

Sites to Help Monetize Your Blog

www.adbrite.com

affiliates.allposters.com/affiliatesnet

affiliate-program.amazon.com

www.apple.com/itunes/affiliates

www.bidvertiser.com

www.burstmedia.com

www.buysellads.com

www.cafepress.com

www.chitika.com

www.cj.com

www.clicksor.com

ebaypartnernetwork.com/files/hub/
en-US/index.html

www.e-junkie.com

www.google.com/adsense

www.google.com/ads/affiliatenetwork/
index.html

www.kontera.com

www.linkshare.com

www.linkworth.com

www.linkadage.com

payperpost.com

www.payu2blog.com

www.printfection.com

www.pulse360.com

www.reviewme.com

www.shareasale.com

www.sixapart.com

socialspark.com

sponsoredreviews.com

www.textlinkbrokers.com

www.text-link-ads.com

www.tribalfusion.com/home

www.valueclickmedia.com

www.vibrantmedia.com

www.zazzle.com

Books

Comm, Joel. *Twitter Power 2.0*. New Jersey: John Wiley & Sons, 2010.

Gunelius, Susan. *30-Minute Social Media Marketing*. New York: McGraw-Hill, 2010.

McFarland, David Sawyer. *CSS: The Missing Manual*. Sebastopol, CA: O'Reilly Media, 2009.

Meyer, Eric A. *CSS: The Definitive Guide*. Sebastopol, CA: O'Reilly Media, 2006.

Willard, Wendy L. *HTML: A Beginner's Guide*. Berkeley, CA: McGraw-Hill Osborne Media, 2009.

Index

C

L

X-Y-Z

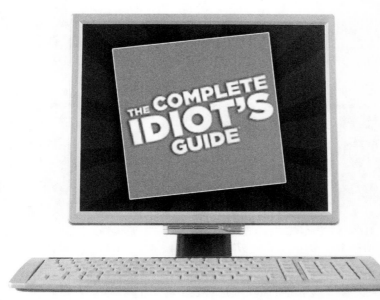

CHECK OUT THESE BEST-SELLERS

More than 450 titles available at booksellers and online retailers everywhere!

978-1-59257-115-4

978-1-59257-900-6

978-1-59257-855-9

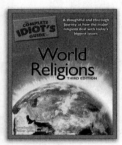

978-1-59257-222-9

978-1-59257-957-0

978-1-59257-785-9

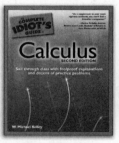

978-1-59257-471-1

978-1-59257-483-4

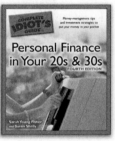

978-1-59257-883-2

978-1-59257-966-2

978-1-59257-908-2

978-1-59257-786-6

978-1-59257-954-9

978-1-59257-437-7

978-1-59257-888-7

ALPHA   **idiotsguides.com**